BABEL'S SHADOW

PETE MOORE writes regularly for *New Scientist*, *The Lancet*, *British Medical Journal* and other newspapers and magazines, and is the author of *Born Too Early*, *Trying for a Baby* and *Pregnancy: A Testing Time*. In 1996 he served on a Commission of Inquiry into Fetal Sentience and was the main author of its report. He gained a PhD in physiology and conducted research into fetal and neonatal development at University College Hospital, London Medical School, before becoming a full-time writer. He lives in Surrey with his wife and two children.

**To Timothy and Joshua**
*My future will be your present.*
*I hope we prepare it for you with care.*

# BABEL'S SHADOW

## GENETIC TECHNOLOGIES IN A FRACTURING SOCIETY

## PETE MOORE

A LION BOOK

Published by
**Lion Publishing plc**
Mayfield House, 256 Banbury Road,
Oxford OX2 7DH, England
www.lion-publishing.co.uk
ISBN 0 7459 4424 8

First hardback edition 2000
First paperback edition 2002
10 9 8 7 6 5 4 3 2 1 0

**Acknowledgments**
Scripture quotations taken from the *Holy Bible, New
International Version*, copyright © 1973, 1978, 1984
by International Bible Society. Used by permission of
Hodder & Stoughton Limited. All rights reserved. 'NIV'
is a registered trademark of International Bible Society.
UK trademark number 1448790.

A catalogue record for this book is available
from the British Library

Typeset in Baskerville
Printed and bound in Great Britain by
Omnia Books Limited, Glasgow

# CONTENTS

# PROLOGUE

Try taking a photo of a fast-moving object. It's not easy. Neither is writing a book about genetic technology. It will always be in grave danger of becoming out of date before it leaves the printers.

When I started, the effort to find the code sequence buried in the middle of most human cells was well underway. While I was editing the first edition in summer 2000, the announcement was made that scientists now had a draft of the code. There is a constant stream of newly found genes and new suggestions for potential uses of genetics. News media seemingly daily herald new therapeutic possibilities and highlight novel ways of scaring people with the power that is being unleashed.

However, within all this change some basic issues will not change. Some questions will not go away. And it is on these that I want this book to focus.

I am excited by science. I am amazed at what is being discovered. I am thrilled at the chance of finding new ways of treating people. But we need to check that we are using our new-found knowledge with wisdom.

Genetics will challenge us personally and will challenge our societies. It will force us to look afresh at what it means to be a human being. It will demand that we look at priorities in healthcare, in employment and in welfare.

Genetic information could be used to revolutionise healthcare, or it could create a divided society. Division is dangerous, as the inhabitants of ancient Babel discovered when many languages destroyed its civilisation. Within this divided system we could find ourselves with a system of medicine that aims to create healthy populations rather than caring for sick individuals in the hope of helping them get well.

The June 2000 announcement from Washington and London that a draft of the genetic code had been completed was also a salutary lesson in the interpretation of hype. The reality is that the scientists have reached a milestone in their quest, but it will take another couple of years before they have accurate knowledge of the three billion letters of human genetic code. In the war against disease, there is also a war to own the technology, and to possess the profits. The wise observer of this technological territory needs to listen hard to hear what is already possible and what is still a pipe dream.

All the same, science and technology are building a tower of knowledge. Those working inside the tower find the task desperately exciting. Many who stand in its shadow remain to be convinced. Because of the pace of change our ethical debate needs to scan the horizons of possibility, anticipating in advance the issues that will be revealed and created. My invitation is to ask technologist and layperson alike to pause from time to time and consider the consequences of genetics, so that the tower can be built with willing consent, proper agreed planning permission and, most of all, wisdom.

# ACKNOWLEDGMENTS

No book is written in isolation and I am extremely grateful to many people who have helped, goaded and encouraged me and to the people who gave me time while I was researching this book. To list them is to risk missing people out, but here goes: Caroline Berry, Sam Berry, Paul Goodridge, Graham Laird, Maurice Lyon, Mandy Little, Oliver O'Donovan, Robert Song and David Wilkinson. If the text is legible and understandable, this owes much to the skills of my wife Adèle and editor Jenni Dutton. Thank you all.

## Mesopotamian Babel

Now the whole world had one language and a common speech.

As men moved eastward, they found a plain in Shinar and settled there.

They said to each other, 'Come, let's make bricks and bake them thoroughly.' They used brick instead of stone, and bitumen for mortar.

Then they said, 'Come, let us build ourselves a city, with a tower that reaches to the heavens, so that we may make a name for ourselves and not be scattered over the face of the whole earth.'

But the Lord came down to see the city and the tower that the men were building.

The Lord said, 'If as one people speaking the same language they have begun to do this, then nothing they plan to do will be impossible for them. Come, let us go down and confuse their language so they will not understand each other.'

So the Lord scattered them from there over all the earth, and they stopped building the city.

That is why it was called Babel – because there the Lord confused the language of the whole world. From there the Lord scattered them over the face of the whole earth.

*Genesis 11:1–9*

# Chapter 1

# TWENTY-FIRST-CENTURY BABEL

Boom-town Babylon had never known it so good. The inhabitants shared a common language and were successfully taking over the entire known world. Trade was up and technology was moving from simple tools for cultivating fields towards the production of manufactured goods including building materials. The natural was no longer good enough. Man-made bricks were suddenly demanded instead of the locally available natural materials of wood and stone, animal skins and dung.

Brick technology was great. It opened up whole new vistas of possibilities. No longer did the simple building materials that they could pick from the ground limit the architects and craftsmen of this burgeoning society. Altering your house was child's play; you simply bricked up a door, or made a hole in a wall and extended through into what had previously been open space. They could let their imaginations run and saw that anything was possible given the resources. But with this unprecedented new-found freedom came unexpected limitations. Archaeologist Charles Pellegrino points out that the flexibility of design resulting from the use of sun-baked mudbricks was so extreme the Mesopotamian civilisations never got around to inventing sewerage systems, because the ground plans of their homes and the street plans of their cities were in constant flux.[1]

Building went on. The city grew and a monument to their

1. Pellegrino, C., *Return to Sodom and Gomorrah*, 1994, p. 156.

power and ingenuity was needed. Nothing too modest, for after all they were supreme. No one had ever been so capable. The city needed a tower. A massive building programme in brick and tar. A focal structure that would reach to the heavens and could become a world-famous temple and the centre for their worship. To people who had never seen any man-made structure bigger than a large garden shed, a multi-layered building that rose from the ground would have seemed incredible. Its dreamers and designers would rise in status to be the high priests of success.

The biblical narrative of the Babylonian tower, or ziggurat, presents a picture of people seeking to display their pride in their own capability and self-sufficiency (see page 8). Their desire was to make a name for themselves, to claim their fifteen minutes of fame and hold tenaciously to it. Up until then, according to the biblical history of the known universe, the only person who was recorded to have made a name for himself was God. So, central to the story is the concept that human beings were seeing themselves as equal to God, maybe even enthroning themselves as God. You can imagine a local peasant wandering into the city after a hard day stumbling along behind an ox-drawn plough and looking at the structure as it rose from the ground, spitting into the dust and saying, 'They're playing God, you know. It shouldn't be allowed. Mark my words, it will all go wrong, horribly wrong.'

Scan your daily paper – you won't have to look hard – and the peasant will be walking by once again, still shaking his head and muttering, 'This genetic stuff, it shouldn't be happening. They're playing God, you know. It'll come to no good. Just you wait and see.' Further down the same page you will find prophetic predictions from the high priests of discovery claiming that all disease will be within reach of their technological sabre within years. Famine could be abolished, weeds destroyed so selectively that they no longer present a problem to farmers, and babies born in a perfect state of health and matching their parents' expectations. In his eye-opening book, *Remaking Eden*, American geneticist Lee Silver speaks in a sort of joyful anxiety of the 'fire of life' being 'tamed'.[2] This fire of which he speaks is the genetic code material stored inside practically each and every cell of our bodies, as well as the cells of every living plant, animal, virus or bacterium.

## A new tower

At the centre of our own society a new tower is being built. The building blocks this time are not brick and tar; they are not even physical. This is a knowledge-based building programme and the subjects of the quest are submicroscopic molecular chains that are so fine and complex that superlatives, while often lavished upon them, fail to do any justice. The material is deoxyribonucleic acid, DNA to you and me. The quest is to uncover the code embedded in its very structure.

The basic ideas underpinning this new 'Tower of Babel' have been evolving slowly. Charles Darwin (1809–82) is famed for collecting evidence that led towards an understanding of inherited traits, an understanding that has grown into the doctrine of evolution. Living on the opposite side of Europe, and consequently unknown to Darwin, an Austrian monk by the name of Gregor Mendel (1822–84) was sorting out the ground rules for genetic inheritance. Mendel had trained for a couple of years in science at Vienna before returning to be abbot of his monastery at Brno. There he observed how physical characteristics of plants were passed from one generation to the next. He developed a particular interest in how combinations of the features 'round' or 'wrinkled', 'green' or 'yellow' passed through generations of edible peas. From his meticulous observations, he drew up his Law of Segregation and his Law of Independent Assortment, setting the scene for others to discover the gene, the physical unit of inheritance at the heart of each cell.

In 1953 Francis Crick and James Watson started to make sense of a growing mass of data when they announced the structure of DNA, the chain-like molecule suspected of being responsible for

2. Silver, L.M., *Remaking Eden: Cloning and Beyond in a Brave New World*, Weidenfeld & Nicolson, 1998, p. 15.

passing information from one generation to another. For this they received a Nobel prize for medicine and physiology, which was awarded in 1962, the year I was born. The pace of change in my lifetime – and I'm not that old – has been remarkable. Soon, enough was known about DNA to confirm its role at the centre of biological control, and technologies had been built that gave access to the stored code.

The scene was set for us to be able to do more than simply watch characteristics pass from one generation to another: we can now influence that passage. To do this we need to manipulate the molecular information, to spot errors or deviations from the norm, to add new sections and to delete or mask old ones. The problem is that to be able to manipulate the genetic code we need to know what it is in the first place. And in the mid-1980s this tower project started in earnest.

The project had a twofold obstacle to surmount. First, the code is huge. Estimates of the number of code characters in human DNA stand at three billion.[3] We are not good at imaging large numbers. Most people can cope with estimating the size of a group of people if there are only ten or so members of it, but once it goes up to 100 or more we become hopelessly inaccurate. This book has approximately 80,000 words. Each word has an average of six letters in it, making 480,000 letters. To get to three billion letters we would need 6,250 books. Given that the book is about 25 mm thick, that is a stack of books over 150 metres high, the height of a fifty-storey tower block.

Secondly, the reading process was slow and expensive. In the mid-1980s the fastest machines could read a few thousand characters per day, so the project was going to demand loads of machines. However, this was being achieved at a cost of about five dollars per letter of code. Finding fifteen billion dollars was not going to happen, so when people started discussing the task they set a threshold of fifty cents per code letter, which would need to be

3. Three thousand million.

reached before a large-scale project could be contemplated. With increased automation this became a realistic target; it was achieved by the mid-1990s and by 2000 had fallen to twenty to thirty cents per letter.

The Human Genome Organisation,[4] HUGO for short, was conceived in April 1988 at a meeting on genome sequencing and mapping at Cold Spring Harbor on Long Island, USA.[5] After a short gestation the organisation was born with a membership of forty-seven scientists from seventeen countries, and in September that year Victor A. McKusick presided over its first council meeting in Montreux, Switzerland. Within five months membership had grown to 220 before exploding to its current list of over 2,000 collaborating people.

HUGO was born out of the desire to discover the human genetic code in the shortest possible time. Drawing from national resources around the globe generated by a multi-billion-dollar budget, HUGO sought to engender an unprecedented level of collaboration and cooperation between scientists. The basic idea was to divide the human DNA into distinct blocks and assign each block to a different laboratory. Each took on the task of decoding a particular section, and in return they hoped to share in the total body of knowledge generated by all of the collaborating labs.

The huge mass of knowledge has revealed a single biological language that has the potential to launch science and technology into a new era. The claims are impressive. Previously unimaginable feats will become possible; we may even reach such giddy heights of human achievement that we feel able to claim equality with God. We may even believe we have surpassed God or the need for God. No longer will we have to make do with the natural – we can now create anything that fills our fancy.

Progress has been impressive. Addressing HUGO's second

4. The word 'genome' refers to the total genetic material within an organism.

5. Cold Spring Harbor was notable for being the centre of the eugenics movement at the beginning of the twentieth century.

international summit in Canberra, Australia, in October 1996, David Cox said, 'In 1990 no one thought we would ever sequence the human genome – the technology was insufficient and the costs prohibitive. We laughed at the scientists with the vision. However, one person with a vision can drive a project like this forward, and there are now enough believers who think that the entire genome can, with international collaboration, be sequenced by the year 2005.'[6] This prediction was made even though only 0.5 per cent of the genome had been sequenced at that time, but the technology being developed and deployed was making the process ever faster.

Since then, predictions have shortened even that time span, and the new 'Tower of Babel' is now due for completion within the first few years of the new millennium. By this point the general sequence of information in the DNA in each human cell will be listed and stored in some computer database. Some believe that the dawning of a new millennium coinciding with the start of a new era in human achievement marks a chance to leave all old myths and superstitions behind. Others see this coincidence of dates as purely poetic, with no particular meaning. However, one thing is certain: the society that gathers around this tower will speak a new language and that language will be used to question previously established core values.

If you don't understand the language or don't join in with the debate then you will be a powerless passenger, or worse still you may even be disenfranchised from true citizenship. In the near future, understanding the peculiarities of your own genetic make-up will influence the type of food you eat, the range of pharmaceutical drugs that could help or harm you, the sorts of jobs available and maybe even your choice of marriage partner – one who is biologically best suited to you.

To be fair to HUGO, the organisation has tried to help people

6. Dr David Cox works at Stanford School of Medicine, California, USA. He is a member of HUGO's Council and sits on its Intellectual Property Committee that keeps an eye on who owns what. More about that in chapter 9.

join in the debate about genetic technology. In its articles and bylaws it establishes one of its three core purposes: 'To encourage public debate and provide information and advice on the scientific, ethical, social, legal and commercial implications of the human genome project.' About one per cent of all funding on the genome project has gone to ethical studies, although questions have been raised about how well this money has been used. Geneticist Steve Jones, a man who has done for the inheritance of patterns on snails' shells what Mendel did for wrinkles on peas, even questions whether any money should have been spent on ethical discussions: 'If you ask me who has benefited from the human genome project, the answer is clearly the ethics industry. There are now great glass towers of ethicists scattered across US campuses that were not there before, that are being funded by genetics... That strikes me as really weird.'[7]

## Science vs technology

The new high priests of the 'tower' are a motley crowd. They mainly consist of venture capitalists, industrialists, technologists and a few scientists. A few scientists – only a few? Yes. One of the main misconceptions is that the world of the gene is one populated by scientists. OK, science used to be at the core of this new religion, but it long ago sold its soul. To see why this is the case, we need to look briefly at what a scientist is and what he or she does.

Science is an intellectual tool that has been developed to help people ask questions. It is much better at asking questions than finding answers. As philosopher Karl Popper famously pointed out, 'Our knowledge can only be finite, while our ignorance must necessarily be infinite.'[8] The idea is to move knowledge forward by setting hypotheses and testing them with the aim of trying to destroy them. If, and only if, the hypothesis cannot be destroyed, we accept

---

7. Steve Jones, cited in Moore, P.J., 'Genethics', *Third Way*, February 1999, pp. 18–21.

8. The Austrian-born, British philosopher and father of modern statistics, Sir Karl Popper, in *Conjectures and Refutations*, 1963.

it as the best current theory and move on. Science, contrary to popular belief, can never prove that something is true. It does not have the intellectual tools to do that. It can certainly show if something is wrong or doesn't happen, or that currently one theory or another is the best understanding we can come up with.

The history of science demonstrates time and again that what is an established understanding one year is often called into question or proved false a decade or so later. One consequence of this is the familiar sight of scientists drawn on to news programmes refusing to give definite answers to probing, or even not so probing, questions. 'Is this safe, Dr X?'; 'Will this work, Dr Y?'; 'Tell us what the outcome will be, Professor Z!' It's not that they are being evasive, it's just that the tool they handle is science, and science lives with uncertainty.

By contrast, technology is driven much more by experience. When we sit on a chair we want to know that it will support our weight. Previous experience tells us that it will be OK. When we put our foot on the brake pedal in the car we want to know that the car will stop. Few of us know the mechanics that make it happen, and the engineers may incompletely understand the precise physics – but they work. When we build a chemical factory we want to know that it is not going to explode. Much of the planning will be carefully calculated, but a lot of the design will be based on safety factors that mask our lack of certainty and our imprecise knowledge. Technologists take the things that scientists discover and make use of them. They build computers that draw on scientific knowledge, but put it to practical use. The dictionary definition of 'technology' is the 'total knowledge and skills available to any human society'.[9] The link between technology and science is that technology uses techniques to apply the fruits of scientific endeavour. Intriguingly a 'technique' is defined as a 'practical method, skill or art applied to a particular task'. In moving from the laboratory to the factory we move from the realm of experimental science to practical arts, where very often a particular action is taken because, well, because that's the way we do it – and it works.

9. *Collins Concise Dictionary.*

This technical/artistic approach is now at the centre of the human genome project, which is currently being driven by the need to discover code sequences and find the locations and orders of genes on chromosomes. One of the prime movers behind the project is Charles De Lisi, the director of the Department of Energy's Office of Health and Environmental Research in the USA. On a BBC television programme he made the following comment about the project: 'My feeling was this was an idea whose time had come. The atmosphere was probably comparable to the type of environment you'd expect when entering a massive project like a Moon Shot. It was not a scientific proposal, in fact. This was a proposal that was more an engineering proposal; it was a proposal to develop a resource that would have general use in the same way that the SSC – Super-Conductor Super Collider – is going to be a resource for physicists, or a space probe is a resource for astronomers.'[10]

The 'Babel' project will probably go through many phases during its development and, while its foundations are in science, the major effort now is much more one of an artistic application of technology. This is not to deny that in the background a few scientists are developing the next generation of ideas, but the main bulk of the work is in pure data-gathering, with no hypotheses in sight.

Who funds these technologically equipped artists? Well, that's where the venture capitalists move in. Research costs money – millions of pounds, dollars or euros. The name of the currency doesn't really matter as long as there is a lot of it. The genetic 'Tower of Babel' has in part spawned, and in part been created by, a new generation of entrepreneurs who are eager to gain financially from their work. University departments, who have found that their traditional sources of funding have been cut off, have set up

10. BBC Television's *Horizon* (January 1989). The Department of Energy's Office of Health and Environmental Research in the USA is heavily involved in this project because they have a remit to monitor inherited damage caused by low-level radiation and other environmental hazards. This grew initially from concerns about the use of atomic energy.

companies to exploit anything that may be capable of generating money. Many mini-companies have been set up to direct a stream of revenue back into their originating department. Others hope to guide the anticipated flow of cash into the founding members' pockets. I say 'anticipated flow', because in reality few of these new projects have generated a profit – yet.

## Calling the tune

What's so important about this analysis of the genome project is that individual people, you and I, are going to be affected by its outcome. As you will discover in the pages of this book, I am excited about some of the potential applications and uses, and sceptical that some of the more extreme prophecies will come to fruition. However, even if the applications don't develop any further than they have so far, and they certainly will, the effect on us will be more than tangible. To have an idea about how it will progress, you need to understand the players, their desires and demands.

It takes two to tango, and in this particular dance there are two key participants, the developer–supplier and the end-user. The first thing to do is identify who is calling the tune – who is setting the pace and giving direction.

The scientists may not like it, but they are not in charge of this particular dance. Not any longer. After all, it's a long-established rule that 'he who pays the piper calls the tune'. It's those in charge of funding who are directing progress. The scientists are more akin to the conductors, giving direction and inspiration to the band, but it is the orchestrated mass of technologists who are making the music, and the sources of funding, the beloved bankers, who are calling the tune. The drive for implementation of new discoveries comes from the need for investors to see rapid returns. No stock market is known for its patience.

This lack of control is simultaneously annoying and convenient for scientists. They would love to be in charge. It would raise their status and power. Indeed some scientists think that they are, as many people who trained initially as biochemists, molecular biologists or geneticists have moved to hold posts as managers of funding organisations or directors of processing plants. Their background education in science is invaluable, but they are no longer performing a scientific job. They are no longer setting up hypotheses in order to try to knock them down. They are using the fruits of science to solve problems and generate income. They are technological artists.

Initially this situation may have been seen as a hindrance for pure scientists, but more recently it has been used by many to claim immunity from ethical, moral and sometimes intellectual prosecution. Steve Jones exemplifies the situation. He is one of the first to acknowledge the potential dangers inherent in some of the areas of scientific, and in particular, genetic research. However, he finds the notion of placing limits on scientific endeavour totally unacceptable. When I interviewed him recently, I asked if he thought there should be any ethical limits to the pursuit of scientific knowledge. He replied:

*I would have to say no, really. Because once you put one on, where are you going to stop? You can put ethical limits on the application of science, but that, I think, is a quite different thing. I think you have to differentiate between science and technology. Take the atom bomb. I'm pretty convinced that on balance it's a bad thing and that it's going to end up causing some kind of global disaster. But it was inevitable that we were going to discover relativity and once we had, nuclear power was almost automatic. You couldn't say, 'Stop now!' because you can't undiscover something.*[11]

The scientists' standard cry is that it is their job to discover, and the politicians' job to establish, what should be done with any discovery. Science abhors the shackles of restriction and, as we will find out, many scientists will go to great lengths to avoid or wriggle out of any regulations placed in their way. At the same time scientists have a tendency to take a teenage attitude towards responsibility, saying that they'll get on with their research and leave the task of

11. Steve Jones, cited in Moore, P.J., 'Genethics', *Third Way*, February 1999, pp. 18–21.

identifying the ethical use of their discoveries to other people. In so doing they abdicate responsibility. In Jones's view, *society* needs to regulate what happens, but then he rapidly acknowledges that 'what tends to be the case is that what can happen will happen'. In reality he is saying that the market, the world's financiers, will be in the driving seat and no one can stop it, nor should they bother about trying to stop it.

Lee Silver would wholeheartedly agree with this analysis. In *Remaking Eden* he paints a picture of the future where the market is so driven by wealthy individuals that a separate human race emerges. He predicts that midway through this millennium there will be two races: GenRich humans, who have been genetically enhanced, and Natural humans, who have been left behind in the race for genetic superiority. By the end of that millennium he prophesies that this GenRich race will have been split by market competition into three differing strains, plus of course the Naturals.[12] Some of the GenRich individuals would even have been given the ability to generate food from sunlight by employing the photosynthetic properties of plants – whenever they needed a snack they would just lie in the sun. The startling prediction is that these four groups would be incapable of interbreeding – the human race would now have become four separate species.

Whether Lee Silver's extreme predictions come true or not, we can be sure that life left to the market place and fuelled by teenage science could be frightening. Genetic technology is sometimes held up in comparison to nuclear technology and it is sobering to see what the fathers of that branch of science had to say when they reflected on their achievements. Having been pivotal in developing the atomic bomb, J. Robert Oppenheimer spoke of his regret in a lecture at Massachusetts Institute of Technology, saying, 'The physicists have known sin; and this is a knowledge that they cannot lose.'[13] Surely they would urge that we proceed, but with caution.

12. Silver, *Remaking Eden*, pp. 240–50.

13. Oppenheimer, J.R., lecture at Massachusetts Institute of Technology, 25 November 1947.

Don't get me wrong. I don't dislike scientists. I trained as a scientist and like to think of myself as having a scientifically oriented mind. I love setting up hypotheses and testing them to see if they can be destroyed. What does worry me, though, is when scientists are pursuing their interests without any pause for thought as to the long-term consequences of their quest.

And what of the end-user? To start with, there is nothing unusual about these participants. This will be a very inclusive club. One thing that is becoming abundantly clear is that everybody alive has many genetic faults. Each of us has undesirable genetic traits that affect either our health, our general physique or our personality. Once any particular aberration has been identified, it will be a short step to providing a test so that individuals can discover whether or not it affects them.

If a test comes on to the market allowing you to know that you are at particular risk from a specific type of cancer, each person will need to decide whether to have the test. A person's right not to have the test will probably be upheld, but experience of numerous antenatal screening programmes shows that many people have tests without really stopping to think about the implications that will flow from gaining the new information. For example, one aspect that we will need to remember is that if a particular genetic disease affects you, there is a high chance that it also affects family members. If you decide to have a particular test you force the information on anyone who is genetically related to you. Without seeking inclusion, many people will be drawn into the genetically informed club.

The anxiety about genetically modified food crops is driven by the realisation that as we all eat food we are all affected by this application of technology. The relaxed attitude towards medical applications comes from the false belief that it will affect only a few – those with some overt genetic disease. Arguably, the medical uses of genetics will be far more profound than the agricultural applications, and it is vital that the users think hard about which genetic tools they want to employ because those decisions will mould our future society.

But what do we want, as individuals, that genetic technology can offer? First, we all want better healthcare: there is the potential for more targeted medical treatments, enabled by more accurate diagnoses. Secondly, we all want new ways of treating old diseases: there is the possibility of a new genre of medical intervention where genetic technology is used as a curative agent rather than as a method of observing what exists. Thirdly, we want our offspring to be healthy: genetics gives us the potential for selecting or changing the way we, or our offspring, are. At the extreme end of this particular spectrum of possibilities is the idea of 'designer babies', babies who match the genetic specifications set out by their parents. At a more realistic point comes the ability to choose not to have a child with a particular disease or physical limitation, such as genetically caused blindness. Not everyone is convinced that this is such a good idea. Indeed many, including some disability support groups, are vocal opponents.

The problem is that once we have the ability to select, how do we make that selection? Caught in the crossfire is a group of health professionals called genetic counsellors, whose task is to equip people to make informed decisions. At present there are few employed within health services, but the need is great and increasing. Users of genetic testing need to tread warily as they enter this particular territory of possibility, because any decision they make will stay with them for their lives. It will also have a direct bearing on the offspring who do, or do not, exist as a result of their decisions. A good counsellor is an indispensable guide and we will consider their role in more detail in chapter 4.

## Today's science – tomorrow's myth

The spiralling tower of genetic knowledge is nearing completion. The so-called draft is finished, although it will take another five or ten years before the majority of the holes in the data are filled in. The shadow is very long. Those who understand its language appear to be very clever and send representatives to speak on radio and television discussion panels. They are held in high esteem. But what of the building itself? How long will genetic technology be held as the pinnacle of achievement? How long until it is superseded?

The problem is that things are more complex than we first thought. At face value, knowing the sequence of the genetic code inside each cell could produce huge effects on health and welfare. However, many of the earlier expectations have been dashed. For example, in terms of tackling disease, many conditions that were thought to have a genetic basis, because they were passed from one generation of a family to the next, have now been found to be tens of separate diseases, each with its own biochemical mechanism. There is no longer any point in looking for a single therapy for all the patients; you now need to find ten or so different approaches to treatment. In shining light on the problem, genetic technology has defined the nature of the disease more fully and in so doing has expanded the task of bringing a cure to individual patients. The positive effect is that each newly developed treatment has the potential for being more accurately targeted to the root cause of the disease, and thus can be far more powerful.

We laugh at people who thought the world was flat, but they were just basing their ideas on the best available information. We pour scorn on the religious leaders who doggedly held to the idea that the sun went round the earth, rather than vice versa, blaming them for having hideous theological blinkers. We giggle at the phrenologists who thought they could determine the nature of someone's personality by feeling the bumps on the outside of their head. The danger is we forget that at one time each theory seemed perfectly logical and the exponents of it were seen as being at the forefront of human knowledge.

Babel's ancient tower aimed to reach the starry vault of the heavens. We laugh. How can a structure a mere hundred or so feet high reach anything? But how were the ancients to know how far beyond their reach the nearest star really was? If you told them that the nearest star was Proxima Centuri and that it was 4.2 light years away (that's 40,000,000,000,000 km) they would have locked you up for insanity. Just as the ancient mudbrick ziggurats rapidly crumbled, so we need to be aware that our current state-of-the-art technologies and understandings will look dusty in years to come. If anything, the pace of change is accelerating and ideas that may have held ground for a century will now be swept away in a decade.

Craig Venter, one of the most ambitious and enthusiastic exponents of genetic technology, puts it this way: 'I'm absolutely certain, that this time at the end of next century, journalists will still be asking scientists to what extent they understand [human genetics].'[14]

Yes, genetics is important. Yes, understanding what genetic scientists are talking about will help you have a greater say in what happens to your life in the future. But let's not get carried away. We haven't reached the pinnacle of knowledge. Like climbers on some infinitely high mountain, each false summit gives way to a distant horizon that is bigger and higher than we can ever dream of.

## Uniformity or diversity?

Returning to the biblical narrative of Babel, let us pause for a moment to see what the narrator might have wanted us to understand from the story. Was he simply painting a picture of a vindictive God who wanted to spoil people's fun and thwart their industrial endeavour? A twentieth-century theologian, Walter Brueggemann, paints an altogether more intriguing picture. He links this with the story of Noah leaving the ark after the floodwaters had receded and being told by God to spread over the earth. 'Be fruitful and increase in number and fill the earth' (Genesis 9:2). This is a command to explore and make wise use of resources, to diversify. Instead of this, the people congregate together and seek to create uniformity – one language, one city – a nervously protectionist mentality. However, the God described by the narrator has other ideas in mind. While wishing to remain the single centre of their attention, he wants people to diversify.

In 1999 there were three nail bombs in London. Each bomb was placed where it stood a high chance of injuring people from

14. Reported in *Bulletin*, the newsletter of the Novartis Foundation, no. 52, September 1999.

minority groups, and 'race-hate' groups claimed responsibility.[15] At the same time Slobodan Milosevic was conducting a programme of 'ethnic cleansing' in order to drive ethnic Albanians from their homes in Serbia, and before him Hitler sought to create a racially pure Germany. Each stands as a graphic example of people trying to force an agenda of uniformity on a society. Standing at a distance from each of these events it is easy to see that the underlying aims are abhorrent.

Diversity is a healthy component of any society and uniformity is boring and dangerous. Populations that lose diversity soon become weak and begin to die out. Groups of people formed around narrow-minded goals often become aggressive towards perceived outsiders. Introversion breeds a belligerent form of fundamentalism that is offensive in its outlook and behaviour.

The desire for uniformity can also be seen within the genetic 'Babel' project – uniformity of health and well-being. The notion that prospective parents will be able to make decisions about some physical characteristics of their children implies that they have preferences. Some of these preferences are more easily determined than others. No one wants to deliberately have a child who will die a painful death within a few months or years of birth, and for the first time parents at risk from this can make choices that massively reduce this possibility.

However, now this particular can of worms has been opened, the issues multiply. Which diseases and conditions would we want to avoid? And what would we deliberately like to select for our children? Geneticist and self-appointed watchdog of the genetic industry Dave King points to a creeping laissez-faire eugenics, in which the dominant concept is consumer choice in reproduction.[16] Now, having warned against expecting too much from genetic

---

15. In June 2000, 24-year-old David Copeland was convicted of all three attacks. He was working alone as a far-right activist, hoping to 'set fire to the country and stir up a racial war'.

16. King, D., *GenEthics News*, issue 22, February/March 1998, pp. 6–8.

technologies, I need to be cautious about overstating this point. But the potential is there and some people think that this sort of power over our offspring is a great achievement. We will look at this in more detail later, but for now it's easy to see how we can reach a situation where diversity is restricted and a move towards a genetic uniformity begins.

In biblical Babel the solution was to confuse the language and scatter the people. The result was diversity. In the future, the genetic 'Tower of Babel' may have a more lasting impact, and the scattering could come from new forms of discrimination and exclusion, or from events as extreme as a split into more than one human race. On the other hand, if controlled and managed with care, it could lead to a world where individuals are treated with respect and enabled to live out their full potential.

Let's look at the technology and then assess its impact.

## Twenty-first-century Babel: the doom scenario

Now the whole world had one database and a common set of genetic codes.

As technology developed they saw great potential for gain.

They said to each other, 'Come, let's make use of this technology to build any organism we want.' They used technological means instead of natural processes.

Then they said, 'Come, let us build ourselves an industry, with a database that encompasses all knowledge, so that we may make a name for ourselves, build future generations to our own specifications and not be afflicted by any disease or illness.'

But the Lord started to look at the science-worshipping populations and the knowledge that the technocrats were amassing.

The Lord said, 'This is so sad. So much effort, so much potential benefit, but so much possibility for it all going seriously wrong. They think that they will be able to ignore me, but the Utopia they hope for will not emerge.'

As the technology developed, the industrial market-led companies started to fight among themselves and hid some of their knowledge from each other and from the people.

Meeting each other only to fight patent applications and move to areas of the world where restrictions were lax, the project began to stall.

That is why it was called Babel – because the language of partnership and benefit became confused as it was usurped by one of market forces and laissez-faire eugenics.

# Chapter 2

# BASIC GENETICS

A good friend asked me recently, 'Now Pete, what's the difference between a nerve and a gene?' I paused for some time before answering. My key problem was knowing where to start, given that the question was akin to asking what the difference is between a telephone cable and an entry in the *Encyclopaedia Britannica*. Yes, if you work hard enough, genes and nerves do have points of contact that would allow some form of comparison, but the question itself pointed to the enormous gap in the questioner's understanding of rudimentary biology.

Whose fault is this? The questioner, who only speaks normal languages, or the science community, which chooses to discuss its subject in unnecessarily complex jargon that obscures the meaning? Well, we could argue that one for days, and some people do. But it's worth pointing out that my friend is an engineer, in other words someone who lives in the realm of applied science, and yet he hadn't enough information to be able to form a particularly meaningful question, much less have a grasp of any brief answer.

In this chapter I don't intend to take expert grannies and teach them to suck eggs. If you really think you understand basic genetics then fine, move on to the next chapter. Having said that though, I wonder how many commentators on the subject really do know the basics, or describe topics in a way that gives full access to interested observers. Writing in *The Independent*, Charles Arthur comments,

*The next time a non-scientist [and for that matter I'd like to add someone who claims to be a scientist] starts spouting to you about genes and DNA, see if he or she in fact knows what a gene does. If they answer 'makes proteins', award half a point; if they answer 'carries the code for protein', the full point. If the answer is neither of those, a kick under the table is in order, to get them to shut up.*[1]

His annoyance is directed at the likes of Richard Dawkins, whose world best-selling books, *The Blind Watchmaker* and *The Selfish Gene*, have done so much to confuse the basic notion of what a gene is and what effect genes have on biological systems. Dawkins treats the notion of a gene, and in particular his concept of the 'selfish gene', more as a metaphysical construct, refusing to be tied down by the discipline of restraining himself to exact descriptions of what one of these things actually is. As you will see in a few pages, if you tie his use of the word 'gene' to the physical construct that geneticists refer to as a gene, then much of his argument becomes distinctly weak.

But first we need to find out what a gene is and how it fits into the biological order of things. After all, to be a qualified voting member in the society of the new Babel, you will need to have an understanding based on the best current knowledge of the fundamental units of genetics, and a few of the biological mechanisms and humanly imposed manipulative techniques. To make them accessible I will try to draw some analogies to more readily conceivable items and concepts, while at the same time being aware that all analogies have their breaking points.

## Required for life

My school biology teacher taught me that to be classified as living, an organism needs to be able to perform seven basic functions. It needs to be able to carry out chemical reactions that make energy available throughout the organism – a process called respiration. It must be able to get rid of waste products from those chemical reactions and clear out any indigestible matter – excretion. It needs to be able to feed, grow, move and respond to external stimuli. And it needs to be able to reproduce.

1. Arthur, C., 'So Why Does Religion Exist?', *The Independent*, 11 March 1999.

The smallest unit that is indisputably capable of performing all of these is a single cell. Some organisms, like amoebae, are no more than single cells, floating around in water and looking after their own business. Lichens that cling to the bark of trees are a union between two types of organism, a fungus and single-celled algae or bacteria. More complex structures, like visually brilliant coral reefs, are in fact huge colonies of tiny organisms that group together for mutual protection and collective advantage.

However, if a plant or animal is going to grow to a large size it needs to develop areas with specific functions. It needs to be made of many cells that group themselves into organs which each play a defined role in maintaining the life of the organism. Trees have leaves, branches and roots. Animals have eyes, nervous tissue and kidneys, among other things. But each of these organs is composed of specialised cells.

Estimates place the total number of cells in the adult human body at 100 million million (one with fourteen noughts after it), give or take the odd million. And while a cell is the smallest living unit, it too is composed of many subunits, organelles, which enable it to perform all of the seven features needed for it to live. A vital component is one or more molecule[2] of DNA. It is referred to as a molecule because at its most basic it is a simple chemical; in itself it is incapable of doing anything other than just sitting there. But within a cell, and with all the cell's weird and wonderful biochemical machinery acting upon it, DNA starts to assume a central role.

Throughout the living world, organisms can be divided into two groups. In one group, the prokaryotes, the DNA exists as a naked molecule floating around in the cell. In the second group, the eukaryotes, DNA is contained in a membrane-enclosed structure called the nucleus (*eu-* means true; *karyo* means nucleus). Human beings belong to the eukaryotes, and so for the most part in this book we will be considering what happens to DNA that is held within a nucleus.

---

2. A molecule is defined as the smallest portion of a substance capable of existing independently and retaining the properties of the original substance (*Penguin Dictionary of Science*, 1976).

With the exception of the red blood cells, which have no DNA, and sperm[3] and eggs,[4] cells that are a law unto themselves, all cells in the standard human body have forty-six chain-like molecules of DNA, called chromosomes.[5] To fit within a nucleus the chromosomes need to be coiled and then 'super-coiled', in the same way that an elastic band first coils and then super-coils when you wind the propeller of an elastic-band-powered toy aeroplane. The result is a staggering level of miniaturisation. Try it with a piece of string. Tie either end to a pencil and then twist and twist and twist. DNA is too thin for anyone to see it using a light microscope, but once it has super-coiled and wrapped itself around proteins to form chromosomes, it becomes bulky enough to be seen.

If you could physically take out the chromosomes from any one cell, unwind them and lie them end to end they would be two metres long, even though the average cell is only a hundredth of a millimetre in diameter.

I'm never sure whether to be amazed at how long two metres is, on the basis that it manages to fit inside a cell, or to be staggered at how short it is, given the amount of information it carries. Normally I opt for the latter, because along this two-metre length of almost impossibly fine strands is stored all of the information needed to create the physical you and me. Remember that this two-metre length of DNA stores the equivalent of 6,250 books. As the human genome project pushes forward, the exact make-up of these strands is becoming more clearly defined, but even now we are still in the realm of estimates. Right now it appears that there are some

3. The word 'sperm' derives from the Latin word for seed.

4. Doctors and other people trying to sound clever call eggs by their Latin name *ova*.

5. One of the problems with getting a basic understanding of scientific subjects is coming to terms with needlessly complex jargon. All too often we think that big words sound as if the person using them has a big brain. However, many of them when decoded reveal the measure of ignorance. Take the word 'chromosome' as an example. Break the word down and we have *chromo*, 'colour', and *soma*, 'body'. It was called a chromosome because it was the part of the cell that early biologists found they could stain and then see down their microscope. We now know a bit more, but in those days it was simply the 'coloured bit'.

30,000 separate pieces of information, genes, collected onto the chromosomes.[6]

No computer matches this degree of efficiency of data storage. In fact the efficiency is even more startling when you consider that about ninety per cent of this two-metre length appears to be inactive, and the vital information is confined to the remaining ten per cent (twenty centimentres, or eight inches if you prefer), a length that would run from your finger tips to the base of your wrist.

It's difficult to get your mind around the scale of which we are talking. The strand of DNA making up each chromosome is only one quarter of a millionth of a centimetre across. Molecular geneticist William Bains calculates that if you magnified the width to that of an audio-cassette tape, the forty-six chromosomes would total more than 2,800 km in length. A cassette tape this long would take over two years to play on a standard tape recorder.[7]

Looking at it another way, if there are 100 million million cells in the human body, and each cell has two metres of DNA in it, that produces a total of 200 million million metres of DNA, which is more than enough to reach to the sun and back 670 times.

## Bookshelves and blueprints

Let's step into the world of analogy for a moment. If the nucleus is our library, then each chromosome is a single bookshelf (see Figure 1). On each of the forty-six shelves stands a series of thousands of files containing carefully constructed code, plus several hundred thousand files that appear to contain rubbish left behind from our evolutionary past.

Other writers have used the analogy of a book or loose-leaf binder to relate to a chromosome, rather than a bookshelf.[8] The problem is that this gives a false impression of how much information

---

6. For a decade or so before the February 2001 announcements in *Science* and *Nature* scientists were anticipating finding 100,000 genes, maybe even more. There is much scratching of heads about the significance of this smaller number.

7. Bains, W., *Genetic Engineering for Almost Everybody*, Penguin, 1987, p. 18.

8. For example, see Dawkins, R., *The Selfish Gene*, 1989, p. 26.

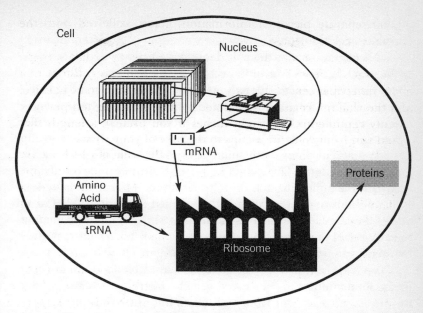

Figure 1: Tracing the flow of information from its storage in the chromosome, to its use in building new proteins in the cytoplasm, the main body of the cell. The chromosomes are represented as forty-six bookshelves, with the genes featuring as books on the shelves. Like reference books, the genes never leave the library, but are copied onto short-lived photocopy paper, messenger RNA, that heads off to the ribosome. These are agents that enable the code to be read and protein produced by linking a string of amino acids together. Amino acids are delivered to the ribosomes fixed to transfer RNA.

is contained on a chromosome. Have you ever seen a book or file that is 3.4 metres thick?[9] In fact the information contained in individual genes is sometimes greater than we find in a standard book.

Going back to the real world, it's time to look at the chromosomes, our library shelves, in a bit more detail. In 1953 James Watson and Francis Crick calculated the structure of DNA from some X-ray-diffraction-generated photographic plates that had

9. Remember that in chapter 1 we saw that we would need 6,250 books to store the three billion letters of code, generating a tower 150 metres high. If this mass of information were divided equally between the forty-six chromosomes each stack would be just over three metres high.

been made by another pair of competing scientists, Rosalind Franklin and Maurice Wilkins. The somewhat clandestine means by which they came across the plates is told in Watson's book *The Double Helix*, but what they concluded was as simple as it was brilliant.

Each chromosome turns out to be made of two strands of DNA that wrap around each other in a perfect double helix. Each strand is constructed of a backbone of identical building blocks, a sugar called deoxyribose. The sugars are linked together by a phosphate group. Within a single chain these sugar-phosphate units have to stack in one direction, much like a child's plastic building blocks, and the two chains are arranged so that they are facing in opposite directions.

This forms the structural unit of the chromosome, but so far no code, much as library shelves form the structure that information-carrying books are placed on. The code is recorded, some say written, in single side-units, one attached to each sugar. These are referred to as bases and there are only four varieties available to DNA: adenine, guanine, thymine and cytosine, normally abbreviated to A, G, T and C. The bases reach out from each chain into the centre of the helix and link with the corresponding bases on the partnering sugar chain. This gives the code on the two chains a weird form of symmetry (see Figure 2). DNA is the molecule that forms as hundreds, thousands and millions of base-carrying deoxyribose sugars link together.

Life would be simple if both of the chains ran in the same direction and the bases reached across to grab hold of an identical unit. But neither of these happens. As I have said, the chains run in opposite directions, and on top of this A always links to T and G always links to C. The two chains form molecular mirror images of each other.

The genetic code therefore stretches out physically along the centre of the helical structure, with its message constructed using the alphabet of four different bases. The language is extremely limited, containing only three-letter words. There are no spaces between any of the words.

The message you receive when you examine the code is therefore critically dependent upon where you start reading. For example, a simple string of letters such as 'youcanseethecatandthedogyes' can be broken up in three different ways:

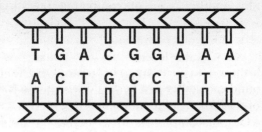

Figure 2: Chemically, the two strands of the DNA molecule point in opposite directions and are held together by weak links between their bases. Because A always links to T and C to G, the two strands form complementary, rather than identical, sequences.

*esy ouc ans eet hec ata ndt hed ogy*

*syo uca nse eth eca tan dth edo gye*

*you can see the cat and the dog yes*

Only one of these starts to makes sense. In normal message writing, we find life is made much easier because we impose on the string of letters a formal syntax. The sorts of sentences that we commonly use start with capital letters and end with full stops:

*You can see the cat and the dog. Yes?*

Genetic code also has syntax. The two most basic ones are stretches of code that spell out 'start reading here' and others that say 'stop reading now'. The space between the start and the stop is basically a gene. A single command. The issue now is, what 'reads' the gene, and what is the product of that process?

By the time that Crick and Watson told the world about the structure of DNA, scientists were well aware that in human cells, almost all the DNA was contained in the nucleus. This was a puzzle, because they were pretty sure that it had a role in directing the production of proteins, and they knew that protein production occurred outside the nucleus.

We tend to think of protein simply as a necessary part of our balanced diet. At a cellular level things are, not surprisingly, more complex. Proteins are made of strings of amino acids that are linked together in chains which fold and wrap around themselves in precise patterns, creating biological blobs with specific functions. Some are needed as structural components of cells; others are involved in chemical reactions, and still others act as messengers within the cell or between cells within a single organism. For example, some proteins act as molecular message-boys, helping information get back into the nucleus which determines when other genes are going to be decoded so that they too can produce a protein.

Then, in 1961, a couple of French biologists, François Jacob and Jacques Monod, working at the Pasteur Institute in Paris, started to put the picture together.[10] They chemically stimulated the bacterium *E. coli* so that it started to produce specific proteins. They were amazed at how quickly the process occurred, because they could see a thousandfold increase in the target protein within minutes of stimulating the bacterium. Furthermore, individual messenger molecules must be short-lived, because when they removed the stimulation, protein production stopped almost immediately. Other researchers found that while DNA was located predominantly in the nucleus, almost all of the RNA (ribonucleic acid) was in the main part of the cell, the cytoplasm. Jacob and Monod then concluded that short lengths of RNA, a molecule that has very similar properties to DNA, must be acting as intermediaries in the process. Jacob and Monod went on to receive the Nobel prize for medicine and physiology in 1965 in recognition of their pioneering research.

With the benefit of a few more years' research we know a little more detail. Floating within the nucleus are bits of cellular

10. Jacob and Monod reported their work in a ground-breaking paper that was published in 1961: 'Genetic Regulatory Mechanisms in the Synthesis of Proteins', *The Journal of Molecular Biology* **3**, 1961, pp. 318–56.

machinery called RNA polymerase. This is a protein complex that acts like a molecular biological photocopier designed to produce copies of gene sequences. Biologists call the process transcription. Rather than making a copy of the section code out of DNA, for reasons best known to itself, it copies the sequence onto RNA, a molecule that, like DNA, comes with four different bases. RNA has two key differences from DNA. First, its backbone uses ribose rather than deoxyribose sugars. Secondly, RNA uses a base called uracil where DNA uses thymine.

RNA polymerase plugs onto chromosomes at a place that says 'start reading here' and then travels along the chromosome one base at a time. Pausing at each base, it waits until the correct RNA unit has been drawn out of the molecular soup inside the nucleus and has plugged onto the growing chain. Rapidly a mirror image of the code forms, attached to a ribose backbone. In cells that have their DNA contained in a nucleus, this piece of 'messenger RNA' (mRNA) travels out of the nucleus into the main body of the cell where it will be put to work.

The photocopy analogy works quite well if you think of the chromosomes as forming a reference library. You can't borrow the book and take it to the office, but you need to copy a page or two of its information. So you open the book, photocopy the pages and then return it closed to the shelf for efficient storage and safe keeping. In the same way, when the cell needs the information contained in a particular gene it separates the two sides of the chromosome, copies the information onto a string of mRNA and then zips the chromosome closed again to keep it safe. The short lifespan of the messenger is similar to that of the old-style thermal paper, still used in small fax machines, except that in the case of the cell it degenerates in minutes rather than weeks.

Once outside the nucleus, mRNA is now ready to act as a template in the production of protein. Now mRNA is a string-like molecule, while proteins are solid little lumps. So the one-dimensional language of the genes needs to be 'translated' into a three-dimensional protein. This translation occurs in factory-like units called ribosomes and the process involves yet another form of RNA, this time called transfer RNA (tRNA). You can think of tRNA as a delivery lorry. It has a section where it carries its load – a specific amino acid – and another section that carries its delivery instructions. These instructions are in the form of three bases, three letters of genetic code. The ribosome enables the lorry to dock onto the mRNA only if its three letters of instruction complement three letters of code in the mRNA (see Figure 3).

The result is that tRNAs gather along the mRNA in a regulated order, each occupying three letters of the gene's sequence. As they do so the amino acids that they carry are brought together in a controlled order, and as these amino acids sit there, side by side, they link together – one amino acid per three characters of genetic code. It is this three-base recognition system of the tRNA molecule that dictates that the genetic code is written in a three-letter language. For example, a sequence on a stretch of RNA of:

*UGU*|*GUG*|*AGU*|*AAG*|*UAA*

would link amino acids together in a sequence of:

*cysteine*|*valine*|*serine*|*lysine*|

The last group of three bases, UAA, is a special sequence that tells the ribosome to stop. Unsurprisingly, it's called a 'stop code'.

As the chain of amino acids leaves the ribosome, chemical forces of repulsion and attraction push and pull the developing protein so that it lies either in sheets or blobs.

Going back to Charles Arthur's comment about knowing what a gene is, we can now see why he says that the essential purpose of a gene is to 'carry the code for a protein'. In *The Selfish Gene*, Richard Dawkins says, 'It is not easy, indeed it may not even be meaningful, to decide where one gene ends and the next one begins. Fortunately... this does not matter for our purposes.'[11] To enable his argument to

11. Dawkins, *The Selfish Gene*, p. 22.

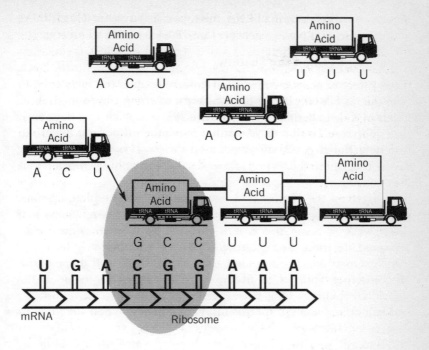

Figure 3: Transfer RNAs carry a specific amino acid and have a three-letter recognition sequence that relates to their amino acid. Proteins form in the ribosome: amino acids are brought in the correct order as the sequence on the tRNA complements the next available sequence on the messenger RNA.

take shape, Dawkins defines a gene as 'any portion of chromosomal material that potentially lasts for enough generations to serve as a unit of natural selection'. This is an interesting idea, but what he is talking about is a significantly different entity to what most people think of as a gene – which is a 'master copy' from which is made a 'blueprint' for the production of a protein. In this case the place where the genetic sequence starts and finishes is of paramount importance.

Dawkins's argument needs this relaxed definition of the 'gene' in order to be able to support the idea that it is DNA that is interested in surviving, rather than the specifics of its code. To be interested in the specifics of the code would start to bring meaning and purpose into play – concepts that Dawkins finds abhorrent.

## Throwing light on the shadow

So why do you need to know all of this? Why do I feel that *I* need to know all this? Well, partly because I want to know. I want to know as much as I can about the way things work and what can happen if they go wrong. But I believe that it is now more important than that. The new 'Babel' is a knowledge-based society. It is our job to throw as much light upon it as possible so that we can know as much about it as possible.

Many of the choices and dilemmas that will be placed before you will come as a result of some form of genetic test. Unless you know what is being tested it is difficult for you to come to an informed decision. Some tests look to see whether you have the standard forty-six chromosomes, others that the overall shape of the chromosomes appears to fit the normal pattern. Some look for individual spelling changes in specific locations on a chromosome, and still others analyse specific individual genes. When we come to look at technologies such as gene therapy, you will need to understand how a gene exerts its influence to be able to comprehend the likely benefits as well as the potential harm.

## Vive la différence

When we walk along the street we instantly recognise other human beings as part of our own species because of their remarkable similarity to each other. On the whole, they have a standard configuration of eyes, nose and mouth set close together within their face, ears tucked away on either side of a head which sits neatly on the shoulders. I could go on. However, that is not what we normally consider as being important. What are important to us are not the points of uniformity between people, but the elements of diversity – the minute detail that makes me different from everybody else in the world, everybody who has ever lived. Of all the millions of people there has never been a Pete Moore before, and there never will be again.

Even identical twins – and for that matter clones (if human clones ever happen) – are not absolutely identical. Every time a cell grows and divides into two it has to place a new copy of its entire set of genetic code into the new cell. Although the copying process is incredibly accurate there will be minor changes that slip through. By the time the embryonic bundle of cells splits to form two individuals, so-called identical twins, a catalogue of minor changes will have occurred. These differences will then be magnified by the fact that each individual will face a different set of environmental challenges and crises throughout life, which, along with the genetic code, influences development.

A critical aspect of these differences stems from our genetic make-up, the precise 'spelling' of each gene in our cells. The human genome project is busily chasing along the chromosomes, listing the sequence of bases as it goes, looking for code sequences that say 'start here' or 'stop now'. We now recognise other sequences that form standard types of proteins. When it is complete it will give a picture, a snapshot, of the DNA sequence of some fictitious individual. That's all well and good and it will have its uses. But that precise sequence will not be present in any individual cell in any real individual human being. What is already becoming more important is to find out which bits of the genome must be static, and which bits can be variable.

Hardly a week, maybe even a day, goes by without some announcement or other that a gene has been found for this or that disease. The sceptic in me wonders why the announcement is given such prominence in the news media, as it may be of interest but normally the news item ends with a qualifying statement that scientists anticipate it will be a number of years before they can do anything useful with the gene. I am always suspicious that it has more to do with a call for funding, rather than an announcement of progress.

Anyway, the gene has been found. What does this mean? One of the confusing points is that the reporting is often in terms of 'the gene for X disease has been found'. This gives the false impression that if this gene was absent the person would be free of the disease. This is not the case. What the statement means is that a gene has been located which if altered, mutated, results in the person being prone to the particular disease. Obviously that phrase is less catchy, but the truth is normally more complex than its presentation in the news.

There are various ways that a gene can be altered. A whole section of it can be missing, a feature called a deletion. This can obviously have a catastrophic effect on the performance of the gene as it may no longer be capable of producing the required protein. It may, however, still lead to some faulty protein being produced so long as the bit that says 'start reading here' is still present and working.

More commonly the situation is that only one base, one letter, of the code is missing, or altered. Returning to our little sentence, we can see what effect this has. Let's start by removing one letter, say the 'a' from 'can', and then re-sort the remainder into three-letter words.

*you cns eet hec ata ndt hed ogy es*

The simple absence of a single character has completely scrambled the code. Removing whole 'words' may be less of a problem as at least the rest are not disturbed. Also, if a few letters are altered, the meaning of the sentence can become very different. Let's replace 'see' with 'eat'.

*you can eat the cat and the dog yes*

So, minor alterations can cause major changes to the sentence. In the cell, equivalent alterations to the DNA sequence can affect either the numbers of individual protein molecules that are built, or their shape. Now each protein performs a particular task within a cell and if it is in excess or deficit the whole cell can be put out of balance. Severe diseases like cystic fibrosis and haemophilia are caused by single bases being missing from the code.

The 1988 edition of Victor McKusick's *Mendelian Inheritance in Man*, the clinical geneticist's bible, lists 2,208 diseases that have been proven to result from single gene defects. A further 2,136 are listed as 'probables', giving a total of 4,344.[12] No one has any idea how many diseases may be caused by faults in combinations of two or more genes, because so far the task of tracking them down is too complex.

How about the news stories that say the genes for long life, good health, intelligence or homosexuality have been found? What has actually happened is that researchers have looked at a group of people who have the trait in question and found that they all share a particular variation in their DNA, what scientists call a single nucleotide polymorphism (SNP), at a particular location on one of their chromosomes. All we have is a correlation between some minor genetic code change and the trait.

How strong is the link? In 1997 Professor Robert Plomin, a scientist based at the Institute of Psychiatry in London, claimed to have identified the first gene which affects intelligence. The gene in question gave the code for building a protein called insulin-like growth factor 2 receptor. Don't worry about its name, the issue is that he believes this gene is responsible for about two per cent of a person's intelligence. If you have a genetic sequence that leads to the production of the optimum amount of this protein, then your intelligence will be marginally enhanced over someone who has a less appropriate version. Plomin says that his research now makes it impossible for people to argue that genes do not influence intelligence.[13] In another piece of research, mice were given an extra gene that caused the overproduction of a particular brain protein. The researchers claimed that these mice subsequently learnt faster and had a better memory than others which had not been genetically 'enhanced'.[14] So, yes, genetics undoubtedly does have an influence over many complex

12. McKusick, V., *Mendelian Inheritance in Man*, eighth edition, Baltimore, MD: Johns Hopkins University Press, 1988.

13. Reported in *GenEthics News*, issue 20, October/November 1997, p. 3.

14. Tang, Y., Shimizu, E., Dube, G., Rampon, C., Kerchner, G.A., Zhou Min, Liu, G., and Tsien, J.Z., 'Genetic Enhancement of Learning and Memory in Mice', *Nature* **401**, 1999, pp. 63–69.

traits, but there are few situations, if any, when a single gene acts alone to control an aspect of a person's character, or their behaviour.

## Subtle difference

Diseases can be different. A single base alteration can dictate that a person will have cystic fibrosis or one of some 2,000 other identified conditions. But not all diseases are so easily linked to a genetic cause.

Cancer is one of the most serious medical issues, partly because we have such little control over it. So the announcements that genes have been found for breast and cervical cancer have been natural headline-makers. However, again we need to use language carefully. Families have been identified in which the women develop breast cancer much earlier than in the average population. These families have mutations in one of two genes. The genes have been called BRCA1 and BRCA2. The names sound pretty technical, until you find out that they mean Breast Cancer 1 and 2. That was about all they could be called when the genes were first located, because all that was known was that they were zones of the genetic code that were related to breast cancer.

The relationship has since been elucidated a little. The genes are now known to code for proteins that are either directly or indirectly involved in repairing faulty areas of chromosomes where the fault has arisen during the copying process that occurs when cells divide – a process called DNA replication. Cancer can occur if damage to a chromosome goes unnoticed, so without this repair mechanism, women are more susceptible to breast cancer. However, this does not mean any woman with this mutation will definitely get cancer, just that her risk is greater.

A similar issue exists for genes linked to cervical cancer, where a change in the coding of one particular gene can leave you at a greater risk of disease, but does not mean that you will definitely succumb. In this case it appears that an additional infection with papillomavirus raises the stakes. A report in *Nature* announced that variations in a gene that codes for a tumour-suppressing protein called p53 could leave a person at an increased risk of getting cervical cancer if they are infected by this virus, relative to people who have the more normal form of the gene.[15] Genes come in pairs, and if both copies of a woman's p53 gene are mutated, then she is seven times more susceptible to virus-induced cancer than a woman who has only one affected gene.

In this case, the person is more likely to get cervical cancer if she has a combination of two features. First, she has the mutation, and secondly, she picks up a particular viral infection. Having the mutation alone is not a problem. Thus we can see that so-called genetic diseases often need to have some environmental trigger. The cervical cancer gene is in fact a gene that codes for a protein that will combat viral infections. If you successfully fight the infection you remove or at least substantially reduce this particular risk of cervical cancer.

But don't fall into the trap of assuming that having damaged genes is always a disadvantage. A group of researchers at the University of Toronto have found that people are protected from becoming tobacco-dependent smokers if they have a damaged version of the gene that provides a protein needed for breaking down nicotine in the body.[16] Another case is sickle-cell anaemia, a disease that is most common in people with an African ethnic origin. The problem they face is that they have mutations in the gene involved in producing proteins in red blood cells, reducing the efficiency with which oxygen can be distributed throughout their bodies. While these changes lead to a blood disorder, they also play a role in protecting the person from infection with malaria. A child with a single copy of a 'sickle-cell gene' has a ninety per cent protection against developing severe symptoms of malaria if he or she becomes infected. Any future scheme aimed at removing the

15. Storey, A., Thomas, A., Kalita, A., Harwood, C., Gardiol, D., Mantovani, F.B.J., Leigh, I.M., Matlashewski, G., and Banks, L., 'Role of a p53 Polymorphism in the Development of Human Papillomavirus-Associated Cancer', *Nature* **393**, 1998, p. 229.

16. Pianezza, M.L., Sellers, E.M., and Tyndale, R.E., 'Nicotine Metabolism Defect Reduces Smoking', *Nature* **393**, 1998, p. 750.

sickle-cell gene from the population would carry the risk of leaving the people at an increased risk from malaria.

## Runs in the family

Back in the 1880s the Polish-born biologist Eduard Adolf Strasberger[17] and the German biologist Walter Fleming were separately studying the way that cells divide. They noticed that each time a cell splits into two, a process needed for any plant or animal to grow, the chromosomes within each cell initially doubled in number and then split equally between the two new cells. Around the turn of the last century, scientists began to think that chromosomes were the carriers of genetic identity. The problem was working out how a chromosome could store information and how this could be copied within a cell and with the incredible attention for detail that was obviously needed.

When Watson and Crick showed that DNA was formed as a double helix they presented a massive clue. They saw that the double-helical chromosomes had the potential to make copies of themselves and in their paper made the following famous statement: 'It has not escaped our notice that the specific pairing we have postulated immediately suggests a possible copying mechanism for the genetic material.'[18]

Once DNA was seen to be a pair of long chains with a series of cross-links, people quickly saw that the pair could separate and then draw in new A-, C-, G- or T-carrying subunits to form two new, but essentially identical, molecules. This concept also fitted with the evidence that various people had collected by watching cells divide under their standard light microscopes. In 1882, Walter Fleming had called the process mitosis, even though he was unaware of why it was occurring.

17. In 1882 Eduard Strasberger named the part of a cell outside the nucleus the cytoplasm, and the material contained in the nucleus the nucleoplasm.

18. Watson, J.D., and Crick, F.H., 'A Structure for Deoxyribonucleic Acid', *Nature* **171**, 1953, pp. 737–38.

Cells can divide at a remarkable pace. In an early embryo you get from one fertilised egg cell to a bundle of sixty-four cells in three to four days. To get to sixty-four means that six separate division stages must have occurred, the first yielding two cells, the second four, then eight, sixteen, thirty-two and finally sixty-four. This means that every sixteen hours each cell has copied all three billion letters of its code.

Not surprisingly, things sometimes go wrong. Errors are made. But the canny cell has machinery that wanders along the newly forming chromosomes and edits them to keep these changes, these mutations, down to a minimum. This is the error-correcting machinery that the breast cancer genes BRCA1 and BRCA2 appear to be involved with. Inevitably, though, a few do slip through and mutations are passed on to the next generation. With each generation of division the number of these changes increases. Most will have no particularly remarkable effect, but others can trigger diseases like cancer.

I recently talked with a man who had discovered that half of his muscles suffered from the disabling condition muscular dystrophy, while the other half were perfectly healthy. The most likely cause of this was that early in his life, as an embryo, one cell made a mistake as it copied its genetic code and damaged a muscle-protein gene. As that cell divided and moved through the embryo it became the ancestor of half of his muscles. With this damaged gene on-board, the muscles failed to operate properly and developed the classic wasting symptoms of the disease. However, all of the other muscles in his body developed from other cellular ancestors and so are free from the disease. Such people are said to have a 'mosaic' condition; they are effectively a patchwork of differing genetic types.

This case history also shows that the earlier in an individual's life a mutation occurs, the greater effect it is likely to have. One place where a lot of variation takes place is actually before an individual starts out – in the creation of sperm and egg. Each of us derives half of our chromosomes from our mother and half from our father.

Now, if egg and sperm were simply normal cells carrying the full complement of forty-six chromosomes, then with each generation the numbers of chromosomes would double. Ten generations later we would have 47,104 chromosomes per cell. Clearly that can't happen.

The solution to this was discovered in 1887 when the Belgian scientist Edouard-Joseph-Louis-Marie van Beneden found that each species had a fixed number of chromosomes. He also found that sperm and eggs had exactly half that number. Cleverly, or logically, this means that an egg and sperm combining gives the full forty-six.

As seems so often to be the case, we now realise that the process by which this is achieved is complex, but basically the cells that are specially adapted to create sperm and eggs initially duplicate their chromosomes before then separating out into four individual cells. Each cell therefore lands up with half the original number. Biologists call this process meiosis.

One thing I haven't explained so far is the business of chromosomes coming in pairs. It is as if the shelves in our library are arranged in pairs. If we think again of genes being individual books on the shelf, each of these two shelves carries the same set of titles stacked in the same order. One shelf is filled with books that came from the individual's mother, and the other with information that originated in the father.

Owing to the separate origins of each member of the chromosome pair – remembering that the genes from each parent will have their own unique combination of minor mutations – the precise information carried within each member of a pair of genes may be subtly different. For example, we all have two genes that bear the code for producing insulin, and they are found in exactly the same place on the two copies of chromosome 11. So far both chromosomes look identical. However, at a finer level of detail, the 'spelling' of the two genes could exhibit some variation – it is possible for one to carry the correct code for building insulin and the other a faulty code.

In human cells, each pair of chromosomes has a distinctive

shape when viewed down a microscope, and twenty-two of the pairs are numbered, according to their relative size, from 1 to 22, with 1 being the longest. (Unfortunately, scientists made a mistake and chromosome 21 is actually shorter than 22.) That accounts for forty-four chromosomes. The remaining pair are called the sex chromosomes. There are two types, named 'X' and 'Y'. If you have two X chromosomes you will be female and if you have one X and one Y you will be male. Because they determine sex they are called the 'sex chromosomes'; the others are collectively referred to as autosomes.

During the division of chromosomes between the forming sperm and eggs, one of each pair and one sex chromosome is drawn into each new cell. This means that each sperm and egg has a complete set of autosomal genes, plus one sex chromosome. Because female cells have two X chromosomes, when they separate to produce eggs the egg can only receive an X chromosome. On the other hand, male cells have one X and one Y chromosome, so in the sharing out that occurs during sperm formation, half of the sperm receive an X chromosome and the other half receive a Y chromosome. If an X-bearing sperm fertilises an egg the resulting embryo will have two X chromosomes and be female. If a Y-bearing sperm fertilises the egg, the XY embryo will be male.

The power of genetics lies in two key aspects. First, genetic information can be handed down from one generation to another, and secondly, when that handover occurs, the genes of different individuals are mixed. This mixing occurs on a number of levels.

We have seen that an individual is formed when maternal and paternal genes combine, but that is not the beginning of the genetic melting pot. As sperm and egg form, the pairs of chromosomes become deliberately entangled, break and form up again. In this 'crossover' process the newly formed chromosomes become a mixture of the two original ones. Where did the parent get these chromosomes from? From his or her parents. The result of this is that a person starts out life with chromosomes that are formed by physically mixing those of his or her four grandparents.

Such 'crossover' is normally very precise and results in the chromosome pair still having complete sets of genes. Even so, the exact content of genes on each chromosome has been mixed. On occasions, the process is not so clean, and errors are introduced into the genes. These errors may have sufficiently minor effects to allow the sperm or egg still to function properly, or they may cause it to become faulty. In this case, it could either not develop at all, or it could lead to the formation of an embryo that miscarries early, or results in a person with some genetic illness that has not been seen in the family before.

A good example of this in action is Duchenne muscular dystrophy. This is called an X-linked genetic disease because the damaged gene, the dystrophin gene, is present on the X chromosome. The dystrophin gene is huge, containing almost two and a half million characters, and because it is so big there is plenty of scope for bits of it to go missing during the copying process. As a result a third of boys with Duchenne muscular dystrophy are born to parents who have no family history of the disease.

Another peculiarity of many X-linked diseases is that females can carry the disease from one generation to another, but only males suffer from it. To complicate the terminology even further, these are called X-linked recessive diseases. If a male receives an X chromosome from his mother, who has a faulty dystrophin gene, he will get the disease. In most cases, the disease is so severe very few or no boys live long enough to have children of their own; consequently they won't pass the gene on. However, a boy would have received the mutated gene from his mother, either because it was a new mutation that formed as the egg was being built, or because his mother's cells had one X chromosome with the damaged gene on it, but the other X chromosome had a fully working copy. The working copy of the gene ensures that she is perfectly healthy, but she is still capable of passing on the faulty copy. In fact, on average, half of her sons will have the disease, and half of her daughters will be carriers. Any daughters will be unaffected, because they receive a copy of the X chromosome from their father, so even if they get their mother's damaged Duchenne gene they will get a compensating gene from their father.

A recessive genetic disease is one where the symptoms only occur if there is no healthy copy of the gene present. If the mutated gene is on one of the paired autosomes, there is normally a second good copy on the corresponding partner. This good copy allows the cell to build functioning versions of the protein in question and so the cell is unaffected. Trouble only starts if both copies of the gene are damaged.

In other diseases, mutations cause the cell to build proteins that are actively damaging. In this case one version of this mutated gene is not balanced out by another healthy copy. The mutation is now called 'dominant'.

I hope that seeing where genetic variation can occur in the biological system, and getting a glimpse of some of the ways that mutant genes can influence things, will help you as we look at how we can manipulate the genetic heritage hidden in each cell.

# Chapter 3

# THE TOOLS
# OF BABEL

It doesn't take much imagination to realise that working with chromosomes and genes is not a simple matter of staring down microscopes to read coded instructions and then using scissors and glue to cut some bits out and stick in others. However, geneticists do have a remarkably efficient set of tools that allows them to analyse DNA, to determine the sequence of codes and then to manipulate that information. Having a broad understanding of the nature of these tools will help us to understand the claims of genetic scientists, as well as have a better chance of deducing what is and what is not likely to be possible in the reasonably near future.

The vast majority of our knowledge about genetics comes from studying bacteria and viruses. These bugs have shown us that the DNA in the centre of each cell is remarkably ready to give tantalising glimpses of its secrets, but highly reluctant to reveal all. However, the pace at which new discoveries can be put to use is rapid, because of the way that DNA behaves. Bacteria have one chromosome; fruit flies (*Drosophila*) have eight chromosomes; onions, sixteen; cats, thirty-eight; humans, forty-six; potatoes, forty-eight; and dogs, seventy-eight, but the chromosomes themselves are all built of DNA and all follow the same basic set of rules and principles, whatever organism they are found in. Therefore, discoveries made while working with bacterial DNA have immediate implications for people working on human genetics, and, as we will see, genes that originate in one species can be moved to another.

When people first started dreaming about the possibility of

reading the code inside human cells the task seemed impossibly large. Let's face it, writing down three billion characters would be hard enough, but making the information accessible to anyone would be tantamount to impossible. Then came the desktop computer and computer-storage technology which makes it possible to access that much information from every laboratory in the world, while providing analysis tools that can search through, looking for patterns.

The pace at which powerful personal computers have marched into the laboratory means that the early predictions of how long it would take to map the entire human genome now seem terribly pessimistic. The American National Institute of Health kicked off the project in 1991 and by 1997 some 10,000 of the estimated 30,000 genes were fully characterised. At that time estimates varied, but some people believed that the full genetic sequence would be mapped out by the year 2005. Others suggested a more conservative figure of 2020. Fact is often stranger than fiction, and a 'working draft' of the sequence has now been written down, with a fully accurate sequence to be completed sometime after 2003. Do remember, though, that this 'draft' is inaccurate and when first announced in 2000 only twenty-five per cent of the code was known accurately.

Whatever the rate of progress, right now we need to concern ourselves with what sort of information the tools are capable of collecting. The first level of detail is obviously a quick count of the number of chromosomes present in the cell. This is fairly simple, though you have to catch the cells when they are in the process of dividing if you want to see them as the classic dumb-bell-shaped blobs that are normally shown on television documentaries and in grainy newspaper photos. They take on the appearance of these tightly packed structures so that the cells can divide, but for the rest of the time they exist as filaments that are too fine to see with a standard light microscope.

## Understanding inheritance

Having counted the chromosomes we now need to work out which genes are on which one. The task is halved in size because chromosomes occur in pairs, each member of the pair bearing the same basic set of genes. But what is needed is a map showing where the genes are and how they relate to each other.

Born in Whitby, Yorkshire, in 1861, William Bateson liked to be known as the 'father of genetics'. Educated at Rugby and then Cambridge, he became Britain's first professor of genetics at Cambridge in 1908 and then moved to be director of the newly formed John Innes Horticultural Institution where he remained until he died in 1926. Bateson was an opponent of the theory that chromosomes were the repositories of genetic inheritance, and opposed Darwin's ideas of natural selection.[1]

However, Bateson produced the first translation of Mendel's hereditary studies and, working with his colleague R.C. Punnet, he pursued Mendel's ideas of inheritance. While Mendel had studied the shape and colour of peas, Bateson and Punnet looked at the colour of sweet-pea flowers and the shape of their pollen grains. They showed that various traits had a tendency to be inherited together. More plants produced purple flowers with long-grained pollen than would have been expected if the traits were being inherited independently of each other. Their conclusion was that the two independent units of inheritance must have been physically attached to each other. The physical location of this information within the cell was, they felt, yet to be discovered.

On the other side of the Atlantic Ocean, Thomas Hunt Morgan (1866–1945) was doing the same sort of work with fruit flies. As the professor of experimental zoology at Columbia University and then at the California Institute of Technology, he started to map his findings onto diagrams of the fly's chromosomes. If traits had a tendency to be inherited together, he placed them near to each other. If they were seldom linked, he separated them

---

1. It is always fascinating to look back at scientific progress and see how it stumbles forward through a series of correct and false hypotheses. Just because we have the benefit of hindsight we should never allow ourselves to be lulled into thinking that our current ideas will survive the test of time any better.

in his diagrams. This major breakthrough in genetics earned him the 1933 Nobel prize for physiology and medicine. Arguably, a lot of his ideas came from a student of his, Alfred Henry Sturtevant, whose interest in genetics had developed from an enthusiasm for devising pedigrees for his father's farm horses.[2] Sturtevant appears to have had the initial idea for chromosome mapping and published a pioneering paper in 1913, showing the relative position of several genes in the fruit fly's genome. He described what happened:

*In the latter part of 1911, in conversations with Morgan, I suddenly realised that the variations in strength of linkage, already attributed by Morgan to differences in the spatial separation of genes, offered the possibility of determining sequences in the linear dimension of a chromosome. I went home and spent most of the night (to the neglect of my undergraduate homework) in producing the first chromosome map.*[3]

So often when geneticists are talking about the location of genes, they are referring to these theoretical maps constructed as a process of studying patterns of inheritance. They are not saying they know the precise location on a chromosome, nor its sequence, and certainly not the protein that it is responsible for building. All the same, these chromosome maps are extremely important in constructing our tower of knowledge, but it is important to be aware of current limitations.

In addition, all this work relies on deliberately interbreeding whole populations of the organism of interest. If the organism is a fruit fly, that presents few problems. When the organism under scrutiny is a human being, we are obviously going to have to take a

2. Alfred Henry Sturtevant was born in 1891 in Jacksonville, Illinois, and died in 1970. From 1928 he worked at the California Institute of Technology where he retained his interest in animal genetics, but also developed a special interest in the lives of social insects.

3. Quoted in *An Introduction to Genetic Analysis*, 5th edition, New York: W.H. Freeman and Company, 1993, p. 124.

fresh approach. Running breeding programmes to test human hybrids would not get through any ethical committee.

## Placing markers

The key to finding your way to information contained in a library is to place plenty of markers on the bookcases and shelves. Some of the markers may be immediately obvious to anyone who can read, such as a notice saying 'Archaeology', 'Paediatrics' or 'Children's Fiction'. Other markers take the form of catalogue codes and are spelt out in combinations of letters and numbers. Different libraries use different systems, but each system covers the entire variety of available books. A couple of letters written on fading pieces of cardboard and hung on the end of each shelf is all that is needed to give a strong lead to anyone searching for information.

In the same way genetic gene hunters have built elaborate systems of markers throughout the human genome. As scientists love to sound clever by using big names they call the markers 'restriction sites'.

The history behind this mapping system has its roots in the work of the Swiss microbiologist Werner Arber. In the 1960s he proposed that when bacteria fight off attacks by certain viruses, they do so by chopping up the DNA inside the invading virus. What he realised was that the viral DNA was always cut at specific places. He found that specific protein units called enzymes did this cutting, and because these enzymes restricted the virus's ability to infect the bacteria he called them 'restriction enzymes'.[4] Once again a Nobel prize was handed out, this time in 1978. The prize was shared by two professors working at the Johns Hopkins Medical School, USA – Hamilton Smith and Daniel Nathans.

Smith's role in the research had been to discover why the

---

4. Restriction enzymes are named after the bacteria they are taken from. For example, all enzymes isolated from *Escherichia coli* strain RY13 start with the letters *Eco*R. The number that follows this simply indicates how many others have been isolated from that strain. So the first would be *Eco*RI, the second *Eco*RII and so on.

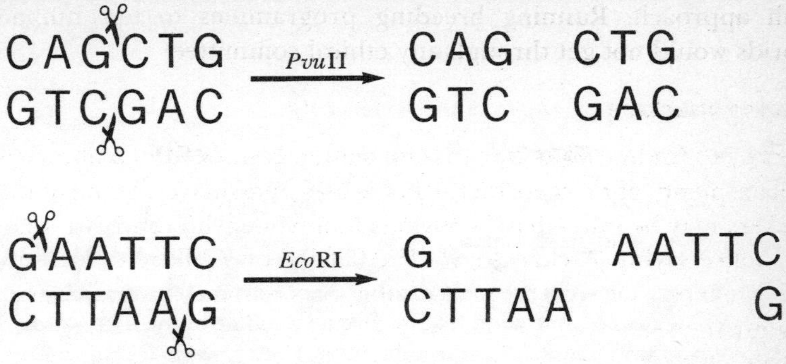

Figure 4: One of the simplest restriction enzymes to understand is called *Pvu*II. This looks for a place where there is a sequence CAGCTG on one side of the DNA and GTCGAC on the other. It locks on and makes a straight cut across the chromosome. Another example is *Eco*RI, which makes a staggered cut.

enzymes always chose to act at specific locations. Working on one particular strain of bacterium, *Haemophilus influenzae*, and one virus called T7 bacteriophage, he isolated one type of enzyme from the bacterium and found that it always cut the bacteriophage DNA into forty fragments. Moreover, each of these fragments had the same small selection of code sequences at the ends. He suggested that this was because the enzyme could only operate by locking onto specific code sequences in the DNA (see Figure 4). His theory appears to be valid. Since this discovery over 500 restriction enzymes have been discovered that each have their own specific cutting sequences.

But what's so exciting about being able to cut up the DNA into pieces? Of prime importance is that scientists have been able to build up maps of each chromosome, showing the various sites where each of a number of restriction enzymes cleave (see Figure 5). Because the scientists can then calculate the size of the bit of chromosome between two cleavage sites they effectively act as milestones, marking out relative distances.

A clue to the mindset of the people who are doing this work comes from the language they use. Like the eighteenth-century

If we think of restriction sites as vowels in a sentence, then this is how we would find the order of the sites in a simple sentence.

**Step 1:** Make multiple copies of the sentence:

the-cat-sat-and-ate-the-mat

**Step 2:** Add a marker molecule to the beginning of each sequence:

**M**the-cat-sat-and-ate-the-mat

**Step 3:** Expose the sequence to an enzyme that chops it up by removing 'a', but use it at a concentration that only removes some of the letters. You get a series of different lengths, all stopping just before each 'a'. However, the only fragments you can detect are those that have the marker attached:

**M**the-c
**M**the-cat-s
**M**the-cat-sat-
**M**the-cat-sat-and-
**M**the-cat-sat-and-ate-the-m

**Step 4:** Now take all the longest fragments and divide them into two groups. Expose one group to the enzyme that removes 'a' and the other group to an enzyme that removes 'e'. You land up with two sets of fragments that can each be arranged in order of their length:

| Remove 'e' | Map | Remove 'a' |
|---|---|---|
| **M**th | e | |
| | a | **M**the-c |
| | a | **M**the-cat-s |
| | a | **M**the-cat-sat- |
| | a | **M**the-cat-sat-and- |
| **M**the-cat-sat-and-at | e | |
| **M**the-cat-sat-and-ate-th | e | |
| | a | **M**the-cat-sat-and-ate-the-m |

**The result:** After all this work you know that the restriction-site sequence – the map – is '**e a a a a e e a**' and you have an idea of the relative distances between them. However, this is still a long way from knowing the full text of the sequence.

Figure 5: Restriction mapping.

navigator Captain James Cook, today's intrepid explorers feel that they are searching an unknown territory, building charts and creating maps. Markers are referred to as mileposts or landmarks and some people call the whole process genetic topography. Some techniques are called 'chromosome walking', where the DNA is mapped out in large paces, and 'chromosome jumping', where even larger steps are taken.

Again we need to take stock of the limitations. Restriction maps in themselves only describe the layout of a series of almost arbitrary points and give no indication of the content or function of the code in that area. However, it is sometimes possible to find which of the fragments contains an individual gene and thereby to start to narrow down the region of a chromosome where the gene resides. A fragment of DNA, and therefore the genes that it contains, can then be chopped out from its original chromosome and inserted into other cells. If conditions are right, the host cell will start to produce the protein that the genes code for, which is a very powerful way of assessing what individual genes actually do.

The host usually used for this process is a bacterium. Bacterial colonies increase in size very rapidly. In some, the individual members can copy their DNA and be ready to divide many times a day.[5] If they have had new DNA added to them, the number of copies of that DNA will increase at the same rate. So not only can this provide information about the nature of the gene, it can also multiply the number of copies of the gene available for research.

If a gene can be identified in a known fragment produced by restriction enzymes, then the gene can be marked on the restriction map. This can then be compared to the previously discussed chromosome map to check that they agree. Double-checking is always a good way of both confirming things and spotting errors.

---

5. Because the process generates multiple copies of identical modified bacteria this process has been called cloning. Don't get confused with this and the sort of clone that most people think of when they talk about reproductive cloning in animals and human beings.

Mouse cells have also proved to be very useful in sorting out which genes are on which chromosome. In a somewhat complex process, geneticists mix human and mouse cells together in a laboratory dish and then add a virus, Sendai virus. This particular combination results in the production of cells that initially contain a complete set of mouse chromosomes along with a complete set of human chromosomes. However, as these hybrid cells grow and divide, some of the human chromosomes are lost. Eventually cells remain that have all of the mouse chromosomes and only one or two human chromosomes.[6] By studying the way that these cells behave, it is possible to work out which genes are on each human chromosome.

## Spotting mutations

In addition, restriction enzymes can sometimes point to the location of a new mutation – a genetic spelling mistake. If a single base is changed in the chromosome, this could create a new area of code that an enzyme can latch onto, or alternatively it could block a previously available restriction site. Such polymorphisms[7] are extremely useful if you can find a group of people with an identical alteration in a single chromosome who also share a common genetic disease. In this case, this is taken as a strong indication of the location of the gene that is at the centre of the condition. The nature or function of the gene remains a mystery, but it is a good start.

A lot of valuable data have been gained from looking for unique polymorphisms in families where a particular genetic illness has spread through many generations. Tracking down the gene for cystic fibrosis is a prime example. The breakthrough was announced in August 1989 by Francis Collins from the University of Michigan in Ann Arbor, USA, and Lap-Chee Tusi and John Riordan from the University of Toronto. By studying the chromosomes from

6. The process is called 'somatic cell hybridisation', because the cells used are standard body (somatic) cells.

7. 'Polymorphism' is Latin for 'many forms'. It is used to describe the variation in physical outcome that is caused by a small genetic difference between individuals.

a 100-member family group that was affected by the disease, they found that a single spelling mistake, a polymorphism, in a 250,000-base gene on chromosome 7, was consistently linked to cystic fibrosis. When the gene sequence was analysed, they realised that it was very similar to genes that build proteins designed to pump salt across membranes. The link between this gene and the symptoms of the disease suddenly became clear as salt movement and water movement in cells is highly linked. In cystic fibrosis, secretions in the lungs, intestines, pancreas and sweat glands are thick and sticky. Damaged salt pumps were preventing secretory tissues from functioning properly.

This sort of work is relatively successful, but it demands that you have a large family with a clearly identifiable disease so that you can obtain enough samples.

## Studying multiple copies

The way I have described things so far (and the way others tend to leave them) gives the impression that a scientist is taking one bacterium and one piece of DNA or a single enzyme and carefully introducing each to the other. While this is indeed possible to achieve, it is seldom done. Most genetic research demands that thousands and millions of identical bacteria are treated with equivalent numbers of identical fragments of DNA. To achieve this we need a method for taking small quantities of the desired section of DNA code and multiplying it.

Thankfully, at about the time that some scientists were developing tools to cut specific sections out of a chain of DNA, others were looking at the cells' own photocopying machinery. In 1959 American biochemist Arthur Kornberg shared a Nobel prize with Spanish-born Severo Ochoa in recognition of their discovery of an enzyme which enables cells to duplicate their own DNA. This 'DNA polymerase' has now been captured and put to work in machines that can take a single copy of a DNA sequence and generate a million identical copies within hours. Throughout the world this is know as PCR – the polymerase chain reaction. The process works by using the original DNA as a template and generating a second copy. These two copies are then used simultaneously as new templates, which thus generate four. From four we proceed to eight, then sixteen, and after twenty cycles you reach one million. Remarkably, each cycle only takes a few minutes.

## Reading the sequence

So far the sort of information collected by all of the tools is pretty vague. We have maps showing the relative locations of places where enzymes can cut through the chromosome. We have indications of which chromosome particular genes may be located on, and snippets of information about the sequence of those genes. We can even deliberately cut out a section of DNA that contains a particular gene and insert it into a host cell so that we can analyse the protein that it builds. But this is still a long way from knowing the exact location of a particular gene, and a huge way from establishing the sequence of the gene's genetic code.

But sequencing is happening. The key to this process is to start with a few thousand copies of a known fragment of DNA, each of which has a tiny lump of a radioactive chemical attached to one end. The DNA is then divided between four test tubes, and a different chemical added to each. In one the chemical attacks the G bases in the code, in another it attacks As and Gs. The third one attacks Ts and Cs and the last goes for Cs only. The amount of chemical is carefully adjusted so that only one in fifty target bases is destroyed. With the base removed the DNA chain breaks.

Consequently a series of chains is built, each starting with the radioactive unit and ending at the point where the target base would have been. This would be useless if there was no method of finding out the lengths of each fragment of DNA. But gel electrophoresis provides the answer. A shallow tray is filled with material much like the sort of jelly that children love at parties; this agarose gel is allowed to set. Then each of the four partially digested DNA samples is placed in its own small well, dug into the surface of the gel. An electric charge is then applied across the plate and, because the DNA fragments have a small electric charge of their own, this causes them to start moving through the gel. The smaller fragments manage to travel faster and so within a few minutes all of the fragments are distributed through the gel according to size. Finding where in the gel the fragments have got to is easy because all you have to do is lay an X-ray plate on top. As the fragments were attached to radioactive molecules, the radioactivity will expose the plate.

We've all seen the result many times in newspapers and TV: it is a translucent X-ray film with rows of dark fuzzy lines that looks reminiscent of a bar code. Normally TV programmes will set the scene in coloured light to try to give an air of excitement and wonder as the white-coated bespectacled scientist pores over the film, pointing with the tip of a ballpoint pen at the columns. The code sequence is remarkably easy to read, and normally a standard computer does the code-breaking. If there is a mark in the G column and the G+A column, then this signifies that G was present at this point in the code. If the mark is in the G+A column alone, then it must have been an A. A similar process is involved in deducing whether a C or a T was present from the information in the C and the C+T columns. The whole process is called base-destruction sequencing (see Figure 6) and, in recognition of the method's usefulness, American molecular biologists Walter Gilbert and Paul Berg and English biochemist Frederick Sanger[8] shared the 1980 Nobel prize for chemistry.

A second system of sequencing has since been developed by Sanger that involves building new DNA chains rather than destroying them. Like base-destruction sequencing, this 'dideoxy sequencing' is easy to automate and can rapidly determine the sequence of bases in specific stretches of a chromosome.

Both techniques are very simple to operate and remarkably effective. The only thing holding back our knowledge of the entire

8. This was Sanger's second Nobel prize. The first had been awarded in 1958 when he worked out the amino acid sequence in insulin and showed that there were minor differences between the insulin from human beings, pigs, sheep, horses and whales.

Use gene cloning to produce many copies of the fragment of DNA to be analysed and attach a radioactive phosphate group to one end of each fragment.

separate the two strands of DNA

**Key stage**
Divide strands into four samples and treat each sample with a chemical that selectively destroys either one or two bases – removing a base causes the strand to break at that location.

removes G    removes A and G    removes C    removes T and C

The concentration of reagent is adjusted so that only one out of every fifty bases is removed. Consequently, some fragments will have only one base removed.

Using gel electrophoresis the fragments of DNA in these samples are separated, and the lengths of any fragments that have a radioactive phosphate group are determined.

The length of each chain is the distance from the marked end to that from which a particular base was removed.

Adding together all the information gained from the four different reagents, a complete account of the sequence can be found.

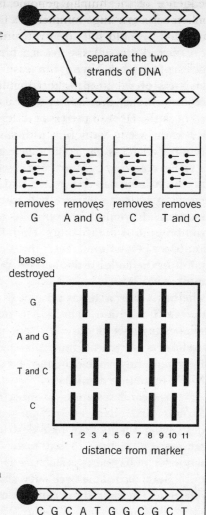

bases destroyed

G

A and G

T and C

C

1 2 3 4 5 6 7 8 9 10 11
distance from marker

C G C A T G G C G C T

Figure 6: Base-destruction sequencing.

sequence of the human genome is therefore its vast size. Three billion bases is a huge number. If a machine could work out one base a second it would still take over ninety-five years to sort it out.

Simple, buy ninety-five machines and it's done in a year. Sorry to disappoint, but it is not that easy. Each section of code needs to be analysed several times to check that the data obtained is reproducible, and to compare the code of several different people. It is important to check the DNA of people of different races if the database is going to give the most complete representation of the code. Hence the need for a concerted effort – the human genome project.

So now we have tools that allow us to identify which genes are on which chromosomes, and to pace up and down the chromosomes placing arbitrary markers that assist our exploration. We can also determine the sequence of sections of chromosomes, and within time will have the sequence of entire chromosomes stored away in a neat computer database.

However, that is the simple bit. The difficult bit is now to work out where in all this code the genes are hiding. Thankfully this task is aided by the fact that genes do not sit there on their own, but are accompanied by a package of coding areas that act as controlling units promoting genes to be copied to mRNA, or restricting the availability of each gene. These areas have common code sequences, so an automated search can identify possible places within the chromosome where a gene may start. Similar codes exist at the end of a gene that act like a full stop in a sentence, and in many ways they can be considered to add punctuation to the sentences.

Another route to identifying the location and sequence of specific genes is to study their product and work backwards. You can study the end protein and work out the sequence of amino acids that makes it and from that make a prediction of the genetic code that acted as its blueprint. Alternatively, it is possible to collect the mRNA that comes out of the nucleus and find the sequence of its bases. Both of these methods would be extremely powerful if genes were simple continuous linear codes. Unfortunately this is not the case. Within many genes there are sections of code that are ignored or cut out at various parts of the process leading from a DNA sequence to the eventual protein. As a result, the DNA base sequence that you would deduce just by looking at the final protein or the mRNA may be significantly shorter than that actually existing on the area of the chromosome.

Still this tool can achieve results. If you can find a portion of a protein that has a unique sequence of amino acids, it is possible to build a section of DNA that corresponds to it. Automated machines now routinely synthesise lengths of DNA containing up to sixty bases within a few hours. Add a radioactive label to this segment of DNA and introduce it to a cell under appropriate conditions, and remarkably it will find its way to the area of the chromosome that has the same code sequence. Because the DNA has a radioactive label attached, you can discover where it has gone and therefore pinpoint the location of the gene.

So we can slowly gather information about the code-carrying base sequence on each chromosome and impose on this a map showing the position of various genes. In time we can determine the sequence of individual genes and that of the protein they allow to be built. However, if that was all, few people would be desperately excited about it.

## New from old

The key to the current heightened interest in DNA and genetic technology is that now we know vast stretches of code we can start to play with it. We can alter the genetic make-up of individual cells and of whole multicellular organisms. The remarkable thing is that you can take DNA from any organism and move it to pretty well any other. Genes that produce proteins which prevent arctic fish from freezing can be moved to tomatoes or other plants to make them resistant to frost. The genes for proteins that make jellyfish fluoresce have been placed in mice, giving them a ghostly green glow in the dark.[9] Genes

9. Perry, A.C., Wakayama, T., Kishikawa, H., Kasai, T., Okabe, M., Toyoda, Y., and Yanagimachi, R., 'Mammalian Transgenesis by Intracytoplasmic Sperm Injection', *Science* **284**, 1999, pp. 1180–83.

for human alpha-1-antitrypsin, a protein needed to treat people with the lung diseases emphysema and cystic fibrosis, have been moved into a sheep named Tracy. The genes have been 'engineered' in such a way that she produces this molecule in her milk.[10, 11] Collect the milk, purify the protein and bingo, you have a treatment, though not a cure, for the diseases. In all other respects, Tracy seems to be completely unaffected by the foreign gene. Clinical trials with this protein have now begun and the company that owns Tracy, PPL Therapeutics plc,[12] hopes to have commercial production of the protein up and running in the early 2000s. Since Tracy arrived on the scene, other sheep have been created that produce a range of different human proteins in their milk, all of which are candidates for use in combating specific human diseases.

To cure the disease you would need to move the gene into the patient, rather than into a sheep. This brings us to the realm of gene therapy, the idea of curing genetic disease by tackling the fundamental genetic error. To an extent it is a wonderful idea, but as we will see it is fraught with difficulties.

Taking a broader look at the possibilities, in theory you might be able to move the package of genes that enables a plant to make chlorophyll and place it in humans. Chlorophyll is the pigment that causes a plant to be green and enables it to trap the energy contained in sunlight, thus making it available to the plant's cells. Dr Richard Seed, who first shot to international fame over his claims to be trying to clone human beings, spoke of this sort of possibility with great enthusiasm at a meeting at the Royal Society in London in March 1999. 'Just think,' he laughed, 'this genetically "enhanced" person

10. Wright, G., Carver, C., Cottom, D., Reeves, D., Scott, A., Simons, P., Wilmut, I., Garner, I., and Colman, A., 'High-Level Expression of Active Human alpha-1-antitrypsin in the Milk of Transgenic Sheep', *Biotechnology* **9**, September 1991, pp. 786–88.

11. Carver, A., Wright, G., Cottom, D., Cooper, J., Dalrymple, M., Temperley, S., Udell, M., Reeves, D., Percy, J., Scott, A., et al., 'Expression of Human alpha-1-antitrypsin in Transgenic Sheep', *Cytotechnology* **9 (1–3)**, 1992, pp. 77–84.

12. The company started out as Pharmaceutical Proteins Ltd, and PPL has survived into its current corporate identity.

would be able to have a snack simply by taking a stroll in the sun. An hour's sunbathing would be a meal.' The idea may seem gross, but it strikes me as mild when compared with his other ideas, such as playing around with genes so as to place an eye on the end of your finger, thus making reading easier.

Stepping back rapidly from the Mad Hatter's Wonderland tea party, let's see what is possible at the moment and what the more immediate future may hold. We have already seen that it is possible to build genes if you know the base sequence you are after. More often, scientists prefer to use genes they have taken directly from cells. Why build them if you can find them lying around for the taking? Using combinations of restriction enzymes and gel plates they have devised ways of snipping out sections of DNA with remarkable accuracy. Using systems like PCR these sections can be rapidly multiplied. Now all you have to do is get them into the new target cell and get the gene to work once it has arrived.

Cells seem to be reluctant to cooperate in this venture, but a bizarre range of techniques has been developed and many have shown a measure of success. One of the first methods to be used involves quite simply firing the DNA into a new cell from a specially adapted gun. Once inside the cell the fragment of DNA seems to join in cellular activity and starts to initiate the production of its protein.

More commonly, genes are added first to modified bacteria or bacteriophages – viruses that infect bacterial cells – and these are invited to infect the target cells. As they do, these 'vectors' carry with them a payload of the gene in question. Other systems involve wrapping the genes in globules of fat and letting these 'lyposomes' diffuse through the cell membrane, thus transporting the gene into the cell.

But getting the gene in is only one of the problems. Another issue arises when the new DNA takes up residence, first within the target cell and secondly within the whole organism. Within the cell the DNA may exist as a free-floating entity. On one hand, circles of DNA from bacteria seem to be particularly stable and capable of existing and functioning inside cells. On the other hand, other techniques cause the DNA to break into the existing chromosomes and become part of the main DNA chain. This has the advantage that the gene is permanently added to the chromosomal material, so that as the cell divides each new copy of the cell will contain the novel genetic material. However, it also has the disadvantage that we have no control over where it decides to break in and make its home. There is every possibility that the gene may insert itself right in the middle of some other gene sequence, therefore destroying the original code, a destruction that could be lethal or at least damaging for the cell. A more major alternative is to introduce a novel chromosome, a huge unit of DNA comprising many tens or even hundreds of genes. This could exist within the nucleus and be duplicated alongside the others.

## Gene therapy

But where in the body? From the geneticist's point of view there are two basic types of cell, somatic and germ line. *Soma* means body, so somatic cells are the cells that make up our bodies, skin, bone and most internal organs. Germ-line cells are those involved in producing sperm in males and eggs in females. The significance is that if you genetically alter a somatic cell then the changes cannot be passed on to any offspring; change the genes in a germ cell and future generations can be affected.

At the moment in the UK, radical genetic modifications are allowed to plants, but regulations forbid any process that will alter the germ cells in humans,[13] though they do allow for experimental treatment that aims to manipulate the genetic content of somatic cells.

13. The 1992 Report of the Committee on the Ethics of Gene Therapy [Cm 1788], which was chaired by Cecil Clothier, reviewed the risks of germ-line therapy:

'Gene modification at an early stage of embryonic development, before differentiation of the germ line, might be a way of correcting gene defects in both the germ-line and somatic cells. However, we share the view of others that there is at present insufficient knowledge to evaluate the risk to future generations...

'We recommended, therefore, that gene modification of the germ line should not yet be attempted.'

This has been the source of a huge debate. If it is possible to use gene therapies to effectively remove a disease from someone, why limit it to that person alone by restricting yourself to techniques that place the new gene only in somatic cells? Why not introduce it into the germ cells? The answer is that right now we have too little information about the long-term effects of any such treatment, and with long-term we need to be thinking not of years or decades, but of family generations. With people choosing to have children later in life, this means thirty or forty years for each generation studied. However, it is noteworthy that the Clothier Committee, which was given the task of drawing up guidelines for the use of gene therapies, said that these techniques should not 'yet' be allowed, leaving the door to future reconsideration of this slightly ajar.[14]

An ideal genetic therapy would allow you to correct faulty genes as they sit there in their chromosomes. To be truly effective this would need to occur in every cell in the body.

A problem with some potential gene-therapy procedures is that genes would be added almost at random to the existing genome. While this would allow them to be passed to future generations of that cell line, this stands a high chance of disrupting the existing code and causing as much damage as it repairs. On top of this, only small lumps of DNA can be added at any one time. To combat this, some scientists have pursued the idea of creating artificial chromosomes. At a biotechnology conference in London in October 1999, Eileen Utterson, the vice-president of Chromos Molecular Systems of Burnaby, British Colombia, announced that they had built an artificial chromosome which, when placed into mice, was inherited by future generations just like any other chromosome.[15] The company intends to use this process to generate large numbers of sheep or cows that could mass-produce pharmaceuticals in their milk, but it also gives rise to the possibility of using it to introduce genes to humans in a form of germ-line gene therapy. This is just the sort of

14. The 1992 Report of the Committee on the Ethics of Gene Therapy.

15. First reported in *New Scientist*, 23 October 1999, pp. 4–5.

process envisioned by Lee Silver in *Remaking Eden*, when he suggests that people will add whole new chromosomes to very early embryos, with genes designed to combat disease and generally enhance the experience of life. The result of that, he surmises, will be a population of GenRich humans who will be unwilling or unable to breed with the standard 'unenhanced' individuals.

While a few scientists are looking into this possibility, it is not seen as a front runner in the race to produce a useful gene therapy. Instead, scientists are concentrating on developing delivery systems that place the gene just in some of the cells of the organs that are particularly affected by the genetic error. The hope is that 'correcting' just some of the cells will substantially reduce the effects of the disease.

Examples of this approach are the techniques being developed to treat people with cystic fibrosis. While the disease affects all tissues that secrete mucus, the effect it has on the lungs is particularly debilitating. However, the lungs also present a wonderful opportunity, because you can gain easy access to them. Suspend a gene in an aerosol and breathe in, and the gene will spread over the airways. This is, in effect, the same sort of inhaler that so successfully delivers steroids to asthma sufferers.

At first sight, cystic fibrosis seemed to be a good starting point for trials of gene therapy because the science of the disease was established fairly clearly. The gene involved had been pinpointed and its sequence was known. The protein resulting from the gene was also known and scientists were sure that they knew its function within the cell. This protein sits in the cell's membrane and pumps chloride ions from one side to the other. In doing so it establishes an electric charge across the membrane which is necessary for the cell to function properly. On top of this the disease is extremely restrictive for people who have it, so any form of improvement would be welcomed. It was therefore relatively easy to find patients willing to join in on experimental trials.

In 1993 I went to a press conference at a scientific meeting in Glasgow where I was told of the exciting developments that would deliver gene therapy for cystic fibrosis within the next five or so years. At the 1999 meeting of the American Society for Gene Therapy people seemed less confident. At the moment the best gene therapies only seem to succeed in getting genes into fewer than ten per cent of cells that line the airway. The reason for this poor uptake is uncertain. And this is not the end of the problems. Based on the initial ideas of the science behind cystic fibrosis, it was hoped that even if only five or ten per cent of cells had the gene on-board, they would be capable of pumping sufficient quantities of chloride ions to make a radical improvement. However, recent work suggests that life is not that simple. It appears that this protein may have many other functions in the cells as well as acting as a chloride pump, and that a higher uptake may be needed. The challenge continues.

On top of this, while the systems in use deliver the genes into cells, these genes do not become incorporated into the chromosomal DNA. Consequently, when the cells grow and divide during the normal process of living, the new genes are lost from the new generation of cells. To make up for this loss, the patient needs to repeatedly inhale new doses of the gene and so 'treat' the new generation of cells. This in turn has consequences on the nature of the vector that can be used to transport the gene. Viral vectors are often used, but if they are repeatedly given then the patient develops a potent immune response that will destroy them before they have delivered their payload.

So why not try to place the new gene within the genome? The gene is deliberately not incorporated into the chromosome, partly because that process is more complex and, more particularly, because of the danger of disrupting other needed genes during the process, and leaving the person with another disease caused by this new genetic accident.

The other problem with building a long-term treatment for cystic fibrosis points to another deficiency in our biological knowledge. Cells like those lining our airways have lifespans of weeks and months and are constantly being replaced by actions of a parent generation of cells called 'stem cells'. However, no one has managed to identify the stem cells that build the airway lining, so no one yet knows what cells really need targeting to provide a long-term cure for cystic fibrosis.

Despite all the current setbacks, cystic fibrosis is an example of a disease that has the potential for being tackled by the giving of a gene that produces the appropriate protein. However, there are times when, rather than stimulating production, you might want to turn off a particular gene. The most famous example of this type of approach comes not from medicine, but agriculture. It is the genetically modified (GM) Flavr Savr tomato, introduced to the world by Calgene Inc. of Davis, California, in the early 1990s, that has now found its way into so much of our tomato purée. The particular modification carried out in this case has been the addition of an 'antisense' gene. The idea is to introduce a gene which generates a piece of mRNA with the mirror-image base sequence of the mRNA for the gene you want to effectively turn off. This mirror-image, or antisense, mRNA will bind to any normal, or 'sense', mRNA and make it useless, because this mRNA can no longer act as a template for protein synthesis. Thus production of a particular protein is prevented.

In the case of the tomato, the gene that is deliberately sabotaged is the one that produces a protein which causes it to soften when it ripens. With the protein made by this gene removed, the tomato has a greatly increased shelf-life. Some ageing processes seem to involve proteins that cause cells to 'commit suicide'. It may be that we could find ways of using antisense genes to turn 'cell-suicide' genes off.

One way of getting around the problem of targeting is to perform the gene therapy on cells or organs that have been removed from the person's body. The modified tissue can then be returned. Seven-month-old Carly Todd, the first patient treated by gene therapy in the UK, had bone-marrow cells removed, treated and then returned in an attempt to rid her of adenosine deaminase deficiency, a disease that left her highly prone to infection. Experiments in the USA have more recently looked at the possibility of combining gene therapy and heart transplant surgery. The idea is that once a heart has been removed from a donor it could be exposed to genes which would increase its chance of being accepted by the recipient.[16]

Another alternative to targeting organs is to perform the treatment when there are only a few cells present – when the person is still an embryo consisting of a bundle of a few cells, maybe even immediately after fertilisation, when there is only one cell. It is conceivable that members of a family who know that a genetic disease has run through their ranks for a generation or more, could opt for a combination of *in vitro* fertilisation and genetic therapy.

In procedures that have almost become taken for granted, fertility specialists take a woman's egg plus sperm from a man, normally her partner, and bring them together in drips of liquid on the floor of a shallow plastic dish. If all goes well the egg is fertilised and starts to grow while still outside the nurturing environment of the woman's womb. In this exposed state it is amenable to testing and possibly treating. However, any change made to these cells would automatically affect all the cells in the body, including germ-line cells. So for the moment it is banned.

In describing gene therapy, I have fallen into the trap of talking about introducing a new gene, or a correctly spelt copy of a gene, into a population of cells. The false impression is that the scientists only need to move one gene. The reality is that a package of genes, often referred to as a cassette, is moved. Genes do not work alone. They need other genes to turn them on and turn them off.

To find out whether a gene has been successfully added to cells, scientists often add 'marker' genes to the cassette, genes that carry some measurable characteristic. In laboratory experiments, genes that render the cells immune to antibiotics are often used. A population of cells that has been treated with the aim of introducing new genes will consist of a majority of unaffected cells, and a minority that have taken up the gene package and are being influenced by it. If the package conveys antibiotic resistance, only

16. This work was presented at the American Society for Gene Therapy in Washington, DC, in June 1999.

these cells will survive once the antibiotic has been added to the nutrient solution in which the cells are suspended.

Not only does the need to have a package of genes make the process more complex to perform, it also introduces new potential dangers. For example, the promoter genes put in to turn on the novel gene may also turn on some otherwise dormant gene in the cell's chromosome set, with unforeseen consequences.

A dark cloud appeared in the blue sky of hope on 17 September 1999, with the death of eighteen-year-old Jesse Gelsinger. Jesse had a seriously dangerous liver disorder[17] and opted to try a new gene therapy. He died four days after being injected with a modified adenovirus. Adenoviruses look as if they might be useful tools for shifting DNA into human cells. These particular viruses are good at infecting many types of cell found in our bodies, and when they attack a cell they place the DNA they carry inside it. The scientists were trying to find how much of the gene-carrying virus they would need to inject to achieve a safe therapeutic dose. It appears that the virus triggered massive organ failure.

Jesse was the eighteenth person to participate in the study and, so the researchers claimed, the only person to develop serious side effects. 'The first time we encountered significant toxicity, it was too late,' comments James Wilson, who led the research at the University of Pennsylvania, Philadelphia, USA.[18] As leading gene-therapy exponent French Anderson explained, most of the people who have so far volunteered have been seriously ill: 'A number of people have died during gene-therapy trials, but they were terminally ill cancer patients. [Gelsinger's death], unfortunately, is the first true gene-therapy death.'[19]

17. The disorder was ornithine transcarbamylase deficiency, a disease that affects about one in 25,000 births in the USA. Currently there are no successful treatments for this disease, and any treatment offered is more in the nature of a stopgap than a cure.

18. Boyce, N., 'Cure That Killed', *New Scientist*, 9 October 1999, p. 11. Wilson is the professor and chair of molecular and cellular engineering at the University of Pennsylvania, and director of the Institute for Human Gene Therapy.

19. Boyce, N., 'First Person to Die as a Side Effect of Gene Therapy', *New Scientist*, 9 October 1999, p. 11.

The admission that a person had died as a result of a side effect from a gene-therapy trial caused quite a stir, not least because it exposed a possible loophole in the regulations, revealing hundreds of previously unreported incidents. A little explanation is needed: in the USA, where this trial occurred, all clinical research on new drugs and gene-therapy protocols requires an investigational-new-drug application to be authorised by the Federal Drug Agency (FDA). Researchers must then follow FDA guidelines. In addition, gene-therapy trials have to follow the National Institute for Health (NIH) recombinant DNA guidelines. The FDA regulations require any adverse event, and this would include a patient dying, to be reported immediately. However, the FDA does not make these disclosures public. On the other hand, researchers claim that the NIH guidelines can be interpreted as suggesting that you only have to report an adverse event if it is clear that it was caused by the treatment. If adverse reactions, such as the patient dying, were thought to be due to causes other than the treatment, they claim that they thought it unnecessary to inform the NIH. You can see why they might have been keen to see things this way as the NIH makes its information public, unlike the FDA, and such disclosures could have an adverse effect on the share price of companies involved in the trials.

After the NIH issued a 'reminder' that it should be notified of any problems, it received 691 reports, 652 of which it had never heard of before. At a Senate subcommittee convened by Senator Bill First, researchers struggled to defend their lack of openness, causing First to conclude that regulation of gene therapy 'is not working, it is failing'.[20]

Clearly there are two issues here that need to be handled separately. One is the politics and regulations that surround research and protect any patients who may volunteer for trials, and the other is whether gene therapy can ever be made to work.

Somewhere around 2,000 trials have been initiated, though none has yet produced a fully fledged therapy. In October 1999, *The*

20. Weiss, R., and Nelson, D., 'Victim's Dad Faults Gene-Therapy Team', *The Washington Post*, 3 February 2000.

*Wall Street Journal* reported that the major pharmaceutical companies, who a few years earlier had poured money into the area, were pulling out: 'All but one of the gene-therapy testing programmes once under way at Genetic Therapy, Inc., and SyStemix [two of the largest research bases] have been scrapped or temporarily halted. And none of the hundreds of human studies conducted elsewhere around the globe so far has offered clear proof that gene therapy works in any significant way to fight disease.'[21] In the same article French Anderson is quoted as saying, 'We were naive to think we could revolutionise medicine in ten years.' He now doubts that any gene-therapy product will reach the market before 2005 at the earliest.

There are a few glimmers of success. The influential journal *Nature Genetics* published a paper describing work in which modified viruses were given to three people who have haemophilia B. The dosage given was so low that the researchers expected to see no effects of the treatment; they were only testing to see if the virus was safe. However, they did observe marginal improvement in the conditions of two of the three patients.[22] The editorial published in the same edition defended the decision to give prominence to such preliminary data on the grounds that 'although it is preliminary, it nevertheless reports modest evidence of efficacy at low doses of virus, and it may prove to be the first report of a clinically efficacious application of gene therapy to haemophilia'.[23]

Gene therapy probably does have a future, but don't hold your breath.

## A new conventional therapy

I'd hate to give the impression that genetics is not getting anywhere. That would be patently incorrect. But the most likely areas for

21. Langreth, R., and Moore, S., 'Researchers Get Dose of Reality as Logistics Stymie Gene Therapy', *The Wall Street Journal*, 27 October 1999.

22. Kay, M.A., et al., 'Evidence for Gene Transfer and Expression of Factor IX in Haemophilia B Patients Treated with an AAV Vector', *Nature Genetics* **24**, 2000, pp. 257–61.

23. Editorial, 'Trials and Tribulations', *Nature Genetics* **24**, 2000, pp. 201–202.

imminent application of genetic knowledge are those which allow conventional treatments to be targeted more appropriately or powerfully.

People respond differently to the majority of drugs, so there is always uncertainty about the potency or side effects of any dose given to an individual. Some people can tolerate penicillin, while others come out in a rash, and others still have extreme and even life-threatening allergic reactions. The reason for the difference is most likely to be found in small variations in the genetic code. Discovering what these variations are should pave the way for a screening test to identify who can safely take the drug, and who will be adversely affected by it. In the same way, some people respond to small doses of drugs, while others need large amounts; find the genetic cause of this difference, and you will be on the way to much more precise prescribing.

Genetic knowledge could also be used to combat cancer. This scourge of current medicine occurs when genetic changes in a cell cause it to grow and divide repeatedly, without pausing to check on how big the cell mass is that is being created. This is in contrast to the organs of the body which have systems of control allowing them to grow to an appropriate size and then maintain that size. Understanding the genetic malfunction will allow new drugs to be designed that can target only cancerous cells, leaving healthy cells unmolested.

The other major Western killer is heart disease. A key problem is that blood vessels in the heart become furred up by cholesterol and blocked, in much the same way that water pipes can become blocked by limescale deposits. Surgery is often used to perform bypass operations: the surgeon splices new vessels into the heart's vasculature, allowing the blood flow to bypass the blockage. An alternative approach is to understand the genetic control of blood-vessel growth, and use that knowledge to stimulate growth of new vessels in the heart.

Similar work has had startling results: researchers have injected the gene that builds a protein which stimulates the growth of blood vessels – vascular endothelial growth factor (known by the science community as VEGF) – into leg and foot ulcers. Ulcers develop when the blood supply to an area is poor and the tissue dies. Allowing the tissue to build new blood vessels eradicates the ulcer.

At the moment the emphasis of research is moving away from taking on what has classically been called genetic disease, but if genetics could be used as a new weapon against cancer and heart disease alone, it would still be considered a mighty triumph.

## Spin in the helix

As we survey the laboratory tools available to people at the centre of the new Babel, we need to keep one eye on the external communication tools that are also being employed. When news stories enter the public domain, they do so because someone has pushed them there. Sometimes it is diligent reporters who, like Bob Woodward and Carl Bernstein in the Watergate affair, pursue a hunch until the ugly truth is uncovered. At other times news stories originate when press releases are circulated by post, fax or e-mail to media outlets by people with some form of axe to grind. The journalist has to try to understand not only the nature of the possible story, but also why this person or organisation is peddling the information. Most media outlets have their own agendas, and if the item seems to be interesting, and fits in with this agenda, then they may choose to give it the oxygen of publicity.

Often scientists complain of unbalanced and sensationalised coverage, saying that the problem is down to journalists who don't understand. But then blame needs to be apportioned fairly. The most extreme example of hype was the 25 June 2000 announcement that the human genome had been decoded. The announcement was highly orchestrated. President Clinton stood in the White House and beamed out the good news with Francis Collins, head of the human genome project, standing tall by his shoulder. At the same time Tony Blair held a similarly cheesy grin as he gave identical news in London.

But it's important to read the wording of their scripts and the accompanying press releases carefully. The White House press release reads, 'President Clinton announces the completion of the first survey of the entire human genome.' The key is in the words 'first survey'. Listen carefully and you hear the experts talking of a working draft.

Now I don't know what this would conjure up in your mind, but I would be tempted to think that this means the vast majority of the genome is sequenced. At the very least. When they stood there, the truth is that only twenty-one per cent was known in detail.[24] The scientists anticipate that the complete sequence will take another three years to work out.

Another example of scientific overselling was the announcement in December 1999 that genetic sequencers at the Sanger Centre in Cambridge, UK, had determined the complete sequence of human chromosome 22.[25] The respected journal *Nature* published a paper and promoted it with same-day press conferences in London, Washington, DC, and Tokyo. The press release announced, 'First human chromosome sequenced.' The result was the standard clamour, as one scientist after another made wild claims about the potential that was now unleashed.

You could be forgiven for thinking this meant we now have a sequence that starts at one end of the chromosome and ends at the other. Sadly, that is not the case. In fact the scientists had produced a transcript of twelve large sections with eleven gaps in between that were 'intractable to sequencing'. So the public statement that it was completely sequenced is not true. What they have is the code of all the bits they think are useful – not entirely the same thing.

Writing a 'News-and-Views' article in the same edition of *Nature*, biochemist Peter Little from Imperial College, London, added hype to the hyperbole: 'As 1999 draws to a close and we approach the third millennium, a new book is being written. It will change the way we see ourselves as profoundly as did the momentous books of the first two millennia – the great books of religion and the *Origin of Species*.'[26] I heard this sort of sentiment being repeated time and again over the following days and weeks and even people who follow the genetic

24. Human genome project web site – www.ornl.gov/hgmis/faq/seqfacts.html

25. Dunham, I., and 217 other co-authors, 'The DNA Sequence of Human Chromosome 22', *Nature* **402**, 1999, pp. 489–95.

26. Little, P., 'The Book of Gene', News and Views, in *Nature* **402**, 1999, pp. 467–68.

debate closely would be forgiven for thinking that the new age of genetic certainty had dawned. But read Little's article further and things get rather more uncertain: 'So what is so revolutionary about all of this? In itself, perhaps not much... it is as a foretaste of what is to come.' Ah, so we are not there yet. I think that that needs to be made clear. Then he asks, 'In more practical terms, what is going to happen next?... First, it will take us to the list of proteins, but not quickly.' Not quickly? How long will this take? Little continues, 'Secondly, will we know the functions of these proteins just because we know their sequence? In most cases we will not, but biologists will have huge numbers of proteins and families of proteins to think about and experiment on.' So it would appear that we are dangerously close to being back to interesting tinkering, rather than forging ahead with solid progress. He then discusses the possibility of being able to analyse which genes are active in any cell, although he admits that 'we do not know what it will tell us about human beings'. Instead he says that we will have a completely new viewpoint of the life of a cell. 'Finally, the DNA sequence will become the framework upon which we will be able to place changes to the sequences which are present in every one of us.' The practical realities seem slightly less exciting than are expected from his opening euphoria.

I'm not knocking the amount of work or effort that has gone into sequencing the genome; after all, 218 scientists were so excited about the result that they were named as co-authors of the paper. I am just pleading that everyone keeps their findings in context and that all people involved are careful not to misinform, even if the result is that the story is less exciting.

Another, more common sort of press release, this time from *Nature Medicine*, claims, 'A single gene determines sleep pattern.'[27] The reality of the research behind this proclamation is that three families have been found that have similar patterns of sleep

27. The reference for the full paper that this press release refers to is *Nature Medicine* 5, 1999, pp. 1062–65. Its title is a much more restrained 'Familial Advanced Sleep-Phase Syndrome: A Short-Period Circadian Rhythm Variant in Humans'.

disturbance extending over between three and five generations. No gene has been looked for, much less found, but there is a pattern to the symptoms suggesting a genetic influence. To give the impression that a single gene has been discovered that controls sleep, as the title of the press release suggests, is stretching the truth.

Debate really heats up if you talk about sex and sexual orientation. And talking about homosexuality sets pressure groups and editors diving for their phones and keyboards. So when in 1993 a group of American researchers reported that they had evidence of a region of one chromosome that gave men a genetic predisposition to homosexuality, the touchpaper for an explosive debate was lit.[28] In the research, biologist Dean Hamer and his colleagues at the National Cancer Institute in Bethesda, Maryland, studied the DNA of forty pairs of gay brothers. They found that thirty-three pairs shared a group of five DNA sequences on the tip of one particular chromosome, the X chromosome. Commenting on the finding, Francis Collins, head of the Centre for Human Genome Research, said, 'all this study is saying is that we may have found part of the genetic contribution [to homosexuality]'.[29] It is worthy of note that seven pairs of the brothers did not share this genetic phenomenon, so even if it has some influence it can't be working on its own. Since then other scientists have failed to reproduce these findings, casting a thick veil of uncertainty over the debate.[30] Nevertheless, as far as the popular press was concerned the 'gay gene' had been found.

28. The research paper was published in *Science* **261**, 1993, pp. 321–27.

29. Reported in Miller, S.K., 'Gene Hunters Sound Warning Over Gay Link', *New Scientist*, 24 July 1993, p. 4.

30. George Ebers, a neurologist at the University of Western Ontario in London, Canada, failed to find the landmarks in fifty-four pairs of gay Canadian brothers, and Hamer and colleagues seem to be having problems repeating their own work. When they increased the number of people in the survey, the strength of the findings started to reduce. Reported in *New Scientist*, 8 September 1996. A full report of Ebers et al.'s research has now been published in *Science* **284**, 1999, pp. 665–67, in which they conclude they can find no evidence in their results to support the idea that a gene on the X-chromosome is an underlying cause of male homosexuality.

But before we get too carried away, let's stop and check the facts, starting with a quick reminder about what exactly a gene is – something that enables the cell to produce a protein. All that Hamer's team had found was a region of DNA, which in some people, who also claimed to be homosexual, had a particular mutation. No one has a clue about which protein this piece of the genetic sequence is responsible for building, and consequently there is no idea why it might influence a person's behaviour. In fact there is no certainty that the genetic variation is in a working gene at all; it could even be in a piece of inactive DNA.

So you can appreciate that a fuller understanding of the background helps us see just how much or little is known. This can help us make intelligent use of the information, rather than simply lying at the mercy of pressure groups and vested interests on either side of a debate, all of whom want to put their own spin on research results.

On other occasions, research groups release press information to try to promote the public awareness of their work in order to put themselves in a stronger position when applying for money. In a slightly different context, it was intriguing to see NASA pushing the story that they had found evidence for life on Mars[31] at just the time when they were likely to have their budgets severely cut. A meteorite that had fallen to earth, having been flung off the surface of Mars fifteen million years earlier, appeared to have some marks suggesting that it might have been colonised by a type of bacterium.

Hype knew no bounds. Among the publicity, the popular science magazine *New Scientist* instantly ran six pages of news stories with the overriding banner heading of 'This week – Life on Mars'. Much less publicity was given to work published the previous month in an equally respectable scientific journal that presented an

---

31. The research was carried out by a team led by David McKay of NASA's Johnson Space Centre in Houston and was published (on 16 August 1996) in *Science* **273**, pp. 924–50. The researchers had found microscopic globules of carbonate that they believe could have trapped and fossilised micro-organisms on the surface of potato-sized meteorite ALH84001.

alternative origin for the microscopic blobs on the rock which indicated that they could never have harboured any life.[32] However, by the time other scientists had poured cold water on that overheated story, NASA had secured its funding. The whole story has now gone very quiet. Call me a sceptic, but I have suspicions about the timing of the publicity.

A similar imbalance of information accompanied the first attempt to cure a disease by deliberately placing a new set of particular genes in infant Carly Todd, whose own set was defective. Carly was initially not named to protect her and her family from publicity, publicity that wouldn't have occurred if they had not pushed the story into the media's spotlight. However, interest soon waned once the treatment had been given and the long wait started to see if it would have an effect. When, a few years later, the doctors and scientists concluded that the genetic therapy had been ineffective there was hardly a murmur.

The society who lives in the new Babel will have tool kits the likes of which have never been seen before. They bring the possibility of giving us new insights into diseases and open the prospect of powerful diagnoses and treatments. However, at the same time the tools are remarkably simple and carry with them their own limitations. Try to analyse any announcement to see through the hype to the reality.

## Making use of the tools

So we can decipher the code, and possibly in the future we will be able to make corrections to it. However, it is not therapy so much as tools for diagnosis that are the massive growth area for the genetic industry. With each weekly announcement of the discovery of the location of a particular gene comes the possibility of a test to see if an individual has a particular variation in this gene. In a few cases, the

32. This work was done at Case Western Reserve University in Cleveland and the University of Tennessee and published in *Nature*: Bradley, J.P., Harvey, R.P., and McSween, H.Y., Jr, 'No "Nanofossils" in Martian Meteorite', *Nature* **390**, 1997, pp. 454–56.

test can lead to diagnosis and appropriate treatment. In the vast majority of cases, the test leads to either diagnosis and no treatment, or to some form of speculation about whether your risk of getting a particular disease is greater or less than the average member of the population.

To start with, our ability to test is racing ahead of any ability to treat. The human genome project is providing information that can point towards genetic errors at a phenomenal pace, leaving those few people struggling to develop therapies lagging far behind. In some cases there is no incentive to spend millions of pounds or dollars on developing cures, because in reality there are so few individuals affected by many conditions that no company is ever likely to see a return on its investment.

What is happening, though, is that people are making choices based on the information. Insurance companies are looking at the tests to see whether their results can influence either their decision-making, or that of their clients. Employers are investigating whether tests could enable them to employ cheaper and more productive workforces. Would-be parents are being offered them to see if their unborn baby has a genetic error, and then offered the option of abortion to remove the problem by removing the baby.

We will see that the dilemma faced is huge. Not only is there the issue of a person's right to terminate the life of an embryo, fetus or baby, but there is also the difficulty of knowing how to handle the information given. Sometimes the diagnosis from a genetic test is clear: the person has a particular disease and the symptoms will develop in a known pattern. In other situations it is less clear: the person has an increased possibility of developing a particular disease, or may develop it earlier than would an average member of the population.

In the past, even the recent past, only a few people have been challenged to think about this sort of information. But in the new Babel everyone will need to make decisions. The reason for this will be the increased availability of tests. Computer chips are being built with thousands of tiny sections of DNA packaged into an area of no more than the head of a pin. Sit a tiny blob of treated blood on top of that little patch and you can look for a thousand genetic mutations in a matter of seconds.[33, 34] The tests, when developed, will be largely automated and once spread widely enough will be relatively inexpensive. A sample of blood taken at birth could soon reveal a profile of every disease you are likely to suffer from, maybe even an indication of how long you are likely to live, assuming that you do not have a premature encounter with a moving bus. We will look later at how much of this information you really *want* to know, but you may well not be given the choice about *whether* you know it.

The last technique in the genetic tool kit that is worth mentioning in passing is the genetic fingerprint so beloved by police forces and crime writers. You might assume that the fingerprint is a mark left by the genes in a chromosome, and that the person-to-person variation in this print is associated with the genetic variation that makes each one of us unique. But you would be wrong. Earlier we mentioned that in between the genes are vast stretches of DNA that appear to have no function. We assume they have no function partly because they consist of sequences that are only 15 to 100 bases long, which repeat time and time again. It is the number and size of these repetitive regions, not the person's genes, that are measured in a genetic fingerprint. This is explored further in chapter 9.

At this point you may well be saying, 'So far, so interesting, but do I really need to know all this stuff?' The issue is that without an understanding of the basic techniques you are in a poor position to judge the validity and strength of so-called expert comments in the news, or press reports about new developments.

Remember that a gene is a clearly defined stretch of DNA, with

33. For example Singh-Gasson, S., Green, R.D., Yue, Y., Nelson, C., Blattner, F., Sussman, M.R., and Cerrina, F., 'Maskless Fabrication of Light-Directed Oligonucleotide Microarrays Using a Digital Micromirror Array', *Nature Biotechnology* **17**, 1999, pp. 974–78.

34. Pollack, J.R., Perou, C.M., Alizadeh, A.A., Eisen, M.B., Pergamenschikov, A., Williams, C.F., Jeffrey, S.S., Botstein, D., and Brown, P.O., 'Genome-Wide Analysis of DNA Copy-Number Changes Using cDNA Microarrays', *Nature Genetics* **23**, 1999, pp. 41–46.

a specific base sequence that enables a particular protein to be built within a cell. When you next hear that a new gene for 'X' has been found, ask yourself a few questions:

- Have the researchers located an area of a chromosome that is different in some people who have a particular condition or disease?

- Is the sequence of DNA in this region known?

- Has a region of this sequence been identified as having the characteristics that suggest it could be a gene?

- Has the gene been spliced out of the human cell and placed in bacteria to see what protein it produces?

- Does it resemble any other known proteins from any other species?

- Do we have any idea what that protein does in individual cells, or within the body?

- Does this tell us anything about the scientific basis of the condition or disease?

I used to service my own car. I could strip the engine down and eventually get it back together again. Now I open the bonnet and have difficulty finding the engine, hidden as it is among a mass of wiring and pipes. At an operating level I no longer know how my car works, but I am still aware of the basic units that make it up and can spot an error in one of them if it occurs. I also know roughly what package of units I want when I buy a new one. Genetic technology needs to be treated in a similar manner. We may never use a genetic tool kit, but we all need to know what tools are available and have an idea about the capabilities and limitations of the ones in common use.

# Chapter 4

# MEDICAL MOTIVES

Kos 400 BC. A beautiful little Greek island lying just off the south-western tip of present-day Turkey. Surrounded by crystal-blue seas and with a gentle breeze blowing, a group of men gather to admit a new member to their ranks: their revered leader – Hippocrates.

*I swear by Apollo Physician, by Asclepius, by Hygiea [Health], by Panaceia and by all the gods and goddesses, making them witness, that I will carry out, according to my ability and judgement, this oath and this indenture.*

*To hold my teacher in this art as equal to my own parents; to make him partner in my livelihood; when he is in need of money to share mine with him; to consider his family as my own brothers and to teach them this art, if they require to learn it, without fee or indenture; and to impart precept, oral instruction, and all the other instruction to my own sons, to the sons of my teacher, and to indentured pupils who have taken the physicians' oath, but to nobody else.*

*I will use treatment to help the sick according to my ability and judgement, but never with a view to injury or wrongdoing.*

*Neither will I administer a poison to anyone when asked to do so, nor will I suggest such a course. Similarly I will not give a woman a pessary to cause abortion.*

*But I will keep pure and holy both my life and my art.*

*I will not use my knife, not even, verily, on sufferers from stone, but I will give place to such as are craftsmen therein.*

*Into whatever house I enter, I will enter to help the sick, and I will abstain from all intentional wrongdoing and harm, especially from abusing the bodies of [fornication with] woman or man, bond or free.*

*And whatsoever I see or hear in the course of my profession, as well as outside my profession in my intercourse with men, if it be what should not be published abroad, I will never divulge, holding such things to be holy secrets.*

*Now if I carry out this oath, and break it not, may I gain for ever reputation among men for my life and my art; but if I transgress it and forswear myself, may the opposite befall me.*[1]

While the language may seem a little formal, smacking even of the back of an insurance document, the concept was novel. Here we had a group of physicians, doctors, who agreed to commit themselves to a basic set of principles that included learning a skill, being in the service of people who are sick, refusing to use their skills to deliberately take human life, protecting the vulnerable and maintaining confidentiality. The idea was to create a profession that could be trusted: a group of people whose members you could feel relaxed about inviting to your bedside when you were at your most vulnerable. You knew they would do you no harm. This was in marked contrast to the general situation in which healers were viewed with great scepticism and fear. The typical physician was seen as a secretive, money-grabbing gossip with loose morals.

Ridding people of disease and illness is given a high priority in most societies, and the people capable of performing that feat are given high status and demand high salaries. In looking at the influence that genetic technology will have on us it is important that we consider the basic driving principles within our system of healthcare. This will help us to establish the underlying motives that will shape our medical systems in the new Babel.

The ancient oath established the idea that, in Hippocrates' mind, the physician's task is more than simply being a clever technician, and is to be governed by a stringent moral framework that

1. Quoted from a translation given by Jones, W.H.S., *Hippocrates*, vol. 1, London, 1923, pp. 299–301.

allows for ethical decision-making. We will see that the physicians working in Babel's tower are in danger of putting that holistic commitment to one side as they practise their technological skills.

The little we know about Hippocrates and the Hippocratic oath has come down to us largely because the values that it espoused matched those of the new branch of religion that swept the world a few centuries later. Christianity had the same concerns for service and, being based firmly in Jewish moral and ethical frameworks, it had a very high concept of the value of human life. In his book, *Matters of Life and Death*, John Wyatt says that 'Christianity did not simply coexist with the old Hippocratic ideal; it brought an enhanced, radical vision of the medical task.'[2] Christianity had a special appeal for people who were sick and in need of healing, and in the first few centuries after Christ it was Christians who set up hospitals within monasteries and saved babies who had been discarded on hillsides to die. Within the Benedictine tradition care for sick people stands before and over all.

Today, few people would deny the basic ideals that this historic understanding has brought to medicine, but as medicine is increasingly infiltrated with scientific revelation and technological innovation we are forced to stand back and ask some hard questions. The most basic one is: *What are we trying to achieve with medicine?*

## Treatment of disease

An obvious answer would be to say that we want to heal people. When you fall down a short flight of stairs and break your leg, you want a system of healthcare that provides equipment and people who can literally come along, pick you up and get you back on your feet. You want someone to help your leg to heal as effectively and as quickly as possible. Alternatively, you wake up one morning with a raging sore throat and feel rotten. Instantly you wonder whether it is possible to get an emergency appointment at your GP for first thing in the morning so that you can grab some antibiotics on your

2. Wyatt, J., *Matters of Life and Death*, chapter 11, Inter-Varsity Press, 1998.

way into work. That way you can continue with the lifestyle that has exhausted you, while hoping that the chemical therapy afforded by the tablets will deal with the infected throat. You want someone, or something, to heal your throat.

But, however noble our desire to use medical technology to heal people, one of the first things we need to do is pause and be realistic about its role in the healing process. In the case of the broken leg, the staff will use an X-ray camera to determine the nature of the fracture, and some chemical anaesthetic to help the patient relax their muscles while the limb is pulled back into shape and then placed in an immobilising physical cast. The body then gets on with the task of rebuilding the bone and repairing any damaged tissues. Not much science, a little bit of technology and a lot of natural bodily healing.

In the case of the dash for antibiotics, many research studies show that people get better from the average infection just as quickly without antibiotics as with them. While each antibiotic has a known chemical action within bacterial cells, no antibiotic can kill all bacteria. A GP therefore tries a suck-it-and-see process. If they give you anything, they start with a lowish dose of a fairly general antibiotic, often penicillin. The hope is that by the time you have finished the course of tablets your throat will be better. But whether the tablets brought about this healing, or whether the body's own defence system prevailed is often unknown. If, however, the throat is still troubled at the end of the course the patient returns. Now we might even see a little science in action. By taking a throat swab and sending it off for laboratory analysis, the GP can discover what species of bacterium is causing the inflammation and then give appropriate antibiotics. Very often, however, the swab will point to a viral infection and you will be told, 'I'm afraid that there is no way of tackling viruses. You'll just have to take things easy for a bit.' Still not desperately much science in evidence, but the aim is to see the person free from the infection – to see them 'healed'.

Some cancer treatments use surgical techniques to remove the offending cells and tumours and thus seek to cure the person. If skin cancer is caught early enough the tumour can be removed and that is the end of the crisis. The patient is on the way to recovery. A lot of intensive care nursing is devoted to supporting life so that the body can use its own powers of restoration to attack disease or repair damage.

In many other cases we don't even bother trying to heal. Instead we try to circumvent the problem. My sight is impaired by the fact that I have an astigmatism, which basically means that there is a trough running diagonally across the surface of the lens in my right eye. So I wear glasses. They are great, they enable me to see, but they haven't healed my sight problem; they haven't healed me. Walking sticks, false teeth and pacemakers fall into a similar category, but so too do highly complex pieces of medical intervention such as coronary artery bypass surgery. Here a team of surgeons and theatre specialists takes a vein from the patient's leg and uses it to build loops of vessel that bypass blockages in the arteries supplying blood to the heart muscle. In this case, no attempt is made to heal the patient by unblocking the vessels and removing the basic problem; instead, the problem is circumvented.

The medical community seldom talks much about it, but the real factor that has given people living in the developed world a healthier life has not been medical technology, but the provision of clean water and sewerage. Travel to any part of the world where these two are absent and you will find people struggling to survive. Providing high-tech healthcare is irrelevant to their needs. Give them disease-free water and the means for keeping their environment clean and the vast majority of diseases go away. The lessons were learnt in nineteenth-century London when the city fathers installed systems to cope with storm water that would prevent sewage being washed around in heavy rain.

Far from being the staple diet of healthcare, medical technology is left to provide the icing on the cake. Having said that, lots of people like icing. And genetic technology has the potential to make that icing thicker and more exciting.

## Cure on demand

In quickly accepting the two examples of treating disease above, we are in danger of narrowing down our concept of healthcare. We are setting our goal for medicine as supplying a simple 'drop-in-and-get-healed' service.

Indeed this would appear to be the direction in which UK healthcare is moving, with drop-in clinics opening for business at railway stations and supermarkets. The idea is that while out buying your groceries you can buy a measure of health. If that is too much we are asked simply to call the telephone helpline. The increased access provided by these initiatives has its benefits, but it comes at the cost of decreased involvement. Previously you would be seen by a GP, who is in a better position to treat you as a whole person because he or she knows something of your personal and medical history.

The current fixation in UK healthcare with waiting lists is also redirecting priorities within the health service. We now give applause for systems that allow lots of patients to be fed in and out as quickly as possible, and lots of operations to be performed in low-cost day-case units. However, providing long-term care for people whose disabilities are not going to go away is becoming increasingly unglamorous. Private medicine would prefer that people who need prolonged treatment did not exist.

We seem to be moving towards a system that tries to be strong on health, but has little time for care.

## Care

The problem at the heart of this system isn't difficult to identify. Just ask your local GP how many of his or her patients have problems that have a purely physical origin, which can be solved by simply signing a prescription and sending them on their way. The majority of people present themselves with problems that need to be talked through. They need to be given a sympathetic ear, the ear of someone who knows about them, preferably because they have been their doctor for years.

This notion of a long-term relationship is part of the reason why doctors and nurses are often said to work within a caring profession – a profession where people are employed to be there in good times and in bad.

We seem to have lost sight of the meaning of caring. This is partly because it is much more glamorous to cure someone than to help them live with their illness or disability.

Now given the choice, of course, most people would maintain that it is better to cure, but that will never be possible for all people. Those who have to live with their illness or disability will need looking after and treating as people who are valued members of society. A medical system that is devoted to curing will be inclined to sweep these difficult people to one side, unless the society that they live in demands that we supply their needs as well.

It will also be in danger of ignoring individual people's aspirations. Many members of the Deaf community do not want healing. They consider that they are part of a different linguistic community, one which uses signs rather than speech. Some extend this philosophy to the point of hoping that their children will also be deaf and therefore become full members of their community, in the same way that hearing parents want their children to learn their birth tongue.

## What is health?

The simplistic view of the ideal situation is that everybody has 100 per cent health for 100 per cent of life. As soon as we deviate from that, we want help to restore the situation, and if you don't think too hard, it is easy to fall into the trap of believing that that is what any health service is there to provide.

The World Health Organisation has a stunning definition of health: 'Health is a state of complete physical, mental and social well-being, not simply the absence of illness and disease.' In September 1978 a WHO/UNICEF meeting at Alma Ata in the south-east of the Soviet Union declared the goal of 'Health for all by the year 2000'. Add these two statements together and it is immediately apparent that, while the aim may have been worthy, it was hopelessly Utopian.

Adverts for private health services and insurance schemes also foster the same impression. Images of smiling nurses guiding people in apparently perfect states of health along gleaming corridors are all very pretty, but do little to establish the real nature of the situation.

Politicians who are involved in healthcare provision all too often haven't thought the issue through. When I asked Dr Liam Fox, the Conservative Party's shadow minister for health, about it he replied, 'I have no problem with WHO's definition.'[3]

However, even the WHO is now cautious about its own definition. In 1984 the WHO Health Promotion Initiative led to an expansion of the original definition: health now becomes 'the extent to which an individual or a group is able to realise aspirations and satisfy needs, and to change or cope with the environment. Health is a resource for everyday life, not the objective of living; it is a positive concept, emphasising social and personal resources as well as physical capabilities.'[4]

Such a definition has much more scope for helping us to see how healthcare can be provided to individuals. Indeed the WHO is now considering including spiritual well-being within the definition, moving the organisation away from one that is solely concerned about the biological workings of the body.

I am also attracted by the brief definition of health proposed by German theologian Jürgen Moltmann: 'Health is the strength to be human.'[5] This makes provision for us to accept that in seeking to make someone healthy, medicine has a high goal, but that seeking health is not the same as seeking perfection. Moltmann explains his definition: 'If we understand health as the strength to be human, then we make being human more important than the state of being healthy. Health is not the meaning of human life.' However, standing alone, his definition asks almost more questions than it resolves – primarily, *What does it mean to be human?* For Moltmann, the answer lies in a Judeo-Christian understanding of humanity and draws a close parallel between health and the biblical concept of shalom: peace, wholeness and well-being.

3. Correspondence dated 15 December 1999.

4. In 'Health Promotion: A Discussion Document', WHO, 1984.

5. Moltmann, J., *God in Creation*, SCM Press, 1985, p. 273. Moltmann's definition is discussed in *Health: The Strength to be Human*, ed. Fergusson, A., London: CMF/IVP, 1993.

In reality we are all ill. I have yet to meet someone who does not have something wrong with them. For the most part, the damage caused is not particularly noticeable. However, it is when a particular illness or accident begins to affect our lives that we start to take notice and seek help. Older people find that years of wear and tear take their toll and leave them in need of help more than younger people.

More problematic is the discussion of what constitutes perfect health. I used to row for my university and we competed with reasonable success. In order to win we needed to be fit, but at the same time many of us had damaged backs and strained knee joints. I was strong, but I was never going to be a weightlifter. I could ride a bike well, but I had no hope of winning a sprinting race. I can see perfectly well to get on with life, but I'll never have perfect vision.

When the National Health Service (NHS) was established in the UK in 1948 there was a wonderful idea that blanket healthcare coverage would not be too expensive. The hope was to run the system on a policy of 'a stitch in time saves nine'. Initial high costs were expected as a background of chronic ill health was swept away, but once that was dealt with we'd be in the clear.

The escalating cost of healthcare provision and seemingly unstoppable waiting lists are witness to the shortsightedness of this Utopian ideal. I'm certainly not knocking the concept of a national health policy, certainly not one that is free to all at the point of use. But I am asking that we carefully consider what we are demanding of it.

It is vital that we take seriously the importance of finding a workable definition of health, because in the era of the new Babel there will be techniques that hold out the illusion of being able to create a 100 per cent healthy society. We need to work out whether our goal is to do everything possible to create health, even if that means introducing genetic changes to us and our offspring, or whether our goal is to use genetic knowledge to give people the 'strength to be human'.

## Designer health

Babel will introduce two key new problems for healthcare providers. First, screening programmes will mean that people are much more aware of their particular collection of disease-susceptibilities and will expect a solution to be provided. Secondly, every person will have to be treated as an individual.

One of the first applications of genetic technology has been in the realm of screening procedures that aim to detect genetic problems so that they can be protected against. The DNA chip that we encountered in the last chapter will make possible tests that look for thousands of potential disease states in a single glance. In addition, such tests on an unborn child could inform you about the developing baby's hair and eye colour; about the future child's potential for growth and indications of his or her intellectual ability; about the likelihood of the resulting adult suffering early heart attacks, and the elderly person's possibility of getting dementia. You may even be able to predict the person's maximum attainable age. And all of this could be discovered by testing an embryo before placing it in the nurturing environment of a womb.

If this sort of testing procedure is implemented, and there is every indication that it will be, then medicine has set off on a very different tack. Rather than accepting a commitment to care for people who are ill, it will be choosing to nurture people who have the potential of being well. We will be in a position to design our own concept of health.

The introduction of prenatal blood tests and fetal ultrasound scans in early- and mid-pregnancy has already set us along this path, giving would-be parents the choice of seeing if there are any detectable abnormalities in their developing child and then offering the possibility of abortion if they are discovered. We are in danger of turning antenatal screening into anti-natal screening. Our society's newly found tolerance of abortion makes this all the more acceptable.

We have long held the view that a parent or guardian has the moral authority to make decisions on behalf of a minor in that person's care. All decisions have to be made in order to protect the best interests of the child. But with the newly available prenatal testing systems it is difficult to see how the best interests of the child are going to be protected, if the outcome of the tests is a decision to discontinue his or her life. The idea is shocking, and fraught with difficulty, but maybe we are coming to a time when these decisions need to be made by a third party.

Formally trained genetic counsellors argue that the purpose of genetic screening is to give information which leaves people with the ability to make informed choices. The process depends on information being imparted in a non-directive manner. If this is the case then the role of this sector of medicine is now about enabling people to make choices, rather than necessarily making them better.

Genetic counsellors also argue that the non-directive nature of any information is vital, so that the person is not coerced into making a decision with which they are unhappy. Yet, in practice, patients are influenced by the kind of information provided and the manner in which it is delivered. People do feel persuaded to make particular decisions. This is hardly surprising given the sort of comments made in a report produced for the UK's Health Technology Assessment programme: 'The aim of genetic screening for CF [cystic fibrosis] is to reduce the birth prevalence of the disorder. This is principally achieved by identifying carrier couples who can have prenatal diagnosis and selective termination of pregnancy.'[6] Such a directive stance is inconsistent with the supposed non-directive goals of genetic services, especially those of many Westernised countries. It's worth noting that other areas of the world think differently. For example, in China and certain South American countries genetic counsellors openly strive to reduce the incidence of affected births.[7]

Again we see the focus switch away from medicine having its primary role in treating unhealthy people to one where it is the prospective parents, or even society, who are the decision-makers and the beneficiaries. Used in this way, the tests are no longer helping to treat the person, but helping the parents maintain their

---

6. *Health Technology Assessment* **3**, no. 8, 1999.

7. Biesecker, B.B., and Marteau, T.M., 'The Future of Genetic Counselling: An International Perspective', *Nature Genetics* **22**, 1999, pp. 133–37.

and their family's lifestyle, while reducing the costs to society of caring for many people whose abnormalities will leave them in need of long-term support.

Using the word 'eugenics' is always liable to get critics throwing their hands up in horror and calling you a crackpot, but it seems to be an appropriate word to introduce at this point.[8] The eugenics movement was born in America at the beginning of the twentieth century out of a desire to create a healthy, law-abiding population by preventing people with undesirable traits from having children. Twenty-five thousand Americans were sterilised in the notion that the common good overrode individual rights. The Nazis picked up the theme and pursued a policy of cleaning up their race with remarkable vigour, inspired by the feeling that the German race was the most evolutionarily developed. Just so that any Brit doesn't start to feel too proud, it is worth noting that the likes of Winston Churchill held similar views. The British Eugenics Society continues to exist, although it changed its name to the Galton Institute in the 1980s, taking the name of Charles Darwin's cousin Sir Francis Galton, one of the pioneers of eugenic ideology.

There are still people who believe that we should have social policies to shape society. Listen to people like Robert Edwards, the force behind the first test-tube baby. In his opinion, we are moving towards a time when it will be irresponsible for any parent to knowingly give birth to a disabled baby. Speaking at the annual meeting of the European Society of Human Reproduction and Embryology in 1999, he said, 'Soon it will be a sin of parents to have a child that carries the heavy burden of genetic disease. We are entering a world where we have to consider the quality of our children.'[9] He believes that we should recognise that fertility treatment and pre-implantation screening will be used as tools of social engineering.

8. The word 'eugene' means 'well born'.

9. Quoted in *Sunday Times*, 4 July 1999,

In addition, west of the Atlantic, key figures such as Francis Crick and Richard Seed expound blatantly eugenic concepts as ways of moving society into a golden age of health, wealth and achievement.

Before we get carried away, we do need to recognise that the drive behind the current development in genetic testing is more civilised than traditional eugenics, but at the same time we must acknowledge that there is a danger the net outcome could become remarkably similar. It is, I believe, this confusion of aims that allows people like Robert Winston to stand up at a meeting held at the Royal Society in London[10] and say that any notion that prenatal screening has any similarity to eugenics is nonsense and a slur, while at the same time other commentators such as Lee Silver say that new ideologies are in fact more powerful than eugenics because they are so subtle. However, Silver too is keen to rid the term eugenics of any of the historically repugnant overtones, saying, 'The Nazi eugenics program was an attempt at genocide. The forced sterilisations in America were wrong because they restricted the reproductive liberties of innocent people... Clearly none of these wrongs can be applied to the voluntary practice of embryo screening by a pair of potential parents.'[11]

Nevertheless, we need to be careful not to miss the point. Individual would-be parents are not the people setting up the screening programmes or building the technology. The permission to use these techniques is being granted by a society that believes it would be a good idea if we could limit the number of babies born with misspelt genes and subsequent illness. Provision of the tests is made by companies who stand to make profits from this permission. The rights, responsibilities and desires of the individual are in danger of being put to one side.

At the same time as acknowledging that this slide towards provision and use of screening tests is occurring, we also need to

10. A meeting organised by the Centre for Bioethics and Public Policy and held at the Royal Society in London on 6 May 1998.

11. Silver, *Remaking Eden*, p. 217.

note that individual would-be parents are not the people holding the purse strings that could provide facilities for any needy children that they 'allow' to be born. Any decision to provide care will only be effective if it is based within a society that wants to care.

The reality is that our society seems to be going the other way and, if anything, becoming less tolerant of people with disabilities, whether they are genetic or otherwise. There is the very real possibility that a society which chooses to spend more time and money on screening will have less interest in caring for people who refuse to join in the programme.

One of the manifestations of privatising the provision of care are so-called 'wrongful-life lawsuits'. These are brought against a health authority after a child has been born with a disability that could have been diagnosed, but wasn't. Parents are able to sue for the cost of raising the child and the sums awarded are considerable. While this provision has been driven by the parental need to supply the additional care that a disabled child will need, accepting the concept of 'wrongful life' endorses society's concept that we have a right to give birth to healthy babies.

In his writing, Dave King propagates the phrase 'laissez-faire eugenics', with the idea that this mode of thinking has crept in by the back door without anyone really intending it. 'The danger we will need to guard against is the development of a kind of eugenic common sense, that it is irresponsible to refuse to undergo tests, and that every child has the right to a healthy genetic endowment. It may soon become common sense that sex is for fun, but having a baby is a serious matter, not to be left to chance.'[12]

## A new era

The current system of running health services expects that you can take standardised treatments off the shelf and give them to a large number of people. In the genetic healthcare era this will no longer

12. King, D., 'The Persistence of Eugenics', *GenEthics News*, issue 22, February/March 1998, pp. 6–8.

be possible. The power of many treatments will lie in their being targeted against specific illnesses in particular individuals.

Philip Noguchi, director of the division of cellular and gene therapies for the American Food and Drug Administration is anxious. Talking of the impact of genetic technology on the medical health system he said that 'we need to envision a future that we can't even imagine at the moment. It is somewhat similar to trying to predict what would happen to computer technology twenty years ago... I believe that we will see some new form of healthcare facility come into being to implement the therapies to patients.'[13]

As this new order comes into being it should solve some problems. A principal reason for the impossibly long waiting lists is that alongside curing short-term illness, we have found treatments for previously untreatable conditions. The genetic fixes that are appearing on the horizon of expectation give the possibility of one-stop fixes for diseases that previously kept people in the healthcare system for years.

One of the more immediate ways that genetic testing may be used is to determine which conventional drugs may be most beneficial to individuals. At the moment there is a staggeringly wide range of effects seen within a population when an individual drug is prescribed. For example, some people have life-threatening allergic reactions when they are given the antibiotic penicillin, while others find that anticholinergic drugs given to relieve uncontrolled muscle contractions in their gut cause blurred vision, dryness in the mouth and urine retention. It is now realised that much of that variation could have a genetic basis. In some cases the unwanted or unexpected effect of a drug may be because the person has a genetic error that prevents them performing the chemical reactions needed to break down and clear the drug, or its by-products, from their bodies. A clear understanding of the individual person's genes gives the potential for avoiding some potentially lethal side effects.

In addition, accurate diagnosis of genetically based disease is

13. Interviewed at the American Society for Gene Therapy, Washington, DC, June 1999.

increasing rapidly. As the genes are pinpointed and then sequenced, many symptoms that were thought to be from a single disease are now realised to have many different underlying causes. For example, Batten disease, a lethal neurodegenerative disorder, used to be thought of as a single illness. A scientific paper describes the current situation in its title: 'Batten Disease: Four Genes and Still Counting'.[14] Four genes means that Batten disease is at least four different diseases that happen to have similar symptoms, but each may need different therapies to treat effectively. Increased knowledge is great, but to make use of this knowledge will require a health service that makes ever-greater financial demands.

Great. These conventional and novel developments in healthcare could enable us to take better care of the vulnerable within our society. They also mean that more people live longer, more active lives. But ageing has not been conquered – we are not about to live for ever. A common myth is that the maximum human lifespan is increasing rapidly. After all, people are living longer, aren't they? However, historical records show many people who have lived for around 100 years. The second president of the USA, John Adams, made it into his nineties, dying in 1829; Italian sculptor, painter and poet Michelangelo died in 1564 aged eighty-nine; Malcolm II, king of Scotland, lived eighty years, dying in 1034. What is happening now is that the provision of good housing, food and healthcare is enabling more people to see in their eighties and nineties. The UK's Office for National Statistics estimates that by the year 2021 the adult population will have increased by ten per cent, although the number of people surviving beyond 100 is unlikely to change very much in the near future.[15]

Evolutionary geneticists and gerontologists like Tom Kirkwood from the University of Manchester, UK, believe that ageing is a consequence of evolution only building a body that is capable of

14. Mole, S.E., 'Batten Disease: Four Genes and Still Counting', *Neurobiology of Disease* **5**, 1998, pp. 287–303.

15. *Population Trends*, vol. 95, Spring 1999.

looking after itself for long enough to reproduce successfully. Thereafter the biological 'expense' of maintenance is great and achieves no benefit. In this 'disposable *soma*' theory, the body – the *soma* – has simply never been designed to last for ever. When its task is complete it is thrown away. Kirkwood, however, believes that as we understand the genetic programming that keeps our bodies healthy in the earlier years of our lives we may be in a position to extend life towards the 200-year mark. In addition, he is keen to stress that we need to be careful about simply aiming to extend life: 'The primary goal of research on the biological basis of ageing must be to enhance the quality of later years of life. If quality is not improved, any increase in quantity might prove to be a Pyrrhic victory.'[16]

There is certainly no indication outside science fiction that we are capable of making people who could live for ever. Babel will not get rid of the problems associated with old age, so at best we will just encounter them after a longer period.

## Reductionism

The primary drive behind medicine has moved from caring for people to fixing them. The holistic concept of care that Hippocrates dictated is being eroded to a relationship between a purchaser and a supplier.

Wyatt believes that medicine should be an essentially holistic process, which treats a person as an entire unit, rather than a kit built from interchangeable blocks. However, current medical science tends to reduce people to biological machines, dismantling them to their component parts, and seeing how each individual unit works. Like a child's construction set, a person is then seen as a combination of these units. The task of medicine is to identify and fix any faulty unit. The process is called reductionism.

At first glance this seems fine, but an important shift in thinking has occurred from the former view that medicine's task was to help people who were ill. The key is that the value of the

16. Kirkwood, T., 'How Can We Live Forever?' *British Medical Journal* **313**, 1996, p. 1571.

individual within the system is becoming diminished. For people like Richard Dawkins this comes as no surprise; after all, according to his model, people have only ever been survival machines that have the sole purpose of preserving their 'selfish genes', and consequently they have no intrinsic value in the first place. Wyatt pursues this argument:

*If I am caring for a being made in God's image, I might have a motivation for philanthropy [the love of humankind], for enshrining the values of respect and compassion. But if I am caring for a survival machine, for 'robot vehicles blindly programmed to preserve the selfish molecules known as genes' then logically why bother? After all, if the mechanisms of this particular survival machine are grossly abnormal, and it lacks the right DNA for the future of our species, why should we not help it on its way to the rubbish heap? There are many better-equipped survival machines which could benefit from medical help.*[17]

Genetic technology raises the stakes even higher with its promise of accurate diagnosis and precision-built drugs. The temptation is now to move away from waiting for a disease to become manifest to predicting whether it is likely to occur in the first place. The more 'Discovery of gene for X' news headlines that get printed, the more people will expect tests to see if they have, or are likely to be affected by, disease X. Rather than waiting for someone to have signs of heart disease, we will try to treat them to prevent them ever experiencing it.

The community that lives in Babel's shadow will have another choice. Not only can we make decisions on who should live or be put away early, but there is also the possibility of altering those who are given the benefit of life. Genetic enhancement is not legal in humans, but the techniques are being developed in agricultural plants and animals. We've already seen that the same genetic principles are involved in all forms of life, so once the techniques are

17. Wyatt, *Matters of Life and Death*, p. 225.

developed there is the possibility of transporting the process into the medical field.

And who would stand in the way? Let's face it, if someone was to offer a way of genetically enhancing your progeny so that it was impossible for them to suffer from viral infections, there would be people queuing at the door. Any attempt to block the process would be seen to be an infringement of personal choice. OK, so this is an extreme example, but it's not beyond the realm of possibility to think of genes that could enhance a person's ability to fight off infections. While there is no single 'gene for intelligence' there are genes that, if present in a particular mutation, improve a person's chance of developing an above-average intellect. Certainly there are genes that influence height, hair colour, facial or other body features... the list is seemingly endless and certainly expanding.

The reductionist way of seeing ourselves as collections of units that plug together allows us to change a unit for a better module without too much concern. If we can introduce stronger muscles, why not? Maybe we will even be able to tackle ageing – now that would be a money-spinner.

Lee Silver sees this as the inevitable way that things will progress. I'm uncertain whether he is excited or worried about the prospect. I think he likes to pretend he is a third-party observer, simply commenting on the process, rather than acknowledging that, as one of the high priests of the system, he is promoting its progress. Intriguingly, he draws his book, *Remaking Eden*, to a conclusion with the implication that humanity will genetically enhance and reframe its own existence to the point that we become all-knowing gods – if so, new Babel's high priests will have reached their ultimate goal.[18]

Returning to the more mundane business of twenty-first-century living, we can see how currently available technology is already used or abused to enhance our capabilities – a situation that is likely to intensify as genetic technologies take hold. Olympic meetings are now more often dominated by press stories about drug misuse than about athletic

18. Silver, *Remaking Eden*, p. 250.

prowess. If a record is broken a shadow of doubt is cast over the victorious athlete and previous track records scrutinised for evidence of sudden steps in times or lengthening distances that would point a finger of suspicion. Spotting an injected or ingested drug is hard enough; spotting an enhancement brought along by the introduction of a new gene could be even harder.[19] This is a long way from the transparent openness of ancient Greek athletes who competed naked, therefore proving that their success was completely unaided.

If we accept that we are no more than biological machines, then what's wrong with taking the machine to a mechanic to see if it can be 'souped up'? We don't like it because at root we believe that we are more than biological machines. It has become unfashionable in some philosophical circles to talk about the sanctity of life, but deep down we have a notion that human life is special and should not be tampered with. It is this that leads to the 'yuk factor' commonly referred to when a new piece of the technological jigsaw threatens the assumed innocence of nature. Reproductive therapies and cloning are particularly liable to heated debate.

A challenging picture is presented by Wyatt, who suggests that the goal of medical practice should be similar to that of the art restorer. He points out that art restorers work by a code of practice that requires them not to change the piece of art in their care. Their task is to return the piece of work to the original design, to the maker's original intentions.[20] Being a Christian, Wyatt sees the maker as the God of the Bible and consequently sees part of his quest to determine what the maker – what God – was planning when he created

19. An article by Christie Aschwanden points out the relative ease with which genes may soon be inserted that boost endurance or build muscle mass: 'Gene Cheats', *New Scientist*, 15 January 2000.

20. In *Matters of Life and Death*, Wyatt quotes the UK Institution of Conservation guidelines, which say that 'Conservation is the means whereby the original and true nature of an artistic object is maintained.' The true nature of an object is determined by 'evidence of its origins, its original constitution, the materials of which it is composed and information which it may embody as to its maker's intentions and the technology used in its manufacture': pp. 87–88.

humankind. And this begs the question, *What was the original intention for this masterpiece?* We'll look at that further in chapters 6 and 7.

## Recognising relativism

The other '-ism' that complicates any discussion of medical policy is relativism – the idea that everyone is entitled to make up their decisions relative to their own set of ethical codes and cultural circumstances. It draws from the principle that there is no such thing as an absolute notion of truth.

Obstetric and maternity wards are perhaps the most extreme places to see relativism at work. A single ward can have two women in adjacent beds – one desperately trying to hold onto the developing baby within her, believing that she should do everything possible to give this little child the chance of life; the other waiting for the abortion that will remove her unwanted baby. Perfectly healthy unborn babies are aborted, while at the same developmental age others lie in incubators with the best efforts of medical science striving to keep them alive, despite the fact that there is a fair chance that if they survive they will do so with some form of disability.

The Australian philosopher Peter Singer[21] notes that this inconsistency occurs not just between people, but also within individuals. For evidence he points to a 1993 survey of senior paediatricians working in the UK.[22] Respondents were asked to say whether they agreed or disagreed with a series of statements, three of which are listed below:

21. On 1 July 1999, Singer was appointed as the Ira. W. DeCamp professor of bioethics in the University Center for Human Values at Princeton University, Princeton, New Jersey, USA. The appointment caused a storm of protest including the withdrawal of financial support from millionaire businessman Steve Forbes. In a letter to the University's weekly bulletin (7 December 1998) Harold T. Shapiro, the president of Princeton University, explained that their decision to employ Singer was based on the scholarship of his work rather than on any notion of agreement with his findings or opinions.

22. Outterson, C., 'Newborn Infants with Severe Defects: A Survey of Paediatric Attitudes and Practices in the UK', *Bioethics* 7, 1993, pp. 420–35.

No. 7: Abortion is morally permissible after twenty-four weeks if the fetus is abnormal.

No. 16: There is no moral difference between the abortion of a fetus and the active termination of the life of a newborn infant when both have the same gestational age and suffer from the same defects.

No. 17: There is no circumstance in which it is morally permissible to take active steps to terminate the life of an infant with severe defects.

Each of these statements gained approval from forty per cent of the people who replied, even though the statements are clearly contradictory. The paper does not make it clear if any individuals ticked all three. However, even if individual doctors are managing to operate by their own particular consistent code of practice, the fact that almost half of the doctors thought that killing disabled newborn babies was morally acceptable, and a similar number said that it was not morally permissible, points to a medical system that is in terrible confusion.

The problem with surveys that assess what people are doing is that they propagate the idea that current practice is what should happen. The everyday life of a hospital will always be fraught with dilemmas that result in different decisions being made in different circumstances, but it is easy to welcome the concept of relativism as an excuse for avoiding hard issues. What we need to do is take a step back and look for some basic ethical principles and then see whether these can direct clinical practice. This need is all the more pressing as the new genetic technologies expand the range of options, some of which are bound to introduce a new genre of ethical complexities.

## Who is the patient?

As we have seen, the problem is that much of the genetic information we can gather does not identify whether a person *will* suffer from a particular condition, but only whether they are more or less *likely* to suffer than the majority of the population who do not have that genetic feature. The value of the information to any individual is doubtful. For instance, does it really help you to know that your risk of developing colon cancer is twenty-five per cent greater than the person sitting next to you on the way into work each day?

However, the value of this sort of information for healthcare strategists is very great. If you can monitor whole populations, this sort of probability data allows you to see whether there are any trends in the numbers of people who are likely to be affected by differing conditions at some point in the future. You are then in a position to plan for that expected demand. You can also see if there is any developing trend in the numbers of people affected by differing conditions. Again, this can aid planning.

The question is, *Who is the patient?* Is it an individual person struggling to keep as healthy as possible, or a population of people who need an industrial style of healthcare provision?

Look also at the language we use. People are no longer classified as patients, but healthcare consumers; hospital and clinic staff are healthcare providers. This is the language of a market economy and marks another recent shift in ideology. Along with this new breed of healthcare consumer comes a vigorous pack of lawyers, eager to check that you get a fair deal out of your treatment. Led on by over-hyped reports of progress, the consumer now expects to be cured after an encounter with scientific medicine, and when this does not occur the assumption is that the system failed.

Now I'm not saying that doctors, nurses, hospitals and any other sector of the health market are free from failure, but very often the fault lies in our lack of knowledge and the limitations of our technology. Having lawyers breathing down their necks is not conducive to helping doctors in their work.

With all the demands that are being placed on health systems throughout the world, there is a drive for efficiency. Departments of health economics are springing up like mushrooms. If you combine the desire for financial efficiency with a Dawkinsesque reductionism, you arrive at a point where the most efficient way to deal with a seriously ill person is to allow them to die. After all, if you have no intrinsic purpose and you could no longer cause your genes to move into a new generation, then why waste money keeping you going.

Singer would agree. He is concerned that we are pretending to run a health system on principles that we have long ago either forgotten or stopped using. Consequently he argues that we should replace the old 'commandment' to 'treat all human life as of equal worth', with a new commandment to 'recognise that the worth of human life varies'.[23] In so doing he opens the possibility of killing people who by the judgement of observers have a life that is not worth living.

We need to make sure that Babel is a society which values individual people and develops an ideology of care which keeps the needs of the patient, the person being tested or treated, at the top of any agenda for change.

## The doctor's role

At the same time that the nature of the patient is changing, the nature of the relationship between doctor and patient is also under review. Initially medicine was aimed at making individual people

---

23. In his book, *Rethinking Life and Death* (Oxford University Press, 1995), Peter Singer presents an ethical system that replaces what he terms the five Old Commandments of the old ethic with five New Commandments that reflect current understanding:

Replace 'Treat all human life as of equal worth,' with 'Recognise that the worth of human life varies.'

Replace 'Never intentionally take innocent human life,' with 'Take responsibility for the consequences of your decisions.'

Replace 'Never take your own life, and always try to prevent others taking theirs,' with 'Respect a person's desire to live or die.'

Replace 'Be fruitful and multiply,' with 'Bring children into the world only if they are wanted.'

Replace 'Treat all human life as always more precious than any nonhuman life,' with 'Do not discriminate on the basis of species.'

He argues that this is a more logical approach and one that fits in more truthfully with healthcare practice. However, it has brutal consequences as we will consider in chapter 6 when looking at what it is that makes human beings into individual persons.

well. In a strongly paternalistic system decisions about treatment were made by the physician and accepted by the patient. In our consumer culture the patient's voice has become more important, and we have entered an age of informed consent. The notion is that the medical expert gives you information about a particular treatment or course of action, and you give your consent, or not, as the case may be.

This step forward is not without its dangers, because now the physician can wash his or her hands of all responsibility: 'Well, you made the decision, we just gave you information.' That's blatantly not fair. How can a person with a limited knowledge of medicine be expected to make rapid decisions, often in a crisis, and why should doctors who have taken thousands of pounds of tax payer's money in their education and training be allowed to duck responsibility?

Wyatt suggests an alternative, an 'expert–expert' relationship. The physician is an expert in medicine, the patient an expert in their own life, their expectations and desires. If both respect and trust each other, then a process of discussion and shared decision-making can safeguard dignity as well as make honest use of hard-won expertise.

The opportunities unleashed by Babel will demand greater degrees of shared decision-making if we are going to use the newly available information, rather than simply allow it to dominate us.

## The challenge

The challenge for the health system is to find a way of honouring people's individuality, without allowing it to degenerate into egocentric individualism. The aim is to give people access to genetic data so that they can make informed decisions about their health. But how do you do this without effectively giving them permission to establish a 'genetic ghetto' that only welcomes those who can prove their genetic righteousness? This could come as a product of overzealous antenatal screening, or by people restricting their choice of marriage partners to those whom they consider to be genetically acceptable.

And what will this new healthcare system look like? Will it be devoted to treating disease and disability, or to reducing the risk of diseased or disabled people entering the population in the first place? Will it give equal access to all sectors of the population, or just to those who have the intelligence and education to cope with its complexities? Will it be driven by the desires and demands of patients, or directed by the companies who want to market their latest invention?

Will we allow a sectarianism to creep into our society, where individuals are invited to buy into the healthcare system that supports their own personal set of beliefs? Could you opt for your money to go to a system that makes maximum use of genetic screening to minimise the risk of health defects in your family, in preference over one that chooses to look after anyone who happens to be born? Or would you prefer to leave the technologists to their little games and instead belong to a system that uses only herbal and Eastern-based 'natural' remedies?

Will the tower of knowledge lead to a society that is united in its basic goals of health provision, or divided between a variety of opposing goals?

# Chapter 5

# CLONING CONFUSION

A wooden-slatted barn in a moderately remote area of the Scottish borders would seem an unlikely birthplace for a world-shocking celebrity. Particularly when that celebrity is a sheep. But on 5 July 1996, at 5 p.m. it happened. Dolly, the cloned sheep, was born. After the announcement of this event, which incidentally was delayed almost eight months until Sunday 23 February 1997, the words 'cloning' and 'yuk' were soon bounding around in a mass of, on the whole, confused hysteria.

Dolly was apparently the clone of a mammal, an adult mammal, what's more. If you could clone an adult sheep, what is to stop you cloning an adult human? Images of multiple Saddam Husseins appeared on the covers of daily papers with stark warnings of mad power-mongers producing armies of their own likeness. Documentaries were broadcast which, while containing valuable information, were deliberately set to threatening music with interviewees filmed in dimly lit rooms or apparently secretive laboratories.

Shock at the announcement wasn't limited to the popular press. Academic and scientific publications were astonished that this feat had been accomplished. The highly respected *New England Journal of Medicine* published a discussion paper in which two scientists took opposing views.[1] John Robertson from the University

1. Roberston, J.A., and Annas, G.J., 'Human Cloning', *New England Journal of Medicine* **339**, 1998, pp. 119–22.

of Texas, USA, argued that human cloning would be unlikely except in rare cases of infertility or genetic disease; that it was little different from the birth of identical twins; and that the important consideration is how a child is treated after its birth. Conversely, George Annas from Boston University, USA, said that cloning would devalue children and treat them as interchangeable commodities; it would radically alter what it means to be human, causing us to lose something vital to the uniqueness of humanity; and that it represents the height of genetic reductionism.

The day after the announcement, American President Bill Clinton performed a knee-jerk reaction and called on the USA's National Bioethics Advisory Commission to undertake 'a thorough review of the legal and ethical issues'. Three months later the commission issued a 115-page report, which did little to clarify the situation.

In fact, the very idea that Dolly was a clone of an adult sheep was so scientifically shocking that for a year or so after the initial declaration a number of scientists held the view that this just could not have happened. They believed there had to be some other explanation for Dolly's existence.[2] Even so, almost everyone acknowledged that a new chapter in the history of life on earth had been opened. The fact that you can create a clone has huge implications for the way we view life, its origins and its value. To that extent, cloning has the potential to become a powerful tool for those people eager to exploit the accumulating tower of genetic knowledge.

## Before Dolly

To see why there was such uniform surprise at Dolly's arrival, we need to have a quick look at the history of cloning. Dolly was not the

---

2. The problem was that Dolly's 'parent' animal had died months or years before she had been born, so there was no parental tissue sample against which Dolly's could be compared. The cells that gave rise to Dolly had been taken at random from tissue samples stored in a laboratory freezer. This particular controversy was basically laid to rest with the publication of two papers in *Nature* showing that Dolly's DNA profile was that of a six-year-old ewe, rather than the two-year-old that she actually was: *Nature* **394**, 1998, pp. 329–30 and *Nature* **394**, 1998, p. 330.

world's first clone. For decades scientists had been making clones of reptiles. In the 1950s American scientists Robert Briggs and Thomas King found that they could take the nuclei of cells from very early-stage larval frogs and place them inside frog eggs.[3] These then grew into full adult frogs. Because they could take dozens of cells from a single donor larva the resulting mass of frogs were all clones of each other. However, they also found that you couldn't perform this trick using cells from older embryonic frogs or adults.

Then, working in Oxford, John Gurdon found that with the African clawed toad, *Xenopus laevis*, the nuclei of cells taken from well-developed larvae could be used to create healthy clones.[4] Later work showed that you could take cells from adult toads and generate clones that grew to be larvae, but did not proceed to become fully developed adults. More recently, techniques have been devised to generate clones from cattle, mice and rhesus monkeys.[5] But there was a fundamental shift in the process of cloning that made Dolly a celebrity.

Prior to Dolly, all mammalian cloning work had involved taking a developing embryo and gently pulling it apart to form a collection of individual cells. Each of these cells would be genetically identical and could then be slipped under the outer membrane of an egg that had previously had its nucleus removed. The egg then behaved as if it had just been fertilised and developed into an embryo. If eight cells and eight eggs were used, this would theoretically produce eight identical embryos. Using standard techniques of fertility treatment, each cloned embryo could be placed inside a female of its own species and allowed to develop until it was ready to be born.

Cattle breeders were enthusiastic about the technique. The possibility was open now to create an embryo from a high-calibre

3. Briggs and King, *Proceedings of the National Academy of Science* **38**, 1952, pp. 455–63.

4. Gurdon, J.B., *Developmental Biology* **4**, 1962, pp. 256–73.

5. Neti and Ditto were born at the Oregon Regional Primate Research Center in Beaverton, USA. Their DNA comes from unspecialised rhesus monkey embryo cells.

bull and prize-winning cow, and then rather than just getting one calf for their labours, they could get up to sixteen, maybe more. But if this was all they could do, they would have been less excited. What makes cattle breeding such a lottery is that just because a calf comes from prize stock does not guarantee that it will be a winner. Until the beast has been born and grown up there is no way of knowing its quality.

However, with this sort of cloning, you can implant one embryo and freeze the rest. When the implanted clone develops you can assess its characteristics, and you then have a much better idea about the chance of the remaining clones performing well or badly. Only the clones of embryos that perform well will be implanted, giving you the opportunity to have a herd containing 100 per cent winners; clones of underachievers need not be given the chance of life.

A more ideal scenario, however, would be to clone the prize-winning bull in the first place, rather than trying to work on his progeny. This would require taking cells from the adult animal and fusing them with an egg. Prior to Dolly this was deemed to be impossible. To understand the main argument against using an adult cell, we need to go back to basics. Remember that pretty well every cell in the body carries within it an entire copy of the animal's genetic code. One of the many things we don't understand about that code is what causes only a fraction of the genes to be expressed in any one cell. The cells in a piece of skin do not use the same selection of genes used by those in the kidney. Similarly the kidney uses specific genes that brain cells don't use. At issue is how does a brain cell know that it is a brain cell and consequently only use the genes that a brain cell needs?

The first cell that is formed at fertilisation has to be capable of giving rise to cells that can become anything. They are 'totipotent' – they have total potential. However, during the formation of the embryo, the cells move in a seemingly orchestrated pattern, so that some groups of cells develop into muscle blocks, while others become nervous tissue. As the cells migrate, they become increasingly specialised and throughout this process the genes that are no longer required are blocked or switched off.

By the mid-1990s the basic feeling was that once switched off, these genes are permanently disabled. One consequence of this would be that it would not be possible to take a body cell, a somatic cell, and use its DNA as the genetic parent of a clone.

## Then the shock

But that is exactly what happened with Dolly.[6] Dolly started out as a single cell that had been removed from the udder of a six-year-old sheep. The cell had been kept in a nutrient-depleted solution, which, for some unknown reason, had reprogrammed it so that it effectively forgot that it had once been specialised. It reverted to being totipotent. At the same time as doing this, an egg had been collected from a donor sheep and the chromosomes inside the egg had been removed by sucking them out with a microscopic glass tube. The reprogrammed cell and the empty egg were then placed alongside each other and a small electric pulse was applied. This jogged the cellular apparatus into action. The two cells fused into a single entity and an embryo started to develop. The two cells acted as one and soon generated into a bundle of cells. Once the embryo had grown in a laboratory it was transferred to the uterus of yet another ewe that was to act as surrogate mother. About five months later a seemingly healthy lamb was born. In her book, *Clone*, journalist Gina Kolata describes the birth as being incredibly low-key, with none of the people involved particularly excited, and blissfully unaware of the scale of response that this event would generate.[7]

One of the first proofs that Dolly was a clone was her colour-marking. To see why, we need to trace her 'parentage'. The udder cell that was used to donate Dolly's DNA came from a Finn Dorset

6. Dolly was initially named as an in-house joke based on the notoriety of Dolly Parton, the American country-music singer who is renowned for the size of her breasts – her mammary glands. I don't think they ever expected the sheep to become an international celebrity herself.

7. Kolata, G., *Clone*, Penguin, 1997.

sheep – a breed that has a greyish-white fleece and a pure white face. The egg cell which had had its DNA removed was from a Scottish Blackface sheep – a breed that, as its name suggests, has a dark-coloured head. The surrogate mother was also a Scottish Blackface. The lamb that flopped to the floor of the sheep shed was clearly a Finn Dorset and not a Scottish Blackface. Her genes must have originated in the cell taken from the Finn Dorset.

The secret to the success of this relatively simple procedure appears to be a stage where the scientists starve the donor cell so that it goes into a dormant stage for a few days. For some reason, this is sufficient to give it genetic amnesia. The cell forgets its specialised history and reverts to an almost embryonic, totipotent state.

No one, least of all the scientists at the centre of the work, claims that they fully understand what was happening during the cloning process, much less that cloning has been tamed. After all, Dolly was the sole survivor from an experimental group that started with 277 udder-cell–egg fusions. But the key to the excitement was the realisation that it could happen. Cloning could be achieved by taking a fully differentiated adult cell and an egg.

So the obvious question on everyone's lips was, 'If you can clone adult sheep, could you do it using adult cells from other mammals? And how about human beings?' Despite much talking, there seems to have been relatively little action since Dolly hit the stage. In July 1998 a group based in Honolulu, Hawaii, and headed by Teruhiko Wakayama, showed that you could perform essentially the same feat with mice,[8] and later that year a Japanese team headed by Dr Y. Kato claimed to have produced eight cloned calves, starting from adult cells.[9] One recently published paper indicates that the success rate for this sort of process hasn't increased, as only 3 out of 274 mouse cloned embryos that were transferred to surrogate

8. Wakayama, T., et al., 'Full-Term Development of Mice from Enucleated Oocytes Injected with Cumulus Cell Nuclei', *Nature* **394**, 1998, pp. 369–74.

9. Kato, Y., et al., 'Eight Calves Cloned from Somatic Cells of a Single Adult', *Science* **282**, 1998, pp. 2095–98.

mothers survived to birth and only one survived into mouse adulthood.[10]

## Human application

As for human beings, things seem less clear. This is partly because it is difficult to see through the dust caused by so much misinformed debate and ethical jumping up and down, and partly because researchers are unwilling to show their hands.

One of the loudest proponents of human cloning is an American engineer by the name of Richard Seed. Within days of Dolly's unveiling, he had announced to the world that he was setting up a programme to clone human beings. He wanted to be the first person to achieve this and volunteers were welcome to get in touch with him. At a meeting held at the Royal Society in London[11] he announced that he had two principal motives for this work. One was to gain the fame that would undoubtedly accompany being seen as the mastermind behind the first human clone, and the second was that as he was getting older his body was not working so well and he was looking forward to starting out again in a new, rejuvenated one. 'A self-clone is an expression of immortality, and the ultimate expression of the selfish gene,' he shouted with a somewhat frightening grin on his face as he limped his huge frame around the podium. Asked how long it would be before he was ready to create his first clone, he was evasive. 'That's a secret,' he responded, saying that he didn't want to give any clues to the 'opposition', and that his greatest fear at the moment was that he would come second in the cloning race.

Claiming to be a Bible-believing Christian, and belonging to the Methodist church, he said of cloning that 'It is now clear that the destiny of man is to become one with God.'

While the public and legislators try to get their minds around

10. Reported in a letter that Teruhiko Wakayama and Ryuzo Yanagimachi published in *Nature Genetics* **22**, 1999, pp. 127–28.

11. The meeting was entitled 'Being human – the science and philosophy of cloning', and was held on 30 March 1999.

the implications of cloning human beings, some scientists are forging ahead. American Jose Cibelli has fused an emptied cow egg to a cell taken from the lining of his cheek. Apparently the human–cow hybrid grew for two weeks before dying.[12] On top of this two doctors at a fertility centre in Seoul, South Korea, Kim Seung Bo and Lee Bo Young, caused an outcry when they took a spare human egg, removed its DNA and fused it to a human adult cell. The resulting clone developed until they deliberately ended the 'experiment' once it had grown to the four-cell stage. And these are the attempts that have been made public; no one knows how many trial runs have never seen the light of publicity.

Attempts at human cloning are not just driven from within science and medicine. A religious group based in Canada, called the Raelian Movement, is offering to supply a cloning service for $200,000 once the technology has been developed. They have based their cloning operation, CLONAID®, in the Bahamas to avoid any anti-cloning legislation. Their web site states that they will 'offer [their] services to wealthy parents worldwide'.[13] In addition they have set up a service called INSURACLONE®, under which anyone who pays $50,000 can have a sample of cells taken and stored. CLONAID® envisages that the cells would be taken from children or a beloved person 'in order to create a clone if the child dies of an incurable disease or through an accident'. Don't laugh. They are serious. They also propose a CLONEAPET® service.

There appears to be no biological reason to believe that the technique which produced Dolly could not produce a human being. But there is every reason to believe that, for the foreseeable future, the process is fraught with danger, the danger of extremely high levels of miscarriage, and the possibility that any child born is more

12. Interviewed on the BBC *Panorama* programme, 'The First Human Clone', first shown on 8 February 1999. We will see later in the chapter that, surprisingly, the hybrid did have some cow DNA even though all of the DNA had been removed from the nucleus of the cow's egg.

13. www.clonaid.com

likely than not to die within days of birth. After all, Dolly was the only survivor from 277 embryo clones.

## A new ~~ewe~~ you

The most powerful lobby for cloning is likely to come from couples who have failed to have a baby by any other means. One in six couples will have some problem trying to have a baby. Many of them find that some minor intervention is all they need to sort things out, but others find that, after a decade or more of tests, treatments, expense and emotional trauma, their hopes have not been fulfilled. Cloning would give one more option.

Even for those who see no particular ethical problem in helping people have babies by any technological means possible, the main argument currently levelled at human reproductive cloning is safety, or rather the lack of it. There is fear in the scientific community that the backlash from a disastrous outcome of a human cloning venture could scupper many other areas worthy of pursuit.

Others say that the possible implications for any resulting child are so unpredictable that human cloning is most unlikely to occur. 'I haven't heard of a suggested reason for [human] cloning with which I'm personally comfortable for ethical reasons... I don't think you can find a reason for doing it that will be fair for the child,' says Ian Wilmut, head of the team that created Dolly. However, Lee Silver thinks this view naive: 'I don't think Dr Wilmut is being realistic because he doesn't understand the powerful force driving human beings to want to reproduce and the fact that infertile couples will want to use this technology as a last resort to have babies.'[14] Silver is thinking of couples who are incapable of producing either sperm or eggs, or both, but are unwilling or unable to make use of donated sperm, eggs or even donated embryos. Cloning gives the hope of another tool in the reproductive tool kit. It could also be of particular use in male infertility where an egg could be taken from the woman

14. Interviews given by Wilmut and Silver were broadcast on BBC *Panorama*, 8 February 1999.

and a body cell from the man. Any resulting embryo would then develop in the woman's body. The result is that both partners would be biologically involved in bringing this child into the world, but all of the child's DNA would have come from his 'father'. Such a technique could overcome one of the drawbacks in fertility treatment, which involves sperm donation, where the nurturing father (as opposed to the biological father) can easily feel uninvolved with the child.

This makes Wilmut anxious. Along with others he worries about the social status of any cloned human being and how well they will be able to cope with the idea that they are quite literally a chip off their 'parental' block. A cloned person would start life not with a blank sheet, but with one already marked with expectations based on how someone else lived their life. While Silver thinks that cloning can't be stopped he is also concerned: 'What happens', he says, 'when you come face to face with your daughter who looks just like your wife twenty-five or thirty years earlier?' I share his anxiety.

Some people argue that it would be plausible to use cloning to replace a fetus or newborn baby who died due to some accident, or was possibly aborted because the embryo was growing outside the womb – an ectopic pregnancy. This, they say, could be of particular use for a couple who had been struggling for pregnancy in the first place. It could be achieved in one of two ways. You could take a cell from the dying child, or take a sample of cells from children as soon as they are born and store them in a tissue bank. This bank would then 'pay out' if there was an accident at some point in the future. The latter could lead to a particularly bizarre scenario of one parent comforting the other with the words: 'Don't worry, honey, we can always have her again.'

You will also hear the argument that single women and lesbians might wish to use the technique to create a child, a DIY baby that does not need the involvement of any male. However, there is little evidence to support this view. Shortly after Dolly was announced, the Wellcome Trust, a medical research charity that also works hard at helping people outside science get an informed insight, ran a consultation exercise to see what people thought about different aspects of cloning. The report made interesting reading. Here is one paragraph:

*One hypothesis suggested – that lesbian women might view cloning as offering a new option to have children without having contact with men – was rejected. The lesbian women consulted in this research dismissed reproductive cloning as unnatural and unnecessary. They respond firmly to the scenario that depicted two women using cloning to have a child: 'I think this is far more dangerous than anything else that we have talked about because it totally excludes the male from any point at any stage of growing a new child.'*[15]

Outside these scenarios are the more hysterically driven notions of dictators building armies of identical human combatants, or visions of factories populated by Epsilon-style workers as was prophesied by Aldous Huxley in his book *Brave New World*.[16] Along with these run the notions of bringing Pablo Picasso, Albert Einstein or Princess Diana back to life.

One argument against reproductive cloning is that the process is unnatural. Personally, I believe that this is a weak point because while it is unnatural, so is much of conventional medicine that relies on synthetic drugs and surgical operations. The glasses I wear in order to see the computer screen as I type are not natural, though I'm not about to get rid of them on that account. We need to be careful of falling into the simplistic trap of assuming that artificial is bad, and that natural is good. On its own the naturalness of an action tells us little about its ethical value.

Cloning to create a new person is also said to defy nature in denying the individual's right to have their own unique set of genes, their own private genetic endowment. People holding this view feel that by creating a genetic rerun you would be removing some aspect of the clone's personal rights and freedoms. However, can we really argue that everyone has a right to his or her own private set of genes?

15. In 'Public Perspectives on Human Cloning – A Social Research Study Conducted by the Wellcome Trust', section 2.4. The study was commissioned in the spring of 1998. The research sorts the opinions of seventy-nine people from five locations in the UK.

16. Out of interest, I wonder how many of the people who say, 'This is just like Huxley's *Brave New World*,' have ever read it?

How about identical twins? Identical twins start out as a single fertilised egg that over the first few days divides into two masses of cells, two embryos. Each subsequently develops into an individual. Many studies have turned to identical twins to try to establish the proportion of a person's personality that is derived from their genetic make-up or from their social and physical environments. In his book, *Twins*,[17] Lawrence Wright points to evidence that genetics has a large influence over who we are, but no one can deny that a pair of identical twins are two separate people with their own individual rights and responsibilities. Sharing hugely similar, even identical, gene sets with another person doesn't mean that you lose your personal identity.

A clone would be as similar to his or her 'parent' as identical twins are to each other. In fact, the two people would probably be less similar, because they would grow up with an age difference of a few decades, and so have very different sets of life experiences.

In a Christian context, the Christian Medical Fellowship also points out that the Bible does not use a language of 'rights'. Instead, it says that 'we have responsibilities and duties towards God and towards other people'. Consequently it says that, in a biblical world-view, the question of a right to a unique genetic identity is fundamentally meaningless.[18]

This leads us to realise that our genetic endowment is not necessarily as precious as we might have thought it. Phrases like 'your genetic blueprint' and 'the molecule of life' give DNA and the genes it carries an overrated status. It strikes me that one of the things that cloning research and the Babel project will do is start to refocus our definitions of what it is to be an individual human.

Anxieties that human cloning would produce a subspecies are also wide of the mark. There is every reason to believe that a healthy human clone would be indistinguishable from any other member of society wandering around. After all, Dolly is basically a normal sheep.

17. Wright, L., *Twins: Genes, Environment and the Mystery of Human Identity*, Phoenix, 1997.

18. Christian Medical Fellowship submission to the Human Genetics Advisory Commission and the Human Fertilisation and Embryology Authority, April 1998.

But that brings us back to the safety argument. Two hundred and seventy-six of Dolly's associate clones were highly distinguishable – they were incompatible with life. Having said that, research into cloning is continuing, and it seems only a matter of time before many of the safety issues will be resolved. What then?

## Public opinion

The argument often given by scientists when defending their research and their desire to implement the findings is that the general public is cautious because it doesn't really understand what is going on. This notion needs to be set against the main conclusion of the Wellcome Trust's commission relating to human cloning for reproduction:

*The public have fearful perceptions of human cloning and were shocked by the implications of the technology. The practice was firmly rejected by almost all of the participants in the research; only a handful were more positive. Understanding of the technical process of cloning was initially limited but the provision of additional factual information did not modify participants' primary concerns. These concerns focused on the likely social consequences of cloning and were often described in the context of popular cultural imagery such as science-fiction films and media stories portraying the lives of public figures. Scientific news coverage appeared to have a lesser impact upon views.*[19]

In this case, understanding did nothing to allay fears. Human reproductive cloning was believed to have no place in our world because it is unsafe and undesirable.

## Novel transplant material

'Not so fast,' shout some commentators. 'Cloning could be a perfect way of finding a donor for a replacement organ, such as bone marrow or a kidney, for a person whose own organs are damaged.'

Organ transplantation has been one of the heralded achievements

19. Christian Medical Fellowship submission to the Human Genetics Advisory Commission and the Human Fertilisation and Embryology Authority, summary, p. 4.

of medicine, giving a new lease of life to one person by making use of organs recovered from another person who has tragically lost their fight for life. Two key features limit the success of organ transplantation. First, there is a shortage of appropriate organs, and secondly, organs are frequently rejected by the body they are placed in as the recipients' immune system recognises that the new organs are genetically different.

Advertising campaigns and social intervention could increase the numbers of organs that are offered for transplantation, but while that is undeniably a difficult issue to handle it is much easier than tackling the science of organ rejection. Donated organs risk being rejected because the body's immune system attacks them in the same way that it attacks disease-causing bugs that may enter the body. To prevent this occurring, the recipient of the new organ is faced with taking powerful drugs that reduce the effectiveness of his or her own immune system. These drugs must be taken for the rest of their lives. Even then many organs are rejected after a few years.

Part of the skill in running a transplant programme is matching donors and recipients. The better the match, the better the chance of long-term success. At root the elements of the match have their origins in the genetic codes of the donor and recipient. If tissue was taken from a patient and a clone produced, the two people would share an identical genetic make-up. So this raises the spectre of embryos, fetuses or babies being brought into existence to be the ideal donor.

The idea is not as far removed from reality as we might like to believe. In June 1991 Mary and Abe Ayalas caused a stir by announcing that they had conceived a child with the sole purpose of providing compatible bone marrow for their teenage daughter.[20] Against the odds, baby Marissa was a good match and, when fourteen months old, she 'donated' some of her bone marrow to her elder sister. At the time, ethicists asked what would have happened had an antenatal test shown that Marissa had an incompatible blood

20. Reported in 'Medical Technology: Handle with Care', *USA Today*, 4 June 1991, p. 10A.

type? Would she have been aborted so that the couple could try again? Journalist Gina Kolata found that the Ayalas' situation was not an isolated case, and that dozens of couples arranged a pregnancy in the hope of generating a donor for an existing child.[21]

## Stem-cell therapies

Yet another possible use of human cloning has been termed 'therapeutic cloning'. This starts in just the same way that reproductive cloning would: take an egg, empty its nucleus of DNA, bring an adult cell alongside it, and give them a pulse of electricity – and the cell starts to grow and divide. So far this is exactly the same procedure as cloning. The difference is that at this stage the embryo is broken into its constituent cells and treated in such a way that these 'stem cells' do not become specialised and lead to the development of organs. Instead they simply self-propagate and produce more of themselves. The embryo has, in effect, been diverted into a developmental cul-de-sac.

These stem cells are valuable because they have the potential for developing into any tissue found anywhere in the body. They are 'totipotent'. Once enough of the stem cells have been harvested, the hope is to be able to trigger them to develop, not into a whole organism, but more likely into a raft of cells of a single tissue type. Some researchers are growing sheets of cells and then forming them into tubes to build replacement blood vessels. It may be possible at some point in the future to cause the cells to develop into entire organs, though there is much work needed before this can happen.

These populations of cells, tissues or organs would have the distinct advantage of being genetically identical to the person who donated the original cell. Using them in reparative surgery or transplantation could then be very attractive as no anti-rejection drugs would be needed. In this way, stem cells could be grown in culture and then be used for skin grafts for burn victims, or possibly

21. Reported in Kolata, G., 'More Babies Being Born to Be Donors of Tissue', *New York Times*, 4 June 1991.

to build new nerves that could patch up the brain damage that conditions like Parkinson's disease cause.

Stem-cell research is counted as one of the most exciting areas of biotechnology and until Dolly was born it was not seen to have any serious ethical dilemmas. After all, everyone really did believe that you couldn't take an old person's cell and create a new person. This was just a clever way of growing cells in culture, and it had nothing to do with starting new individuals. However, all that has changed and now the first part of the stem-cell process is the same as that used to create Dolly. Therefore we have to ask whether stem cells are obtained by creating a new human life, and then diverting it into a developmental cul-de-sac.

Realising the anxiety that the word 'cloning' brings, there is now a desire among the technique's proponents to move away from calling it 'therapeutic cloning' and concentrate on using the term 'stem-cell technology'. However, the technique undoubtedly begins by creating a clone.

When asked to consider therapeutic cloning there was an interesting response from the people involved in the Wellcome Trust's consultation exercise:

*Unlike reproductive cloning, this concept did not arise spontaneously during discussions and required prompting and explanation. At first, participants saw cloning in this context as 'good' as it would be beneficial for health. After more information and consideration, reservations were expressed and caveats on the type of research and the uses to which it would be put were drawn out.*[22]

And:

*Participants were not fundamentally opposed to the principle of using cloned human embryos for medical research, although as they gained more information and considered the issues, significant reservation and conditions were stipulated.*[23]

22. 'Public Perspectives on Human Cloning', summary, p. 3.
23. 'Public Perspectives on Human Cloning', section 6.4.

Proponents of this technique say that there are no ethical problems, because the embryo is diverted from its natural development before it is fourteen days old, the age at which a rudimentary nervous system starts to develop. This is the age that the Human Fertilisation and Embryology Authority (HFEA) uses as a cut-off for experiments on human embryos, deeming that without a nervous system the embryo has no claim to be called a 'person'. However, giving the participants this information did little to allay their fears:

*Increasing knowledge of the science and related issues around these uses of cloning technology brought about greater sophistication in the debate, but as the participants' awareness increased, so did their concern and apprehension. While the potential value of using cloning technology for therapies was accepted initially, participants became more critical as they considered the implications further.*[24]

Again the more people knew, the more cautious they were about using the techniques.

## Pretty Polly

Peering into the future, we see some other possible uses for cloning. They would be of particular interest to families who have identified genetic diseases passing from one generation to the next. If you took a cell from an adult who carries a genetic disorder and cultured it in a laboratory petri dish, you could apply some yet-to-be-invented gene therapy to it in the hope of fixing the genetic problem. The aim might be to correct the spelling of an existing gene or add new genetic material.

Tests on the newly altered cell could show whether the therapy has been a success or whether it has created additional problems. Cells that have had their genetic code corrected could then be used in a cloning procedure and a new healthier individual could be on his or her way towards being born.

24. 'Public Perspectives on Human Cloning', section 3.3.

Such a procedure would alter every cell in the new individual's body, including the germ cells – those that produce eggs and sperm. It would therefore introduce a potent form of germ-line gene therapy.

You might have noticed that I said 'could' and 'might' an awful lot in the previous few paragraphs. It might not happen, but it could. And if it did would that be good? Again we have all the problems of bringing a baby into the world with the added baggage of expectation that would come from being a genetic replica of an existing individual, and this time there is the extra burden of elevated expectation.

More than ever, this sort of approach would make way for all sorts of potential manipulation. Why stop at adding genes that remove genetic illness? Why not add a gene to give the person increased immunity against the common cold? Quite soon we could be on the way to the much-talked-of 'designer baby'. Medicine would have moved to a point where, rather than treating people, it was trying to create a superior design. In Wyatt's terminology, we would no longer be setting out to restore the damaged masterpiece, but trying to improve it.

And how far-fetched is this idea? If you like conspiracy theories, Dolly is a superb smokescreen, but Polly is the real force to be reckoned with. While Dolly is pretty much a rerun of an animal that has existed before, Polly is a sheep with add-ons. And the add-ons make all the difference. Dolly led to a stream of questions about the desirability of producing genetic reruns, but Polly introduces a world where cloning meets genetic engineering.

So who, or what, is Polly? In the summer of 1997, about a year after the birth of Dolly, the same team of scientists backed by PPL Therapeutics announced that they had another woolly world first. On this occasion they had taken skin cells from a sheep fetus and grown them in a laboratory. To these cells they then added genes that produce proteins normally found only in humans. A few of the fetal cells took up and started to use these human genes. The scientists fused these adapted cells to enucleated egg cells (cells with the nucleus removed) and triggered new embryonic development with an electric pulse. Some of the embryos developed to birth. The first was called Polly and two similar lambs were born a few days later.[25]

The result is that we can now take mammalian cells, add a gene to them, check that the new gene has been added properly, and then use these quality-controlled cells to create a new genetically manipulated individual.

Why bother? The creators of Polly are primarily interested in generating pharmaceutical products in animals' milk. In this case the protein was human Factor IX (sometimes called Christmas factor), a protein that is missing in some people who have haemophilia. Without this protein in their blood any cuts or bruises that they may get in day-to-day life bleed for many hours. Conventional ways of obtaining clotting factors from donated human blood are costly and carry the risk of introducing some new infection into the recipient. A friend of mine, and fellow Ph.D. student at the University of Reading, UK, died of HIV-AIDS as a result of receiving the virus through supplies of the clotting factors that he needed to control his haemophilia. Getting this protein from sheep's milk could be a lot cheaper and safer.

But if you cast your mind back you will remember that we have already met Tracy in chapter 3 – the sheep who produced alpha-1-antitrypsin in her milk – and she was announced in 1991. So what is the big news about Polly? The difference is that the technique of cloning used for Polly is potentially a lot more effective and controlled than the much more hit-and-miss technique used to place the desired gene in Tracy. PPL Therapeutics believe that this transgenic cloning could halve the number of animals needed to achieve successful results compared with the systems used to create Tracy. From a commercial point of

25. Schnieke, A.E., Kind, A.J., Ritchie, W.A., Mycock, K., Scott, A.R., Ritchie, M., Wilmut, I., Colman, A., and Campbell, K.H.S., 'Human Factor IX Transgenic Sheep Produced by Transfer of Nuclei from Transfected Fetal Fibroblasts', *Science* **278**, 1997, pp. 2130–33.

view this is great news, and from the point of view of a patient looking for a good source of pharmaceutical agents this brings real hope.

The problem is when you start looking a little further into the future. Transpose this technology into a human environment and add a pinch or two of imagination, and the designer baby comes into view. For instance, a couple wanting their child to achieve in sport could provide sperm and eggs which could be used to generate an embryo. This embryo could be dispersed into many individual cells and these cells grown in a laboratory. Genes that can enhance size, strength, maybe agility, could be added and those cells that had taken up the genes could be easily detected. The last stage would be to turn these cells into clones and implant them in the mother's womb. Nine months later you would have your baby, modified to your specification.

To an extent you could argue that these are no longer clones as they now have a set of genes which is not identical to that of the donating 'parent', but the process involved is that of nuclear transfer – the technique currently called 'cloning'.

You might dismiss this on the basis that no one is that concerned about sport. Maybe, though, the current use of growth hormone in the USA by parents anxious that their sons should win trophies indicates the lengths some people are already taking to pursue that goal. But how about giving a gene that would provide the resulting child with an increased ability to fight off infections? How about giving a gene that removed cystic fibrosis from your family line for ever? How about increased protection from cancer?

How about thinking through the possibilities before companies like the UK's PPL Therapeutics and the US biotechnology company Geron have developed the technique to the point that it is conceivable to use it with human beings?

## The ultimate commodity

The problem, to my mind, with all of the potential uses for cloning is that, to a greater or lesser extent, they turn the embryo or child into a commodity. It is all too easy to drive fertility programmes from the point of view of solving the couple's desire to have a child, without pausing to think about the possible consequences for any child born of the process. Some fertility experts even go so far as to argue that it is irrelevant to consider the child during the fertility programme, because at that point the child does not exist. Also, developments in treatments can seem so exciting that it is easy to overlook the means that bring about the particular end.

Writing in *The Times*, Alan Colman, director of PPL Therapeutics, said, 'These uses [human reproductive cloning] are unethical; they dehumanise the new individual because he or she can be considered the product of an assembly line.'[26]

But what of an adult's right to have children that is enshrined in our underlying legal structures? For instance, the United Nations' 1969 declaration of Social Progress and Development says, in Article 4, 'Parents have the exclusive right to determine freely and responsibly the number and spacing of their children.' The European Declaration of Human Rights also asserts the right of a person to have a family. However, these rights to be free from imposed restrictions placed upon our reproductive freedoms should not be interpreted as carte blanche permissions to create children by any means.

Indeed the European Parliament reacted strongly to the news of Dolly by passing a resolution that contained the following statement:

*The cloning of human beings, whether experimentally, in the context of fertility treatment, pre-implantation diagnosis, tissue transplantation or for any other purpose whatsoever, cannot under any circumstances be justified or tolerated by any society, because it is a serious violation of fundamental human rights and is contrary to the principle of equality of human beings as it permits a eugenic and racist selection of the human race, it offends against human dignity and it requires experimentation on humans... each individual*

26. Colman, A., 'Why Cloning Would Be Inhuman', *The Times*, 15 June 1998.

*has a right to his or her own genetic identity and human cloning is, and must continue to be, prohibited.*[27]

Colman is also worried about the effect that being a clone might have on the child. He points out that although Louise Brown, the first test-tube baby, has been allowed a media-free childhood, he does not believe that that would happen for the first clone: 'I just do not believe that man-made clones would be granted the same freedom to develop and, therefore, I say that human cloning is unethical... A child so "manufactured" – and that I believe is the appropriate term – could be a twenty-first-century circus act.'[28]

It would be wholly incorrect to assume that using cloning would be the first instance when children are born for less than entirely unselfish motives. Throughout history, people have had a mixture of motives for having children. Some who lived in less-developed times or places preferred large families – having children was seen to be the best way of providing for yourself in old age, a type of self-help social security. This, of course, still happens in less-developed countries. Children have also been born and then given in marriage to solve territorial disputes. In the developed world, a successful child is all too often seen as a part of the trimmings of social achievement. None of these are particularly appealing concepts, because they all place on the child expectations and duties, making the child into a being who has been born to serve a purpose.

Commenting on the ethics of human cloning, the UK's Christian Medical Fellowship acknowledges that most people hoping to become natural parents do not have entirely unselfish motives. Even so, it believes that with human cloning 'the child would be

27. The European Parliament Resolution on Cloning (1997). By June 1999, twenty-eight states out of the forty-one potential signatories had signed up to this declaration including France and the Netherlands, although the UK and Germany are notable absentees. Only Greece, Slovakia and Slovenia have gone on to ratify this treaty.

28. 'Why Cloning Would Be Inhuman', *The Times*, 15 June 1998.

being created to fulfil a function, not to be loved for himself or herself'.[29] Such a 'carbon-copy' child would be a commodity.

The most extreme example of commodification is the suggestion of creating a clone to supply organs for a living child or adult. While the new individual will have a life of his or her own, the motive behind creating that life was to solve someone else's problem. No human should be born with the express burden of satisfying another's need. This would be a new and very nasty form of slavery. Justification for this sort of procedure is drawn from the fact that some like the Ayalas have already had children via natural mechanisms in the slim hope of generating a donor for a sick family member. But just because a few people are already creating children to serve others does not mean that it is morally justifiable.

Many of the concerns about cloning, be it for reproduction or therapy, hinge on the ethical status of early human embryos which we will discuss in the next chapter, but for now we should record that destroying embryos, for whatever purpose, raises ethical questions.

## Reaching a consensus

So where does this leave human cloning? The consensus view is that cloning which aims to produce a new human being has so many technical problems that it should be banned. In addition, the majority of people say there are so many ethical and moral issues that, even if these problems were solved, the procedure should never be used.

A joint report by the HFEA and the Human Genetics Advisory Commission (HGAC), the two bodies charged with the task of overseeing this area of technology in the UK, noted the lack of public support for reproductive cloning. In the words of Sir Colin Campbell, chairman of the HGAC, 'It is quite clear that human reproductive cloning is unacceptable to a substantial majority of the population. A total ban on its use for any purpose is the obvious and

29. Submission from the Christian Medical Fellowship to the HGAC and the HFEA, 'Cloning Issues in Reproduction, Science and Medicine', April 1998.

straightforward way of recognising this.'[30] This gives the impression that they were being reassuringly tough, but, in reality, there was not going to be a mass dash to clone babies.

In contrast to the almost uniform rejection of reproductive cloning, the potential for using cloning techniques to generate cells, tissues or organs to treat patients leaves people more divided. Acceptance of it can only be based on an understanding that before fourteen days of gestation the value of a human embryo is so slight that it can be broken into individual cells and used for the benefit of the person who donated the original cell.

At the moment, the HGAC and HFEA seem unwilling to take on-board evidence of concern about therapeutic cloning, saying that 'we believe it would not be right at this stage to rule out limited research using such techniques, which could be of great benefit to seriously ill people'.[31]

Ruth Deech, chairman of the HFEA, added to these comments, saying that 'much needs to be done to encourage public understanding of the complex issues involved'.[32] The implication being that if only people fully understood the science they would be more excited. However, this ignores the evidence from the Wellcome Trust exercise, in which the more people were helped to understand the issues and the science, the more anxious they became. If she is not careful, Deech is in danger of appearing to have her sights set on encouraging *acceptance of* rather than *understanding of* the technologies.

Whatever uses we make of cloning, one thing is sure: the fact that a set of old genes can be rejuvenated and used to start a new individual has radically altered the way we view life itself.

POSTSCRIPT ONE – THE TELOMERE TIME BOMB

Before cloning could be moved into the human market, everyone involved would surely want it to be safe. In particular, it should be

30. Press release accompanying the HGAC/HFEA report.

31. Press release accompanying the HGAC/HFEA report.

32. Press release accompanying the HGAC/HFEA report.

safe for any potential offspring. With this in mind, one unresolved issue is telomeres. These are the end tips of chromosomes, and as a person gets older these tips appear to get shorter. No one quite knows what these regions do, or what would happen if they became so short that they disappeared entirely. The assumption is that this is part of the body's ageing process.

Using the Dolly approach to cloning, a new individual starts life as a single cell taken from an adult. That cell will have shortened telomeres, so as the individual grows there will be aspects of its genetic make-up that point to the individual being decades older than he or she really is. Tests on Dolly, published in 1999, showed that the telomeres in her cells were the length you would expect to find in a sheep of six or more years old, not in the one-year-old she was when the test occurred. Time will tell whether her life is suddenly cut short or whether she suffers prematurely from diseases normally associated with ageing, although at the moment Dolly appears perfectly healthy and has undergone two normal pregnancies, each time delivering healthy lambs.[33]

At the same time as we are discovering about telomeres shortening throughout an individual's life, scientists are working out ways of rebuilding them. The US company Geron has developed methods for using telomerase, a naturally occurring protein that rebuilds broken-down telomeres. If the shortening does prove to be linked to diseases of old age, then this technology will be grasped as a potential elixir of youth.

POSTSCRIPT TWO – BUT DOLLY ISN'T A CLONE

Intriguingly, it now turns out that Dolly isn't a clone. Not in the fullest sense of the word. To be a clone you need to share 100 per cent of your DNA with your genetic 'parent' and fellow clones. And Dolly doesn't.

To see why not, we need to take a brief step back into basic

---

33. Shiels, P.G., Kind, A.J., Campbell, K.H.S., Waddington, D., Wilmut, I., Colman, A., and Schnieke, A.E.; 'Analysis of Telomere Lengths in Cloned Sheep', *Nature* **399**, 1999, pp. 316–17.

science. Sadly, or at any rate sadly for anyone who would like life to be simple, DNA is not exclusively located in the nuclei of cells. There are intracellular packages other than the nucleus called mitochondria – a type of organelle – which also contain this wondrous molecule. Mitochondria are the powerhouses of the cell, and play a key role in metabolism, taking energy derived initially from glucose and converting it into an energy-laden molecule (adenosine triphosphate – ATP for short) that the cellular machinery can use.

Arguments rage about how DNA comes to exist inside mitochondria, and its presence has had many fascinating forensic uses. But for our purposes we need only know that DNA-containing mitochondria are present in all cells.

If we go back to Dolly's creation, we find one egg (a particular type of cell), with its nucleus removed, being fused to a rejuvenated cell. Both of these cells will contain mitochondria. Both of them will therefore contain DNA that has come from their own genetic line of heritage. What has now been discovered of Dolly is that, as she has developed, she has lost all of the mitochondria that came packaged in the donor udder cell, and so her cells are populated solely with mitochondria derived from the egg.

Looking at her total genetic complement, therefore, she has DNA in the nuclei of her cells that hails from the sheep that provided the donated udder cells and DNA in her mitochondria that has its genetic origin in the animal that supplied the egg.[34] The consequences are not necessarily extreme, in that both sets of genes have come from sheep, albeit from two different breeds of sheep. And they have come from breeds that would be quite capable of breeding

---

34. Ian Wilmut and his colleagues have looked at cells from Dolly as well as those from nine other cloned sheep that were generated from fetal cells. 'The mitochondrial DNA of each of the ten nuclear-transfer sheep was derived exclusively from recipient enucleated oocytes [eggs], with no detectable contribution from the respective somatic donor. Thus, although these ten sheep are authentic nuclear clones, they are in fact genetic chimeras, containing somatic-cell-derived nuclear DNA but oocyte-derived mitochondrial DNA': *Nature* **23**, 1999, pp. 90–93.

together naturally. However, it can easily become more questionable, as was shown when Cibelli created the cow–human hybrid embryo that we encountered earlier in this chapter. The egg that donated the mitochondrial DNA was a cow's egg and the cell donating the nuclear chromosomal DNA was human. The embryo would therefore have its predominant features directed by its human chromosomal DNA, but a critical component of its metabolic activity would be conditioned by its bovine heritage. If the embryo had grown to term, you could look on it as being basically human, but with a little bit of cow on-board. We have a long way to go before we know how well cow mitochondria would work in the full range of human cells.

But so what? If the mitochondria are only concerned with the cell's metabolism – in other words, how well they supply energy to the cell – then does it matter where the instructions in it come from – assuming they are human? After all, if the experiments using human cells and cow eggs ever worked, you could land up with a human powered by bovine mitochondria. This starts to shed light on the complex nature/nurture debate. Are we who we are because of our genes (our nature) or our upbringing (our nurture)? To my mind the answer is that quite obviously both are involved.

In the mitochondria, mutations in certain genes may make them slightly better at supplying the cell with its energy. This is likely to enable the owner of these mitochondria to perform slightly better as an athlete than a competitor with a less favourable mitochondrial genetic endowment. In our society being a strong athlete can lead a person to have increased self-confidence. Winning is good for morale – learning to cope with failure could generate a steely personality or could leave someone with low self-esteem. Athletic talent will certainly affect how much time the person has available for developing other areas of his or her personality.

About half of people with an oriental background have a mutation in a mitochondrial gene that helps remove alcohol from their bodies.[35]

35. The enzyme is called mitochondrial aldehyde dehydrogenase and is the first line of defence in breaking down acetylaldehyde, a by-product of alcohol metabolism.

The consequence is that, for them, alcohol is much more potent than for people with the active version of the gene. It's easy to see how this could influence behaviour and personality.

So Dolly is really a weird genetic mixture. Certainly not a genuine clone. In the letter to *Nature* announcing this finding, Wilmut describes her as a 'chimera'. But even this isn't quite right. A chimera is an animal that has cells derived from more than one genetic source. The classic was the 'geep', an animal generated by fusing together a sheep embryo and a goat embryo. The resulting creation had the standard one head and four legs, but it had patches of goats' hair and patches of sheep's wool. Some of its cells were genetically goat, others were genetically sheep. But look at any one cell and it had a single basic origin.

Not so with Dolly. All of her cells have the same curious mixture of DNA from the cell donor and DNA from the egg donor.

So where does this leave the debate? Certainly more confused, but possibly only by a little. Dolly, after all, is not the be-all and end-all of the debate. Dolly might not be a pure clone, and so does away with the argument that this sort of process is not acceptable because we have no right to create a person who is not genetically unique.

But at issue is whether we want to put boundaries around a science which, if left uncontrolled, could turn human life into a designer commodity. Dolly has opened up new horizons, and at least she has encouraged us to start asking questions.

## Chapter 6

# GENETICS AND THE PERSON

*What are little boys made of?*
*Frogs and snails*
*And puppy-dogs' tails*
*That's what little boys are made of.*

*What are little girls made of?*
*Sugar and spice*
*And all that's nice*
*That's what little girls are made of.*[1]

At the centre of debates about medical applications of genetics is the anxiety that, if we are not careful, we will change humanity – we may even alter what it means to be a human being. The issue is important because most people accept that it is all right to deliberately breed animals to perform specific tasks – dogs as pets, cows to produce milk, horses to ride on – but that it is not all right to do the same with members of the human race. In addition, we find it acceptable to put a horse with a broken leg out of its misery by shooting it, but we take rather more care of members of our own species, preferring to care for a person up until his or her death. Even after death we believe that it is appropriate to treat their bodies with respect.

The division between *Homo sapiens* and the rest of the living

1. From Halliwell, J.O., *Nursery Rhymes*, 1844.

world seemed fairly straightforward until genetics revealed our similarity to other species. Our new knowledge of genetics shows that we share at least ninety-eight per cent of our genetic code with chimpanzees. But more than that, we have a seventy-five per cent overlap with animals like nematodes – millimetre-long soil-dwelling worms. Using a scientific argument to assert the unique value of our species has little credibility.

For this reason, my toes always curl with mild embarrassment when I hear people talking about humanised animals: animals such as Polly that have a gene from a human being inserted into their chromosome. If we classify that as a human gene, what do we call all the other genes that we have in common with sheep? While some people use it as shorthand, others use it to stir up fear and ask whether sheep with a 'human gene' should now be given increased ethical status.

Genetics, if taken as the only point of reference, has no grounds for justifying the moral supremacy of human beings over other animals – a position that most people find to be incompatible with their experience of squashing a fly. If, as I believe, we are more than animals, then we will have to look beyond our DNA to find out where that difference comes from.

## I am my brain

The most common argument used to give credence to our notion of superiority is that we have higher status because we are more intelligent. And it would appear that, as far as intelligence is concerned, size matters, although the relationship between brain size and intelligence is not totally straightforward.

Anatomists have shown that there is a clear relationship between the size of an animal's body and the size of its brain. The bigger the animal, the bigger the brain. A pigmy tree shrew's brain weighs about a tenth of a gram, while a whale's brain weighs eight kilograms. This doesn't mean that the whale is thousands of times more intelligent that the shrew, but that the whale has a lot more body to look after, muscles to control and surface area to monitor than a shrew. However, primates, and human beings in particular, are different – they break the rule. A chimpanzee's brain is larger than can be explained simply by looking at the size of its body, and our brains are about twice the size that you would expect for our size. So this is a clue to the biological basis of our exceptionally high level of intelligence.

Australian philosopher Peter Singer believes that we should drive these observations to their logical conclusions. He points out that if our kidneys are dead we continue to survive using the services of a kidney machine. But if a person's brain is destroyed he or she is considered to be dead, even though at the time of the pronouncement, the rest of his bodily organs may be very much alive. He would see individual animals, including human beings, ranked according to how well they can think. The better your ability to think, the higher in the ranking you are placed, the higher your status and the more your life should be protected. He maintains that to place human beings in a rank of their own is 'speciesism' – a particularly nasty form of discrimination.

In *Remaking Eden*, Lee Silver attempts to describe human existence by saying that there are two types of life: 'life in the general sense', and, 'life in the special sense'. The general is our biological bodily function, the everyday life of our cells. The special is 'localised in the region between our ears, but it lies far beyond the level of any individual nerve cell'.[2] This is classical Cartesian dualism.[3] For Silver, life in the special sense is identified in a human being's ability for 'reflective self-awareness'.[4] In effect he adopts Descartes' position of *cogito, ergo sum*[5] – 'I think, therefore I am.' A person is thus defined by their ability to think and realise that they exist. It fits in well with the debate that has followed the eighteenth-century Enlightenment,

2. Silver, *Remaking Eden*, p. 22.

3. One of René Descartes' (1596–1650) fundamental doctrines is that we are made up of two elements: mind and body.

4. Silver, *Remaking Eden*, p. 22.

5. Descartes, R., *Le Discours de la Méthode*, 1673.

in which reason, knowledge, education and intellect were first recognised as being of great value.

Singer's horrific genius is to take concepts to their conclusions. If thinking is needed for a human animal to be given the status of a human being, then this status can be logically withheld from newborn babies, because, after all, babies are basically incapable of thinking. Most people shy away from this concept. Try suggesting to a mother who is cradling her day-old baby in her arms that the sleeping or crying infant is not fully human and you are unlikely to be taken seriously. Recognising this problem, Silver hesitates at this thought,[6] but intriguingly still continues to use the idea that reflective self-awareness is the critical feature of a human being as a central plank of the thesis he develops throughout the rest of his book.

Silver's hesitation exposes the flaw. In arguing that our intelligence alone gives us value, we arrive at a situation where dogs should be given higher status than human infants, and people with mental disorders soon find that they have less status. At its extreme, some researchers have argued that it should be ethically permissible to perform experiments on babies born without a cerebral cortex – anencephalic babies – because they cannot really be described as living human beings.[7] Singer extends this further to the cortex, the part of the brain where cognitive activity is purported to occur. Again, 'I think, therefore I am' – *cogito, ergo sum*. Wyatt terms this argument one of 'corticalism',[8] saying that it is a mode of thinking that makes value judgements about a person based on the ability of their cortex to perform.

You can see this thought process in action in medicine, where intensive care practitioners use the presence or absence of a functioning cortex as evidence of life or death; but we need to

---

6. Silver, *Remaking Eden*, p. 58.

7. Shewmon, D.A., Capron, A.M., Peacock, W.J., and Schulman, B.L., 'The Use of Anencephalic Infants as Organ Sources: A Critique', *Journal of the American Medical Association* **261**, 1989, pp. 1773–81.

8. Wyatt, *Matters of Life and Death*, p. 45.

recognise the distinct limitations of using this as the sole criterion of value.

## A matter of respect

We can't just ignore the fact that we give babies high moral status even though they can't think and are not able to reflect on their own existence. To do so would be to miss some critical issues. Human beings have value because it is given to them. This concept is not unique to people. Paper currency has its value because we respect it. You walk into a shop and hand over a few bits of paper and come out carrying bags of food, clothes or maybe even jewellery. No one is shocked that little bits of paper can have such power.

One of the calls from people who have disabilities is that they would like to have dignity, and they can only get it if those who meet them give it to them. Dignity can't be demanded; it can only be received.

Babies have high value and status because we give it to them. They may demand to be fed and scream out for attention, but they can't force anyone to give them dignity. It is a dignity that is reciprocally given and received by people as we meet and interact with each other.

I am intrigued that the creation story told in Genesis starts off by recognising that humankind shares almost everything with animals. They are all made as living creatures, made from the raw fabric, dust, of the earth, with life 'breathed' into them.[9] Theologians refer to it as a 'solidarity with the sixth day'.[10] According to the Bible, the only difference we find between human beings and animals is that we have been made 'in the image of God' – *imago Dei*. Unravelling the meaning of this phrase has taxed theologians and

---

9. In the Bible the Hebrew word translated as 'living beings' is *Nepeš* and is used for both non-human animals and human beings. Also the word *rûah*, which is translated as wind, breath or spirit, is used of all living creatures.

10. Sherlock, C., *The Doctrine of Humanity*, Inter-Varsity Press, 1996, p. 74. Dr Charles Sherlock is a former lecturer in theology at Ridley College, Melbourne, Australia.

philosophers for millennia, but it is certainly not meant to inform us about our physical nature. Instead it is a statement about our ability to reason, form relationships and take responsibility for our actions.[11] The dignity that we want to feel for ourselves and attribute to others is a product of the relationships between people and our joint responsibility for each other's welfare.

Christian theologians refer to this as a horizontal social relationship, but add to it a vertical dimension, that of a relationship with God. I believe that this close relationship with our creator is the foundation principle of our elevated status.

Applying this thinking to the anxiety that genetic technology threatens the fundamental nature of humanity, which I raised at the start of the chapter, we can see two opposing principles that need to be kept in balance. On the one hand, we are much more than a product of our genes, because our status has a highly relational element. This realisation can enable us to take a relaxed view of genetic adventures, because they cannot threaten what it is to be human. On the other hand, we can see that genetics gives us the power to ask new questions of each other, and to try to manipulate or modify individuals. Going back to Richard Seed's notion of putting chlorophyll in human beings, I think that it would be distinctly inadvisable, even wrong, but the resulting person would still be human. The problem is that, if used incorrectly, genetic technologies can treat individuals as if they have no value, and in so doing damage, and possibly even demean, the whole of humanity.

## The gene is the machine

Another way of viewing humanity, and any other living thing, has been proposed by Dawkins in coining the phrase the 'selfish gene'. He doesn't claim that there is a gene which makes us selfish. He

---

11. 'Ancient texts such as the Babylonian *Epic of Gilgamesh*, and modern groups such as the Mormons, hold that humans bear a physical resemblance to the god(s), based on ideas such as our walking upright rather than moving on all fours... Some seek to define what it means to be human by way of contrast with animals; at a popular level, reaction to Darwin's postulation of human descent from the apes revived these sorts of notions': Sherlock, *The Doctrine of Humanity*, p. 74.

doesn't even claim that genes in the way that most people define them are selfish, wanting to propagate copies of themselves. Dawkins's theory is that DNA itself is solely concerned with the task of replicating itself. Because Dawkins uses his own loose definition of genes, as lengths of DNA with no particular boundary, this allows him to say that 'genes' are intrinsically selfish.

Taking reductionism to an extreme that I and others find to be distinctly absurd,[12] Dawkins maintains that microbes, plants and animals are machines built by DNA to propagate itself – the DNA, that is. He refers to living things as 'survival machines – robot vehicles blindly programmed to preserve the selfish molecules known as genes'.[13] In other words, you and I are simply machines built to enable genes to survive. We have no greater purpose, and any illusion of purpose is something we create through our own accidentally evolved powers of imagination.

To be fair, even Dawkins sees the idea of a gene being selfish as silly, but he holds to the phrase by seeking to redefine the use of words. It is a favourite game of his. Earlier, in chapter 2, we examined how he redefined the concept of a gene, and now we see him set to work on the notion of selfishness. For him, 'selfish' describes the fact that biological systems are set up in a way that just happens to focus around propagating DNA, and as such has the appearance of self-seeking intention: 'When biologists talk about "selfishness" or "altruism" we… do not even mean the words in a metaphorical sense. We define altruism and selfishness in purely behavioural ways… In effect I am saying: "Provided I define selfishness in a particular way, an oak tree, or a gene, may legitimately be described as selfish."'[14] Actually, Dawkins's idea of selfishness is something along the lines of self-preserving, self-replicating or self-perpetuating.

12. A series of articles in *Science and Christian Belief* follows a debate between Michael Poole and Richard Dawkins, in which Poole sheds light on the flaws in the reductionist argument: **6**, 1994, pp. 41–59; **7**, 1995, pp. 45–50; and **7**, 1995, pp. 51–58.

13. Dawkins, R., preface to the 1976 edition of *The Selfish Gene*.

14. Dawkins, R., 'In Defence of Selfish Genes', *Philosophy* **56**, 1981, p. 557.

This need to redefine the use of common words stems from Dawkins's drift away from the science that he is seeking to explain. DNA can only function in the midst of a cell, which in turn provides a protective environment for the DNA. The relationship is circular. Without DNA, the cell would not exist; without the cell, DNA would have no role or function.

But taking Dawkins's argument at face value presents a picture that even he finds distasteful and difficult to reconcile with reality. In the first chapter of *The Selfish Gene* Dawkins states that he is 'not advocating a morality based on evolution... Be warned that if you wish, as I do, to build a society in which individuals cooperate generously and unselfishly towards a common good, you can expect little help from biological nature. Let us try to teach generosity and altruism, because we are born selfish.'[15]

On the one hand Dawkins is arguing that we are nothing but machines to propagate our genes, but then seeing the bleakness of this view he calls us to climb above the bland fate set by our molecular genetic masters. He calls us to create a sense of purpose for ourselves by using our accidentally generated intellect to espouse generosity and altruism. His request is that we strive to try to let nurture rise above nature.

To defend his position he also includes two additional riders. First, that the notion of the selfish gene 'is not an advocacy of one position or another in the nature/nurture controversy', and secondly, that the book 'is not a descriptive account of the detailed behaviour of man or of any other particular animal species'.[16] Looking at it another way, Dawkins limits this line of thinking to describe how he believes that the physical process of evolution may have occurred, but acknowledges that it has nothing to say about the nature of the beings that are the end-product of that evolution. For that we need to look at behaviour and relationship.

Realising that his notion of a gene bent on its own self-

15. Dawkins, *The Selfish Gene*, pp. 2–3.
16. Dawkins, *The Selfish Gene*, p. 3.

replication is insufficient to account for the creation, order and working of societies, Dawkins has now introduced the notion of a 'meme'. He describes memes loosely, but sometimes refers to them as parasites that live in the environment built by genes. In effect Dawkins is trying to show how ideas are passed around a population of people or animals, and in so doing create a recognisable culture that passes from one generation to the next, evolving gently as it does so. It's a nice idea, and as a meme has no physical existence it is very hard to prove or disprove it.

So, as far as Dawkins is concerned, a gene is a purposeless stretch of DNA sequence that has no particular beginning or end, but builds our bodies, as well as the structures of all living organisms, so that DNA can replicate. As far as I can see this has the effect of reducing life in all its wonder to less than the sum of our parts; all purpose is removed.

A consequence of this line of debate would be that there can be no reason for placing any limits on genetic technology. As nothing had any real purpose in the first place, nothing can be damaged. If the propagation of lumps of genetic code is the only reason why life forms exist, then no one needs to worry about esoteric issues such as the nature of a person.

The concept might work well in an academic debate, but it struggles to provide a convincingly watertight argument in the warm light of reality.

## Honouring our beginnings

It's important that we stop for a bit and ask, *At what point did we begin?* This is demanded by the convergence of two themes: the need to give dignity to all human beings, and the reality that many genetic techniques require human embryos to be created with the purpose of using them in experiments, or possibly modifying them. As we hold that it is unethical to experiment on living human beings, and are cautious about modifying them, we need to form a view about whether an embryo is human. Forming an opinion about the nature of the start of life is vital if we are to develop a society that uses its technology to serve humanity, rather than vice versa.

Again we will find the answer is not as clear as we would like, and we can argue that genetic knowledge has both clarified and confused the situation.

If, according to Dawkins, the purpose of our existence is to propagate genes, and we are in effect no more than a staging post for our genes to reside in, then asking when our existence started is impossible to answer. You can ask when this particular survival machine came into being, and the answer would be when the sperm and egg combined. But to ask the question at the level of purpose would require you to look at the genes, and their origins are lost in the mists of time.

This is all very clever, but for most of us the questions we are really asking are, *When did I start to exist? When did I start to be a person? When did I become a valuable member of the human race?* Or, for that matter, *When did I become a member of the valuable human race?* Let's look at some biology.

## Biology of a birth

The best place to start the search is at the time when a sperm and an egg combine. From now on we have a new individual. At face value there should be no controversy in that statement, but because of the pressures and tensions brought about by the pro-choice (or pro-abortion) and the pro-life (anti-abortion) lobbies I can feel the air begin to crackle already. I will try to choose my words carefully to avoid confusion.

I'll put it another way. When a sperm and an egg join, a new lump of humanity is created. This is indisputable. Fertilisation is the period when the half sets of DNA present in the sperm and egg start to act together to create a new set of variants that has never been seen before. I use the word 'period' rather than 'moment' because this coming together does not occur in an instant, but is a process that takes some twenty-four hours. In fact, the mingling of the two sets of DNA is not complete until the first stage of cell division has occurred and a two-cell embryo exists.

Let's pause for a moment to consider the genetics, because

there is nothing new about the DNA and the genes. Their history reaches back through countless generations. At a genetic level, asking, *When did I start?* is like standing in a hall of mirrors and trying to find the most distant image. Genetic counsellors are fond of drawing family trees and marking on them any known occurrence of an illness that could have a genetic factor. Your appearance, health and many other personal attributes will be influenced by mutations and genetic accidents that occurred many generations before. Viewed this way, 'you' started long before sperm met egg.

It's equally intriguing to realise that the cell forming the egg that created half of each of us was present in our mother's ovary when she was a fetus inside her mother. You can trace your biological roots back and back in highly tangible ways.

But, interesting though this may be, a newly formed embryo has a unique variation of genetic mutations, and has the potential of developing into a fully fledged human being. Because fertilisation is a process rather than an event I have difficulty with those who say that life starts at that moment. Biologically that moment doesn't exist. Once we have reached two cells we definitely have a living human entity. The difference between these two cells and any other pair of cells that you could get by, for example, scraping gently on the inner lining of your mouth, is that they have the potential to become a full individual. However, they have many hurdles to get over to fulfil that potential.

The first major hurdle is implantation. This starts some six days after egg and sperm have come together and the process takes six or seven days to complete. While reptiles and birds reproduce using large nutrient-filled eggs that are deposited outside the female's body, a mammalian egg is basically a single cell and the first thing to leave the female's body is a highly developed progeny. Mammalian embryos therefore need to tap into a source of oxygen and nutrients. They also need to plug into an effective waste-removal system. Both of these functions are achieved by invading the lining of their mother's womb, literally burying themselves inside the blood-vessel-rich surface and building a placenta.

The process has been likened to a parasite, such as a leech, locking onto its host, and although it has some validity as an analogy it gives a few false impressions, in particular that this is a pathological event. Far from this, it is a very healthy event and the mother's body is enabled to make many adaptations to accommodate the growing baby.

One thing is certainly true: the invading embryo is an individual, with a separate identity from the mother, and one who in fact lives on the outside of the mother's body. The lining of the womb is an external body surface that is folded in on itself, invaginated, inside the woman. An obstetrician friend described how you can achieve a similar effect by pushing your finger into an inflated balloon. Your finger goes into the inner space of the balloon, but it is still on the outside.

A remarkable feature about pregnancy is that the woman's body doesn't instantly reject the newcomer in the way that it would reject any other 'foreign' body. Then again, maybe quite often it does. It's difficult to arrive at firm figures for the success rate of implantation in human beings, partly because of the way that facts are all too often clouded by politics, and partly because it is hard to investigate. But somewhere between twenty-five and seventy-five per cent of embryos fail to implant and are lost before their mothers are even aware that they existed. Most probably a large proportion of these lost embryos have some major genetic defect that is confounding their development. However, the large rate of loss causes many people, myself included, to question whether it is sensible to afford full human status to these very young beings. I do not maintain that this is a conclusive argument, but it is one that needs considering.

One of the UK's senior experts on contraception, and a devout Christian, John Guillebaud, sees fertilisation as a process, a continuum, that starts with the fusion of sperm and egg and continues through to the point at which implantation is successfully completed.[17] Such a definition enables us to create a clear distinction

17. Guillebaud, J., *Contraception: Your Questions Answered*, Churchill Livingstone, 1993.

between fertilisation – the uniting of sperm and egg – and conception – the implantation of a new individual in a pregnant woman. Implantation also initiates a new maternal-embryonic relationship. Hormones from the embryo start to direct change in the mother's physiology, and the mother's body starts catering for the embryo's needs. The relationship is tenuous, and may not even be recognised for many months, but, at the very least, a physiological relationship has begun.

## Increasing capability

As the embryo is implanting in the lining of the womb, it[18] continues to develop. Starting as a solid blackberry-shaped lump of cells, it soon develops into a hollow ball surrounding a fluid-filled space. From now on an embryologist would be able to identify the area that will develop into the placenta and the area destined to become the person. By about fourteen or fifteen days after fertilisation, a structure called the primitive streak has formed. This is the first clearly visible sight of the developing embryo.

Occasionally two separate primitive streaks develop, and in this case the result will be identical twins. This begs the question, what was the embryo before this point – one person that divided into two, or two crammed into a single ball? The question is almost nonsensical, but it must be answered by anyone wanting to find a scientific basis for his or her claim that full personhood starts at fertilisation.[19]

Much less frequently, but at the same time much more bizarrely, is the situation where two embryos combine to form one.

18. Deciding how to refer to an embryo in a book like this is difficult. The terms 'he' and 'she' hardly seem appropriate, but 'it' seems to relegate the embryo to the status of an item. However, 'he or she' is clumsy, so I'll use 'it'. Please forgive me if this offends you.

19. Roman Catholic and many Protestant Christian groups maintain that the Bible indicates that full human status is achieved at conception. In *Issues Facing Christians Today* (pp. 315–17), the theologian John Stott says that the strongest evidence for this is found in Psalm 139, where the writer talks of the continuity of God's loving relationship extending to the person as they existed in their mother's womb.

The resulting 'mosaic' develops as one biological entity with no evidence of a split or dual personality that could be expected from his or her genetic origins. Many people who have a mosaic genetic endowment are completely unaware of the situation, while others only know because they have patches of hair or skin that have one colouring originating from one embryo and different coloured patches emanating from the other. It will be intriguing to see whether the world of increased genetic screening shows more of these individuals. I use the word 'individuals' deliberately because they are certainly not 'two-in-one' people.

Going back to the embryo, by day seventeen the neural tube is forming – a structure that rapidly develops into a rudimentary spinal cord – the nervous system's equivalent of its principal motorway. Genetics now shows us that many of our genes are solely concerned with these stages of embryonic development and are then turned off, never to operate again during the lifetime of that individual.

This is another stage that some people look to as a potential starting point. The argument is that consciousness needs a functioning brain. A functioning brain needs nerves. Before the embryo has any nerves it can't have any form of consciousness, but once it has nerves you never really know what it is capable of.

By the time the embryo has been growing for about seven weeks all of the internal organs are in place and it has taken on a distinctly human appearance. Arms, legs, fingers, toes, head, eyes, nose, etc., are formed. This physical completeness caused early biologists to call it a fetus from this point forward – the word is Latin for 'offspring'.

Early thinkers such as Aristotle (384–322 BC) and the Catholic theologian and philosopher Thomas Aquinas (1225–74) decided that this physical maturity signalled the time when the embryo became 'ensouled', became a person. According to Dr A. Majid Katme, a Muslim health advisor and spokesman for the Islamic Medical Association in Britain, their holy scriptures teach that from day one the embryo is sacred and deserving of protection, but that

God breathes in the person's soul at about six weeks after conception. From this point the embryo is a full human being and many features of its life are already 'written down', including the dates of birth and death, and social aspects such as the extent to which the person will be law abiding, and the amount they will earn.

Recent data have poured a little cold water on the scientific logic that Aristotle and Aquinas used to underpin their seven-week notion, as we now know that, although the organs are in place, many are not working, or are performing different functions from those they will perform after birth. For example, the lung material might be in place, but it has minimal airways until twenty-three to twenty-four weeks of gestation and doesn't start to form proper air sacs, alveoli, until just before full-term birth. So the notion of seven weeks being a good developmental stage to attribute with special importance does not seem terribly strong.

It is intriguing to note that so often both the arguments for and against this stage being seen as the start of personhood are based on a notion of utility. The fetus is a person because it now has all of its components, says one camp. The fetus is not a person because its components, while present, are not capable of functioning, claims the other camp.

Quickening, the moment when a mother feels the fetus move for the first time, is undoubtedly of emotional significance, but again it is of no help in defining when the person starts to exist. In reality the fetus has been bounding around inside for weeks, but has just been too small to feel. The purpose behind fetal movements appears to be to aid nerve and muscle development, so the womb is in many ways a live-in gym.

By twenty-three weeks of development the fetus is capable of surviving outside the womb, so long as he or she is given intensive support, and at somewhere around twenty-five weeks the nerves that make up the cerebral cortex, the thinking part of the brain, start to function.

Of all the stages in development, birth is in many ways the least significant. The baby moves from a protected fluid-filled environment, where food and oxygen are supplied via the umbilical cord, to an air-filled environment where food and oxygen now come in through the mouth. Birth is certainly an event to look back on, but in reality it can occur anywhere from twenty-three to forty, or more, weeks from the time the egg and sperm first met. However, the legacy of our former lack of scientific understanding is that birth is still taken as the legally accepted time when personhood starts, but as we have seen it has little scientific credibility.

So, when does life start? Well, new humanity starts as egg and sperm fuse, and implantation starts a new relationship. The following months see that relationship increase until the new person is delivered into the world to commence a life of increasing independence. As I have previously stated that being a person requires aspects of relationship and responsibility it seems inappropriate to say that a day-one embryo is a person. However, the value of humanity is something that is given to individuals and I believe that we should give the embryo a high sense of dignity because it is part of the story of a person's existence. The very uncertainty over the question of when a person comes into existence should instil in us a sense of caution rather than licence.

I discussed this with theologian Oliver O'Donovan. He described the situation thus: you go to sleep and wake to find a rose has been placed on your pillow during the night. You have no way of knowing precisely when the rose arrived. You know it wasn't there when you went to sleep, but was there when you woke. Similarly, the embryo at day one does not exhibit the characteristics of a person, but by birth it has formed relationships and can respond to others. It is extremely difficult to put any firm conclusion on the moment of origin.

The consequence for human genetic experimentation is that this doubt and uncertainty should cause us to be extremely cautious in the way we view and handle human embryos. Acting without caution or concern will, I believe, in the end damage ourselves. At the moment the UK is out on a limb, being almost the only country to allow embryos to be deliberately created for the purpose of experimentation. Most other countries that have considered the situation believe that this is throwing caution to the wind, and I would agree.

In the realm of fertility treatments, I believe that treating the embryo with respect means bringing the minimum number into existence. The recent advances in the ability to freeze eggs should help with this, as a large number of eggs could be 'harvested' and stored, only enough fertilised for a single treatment cycle and the rest kept for a later day. Prior to this, there was no way of storing eggs, but embryos could be frozen. This has led to the bizarre situation of families having 'embryos on ice' – and a confusion breaking out as to whether these are people or property. Again, I think the cautionary principle should guide us away from freezing embryos, unless there is clear indication that they will at some point in the future be given the chance of life.

## Fertile ground for thought

To try to address the issues surrounding fertility treatments, a committee established in 1984 by the UK's Department of Health and Social Security and chaired by Dame Mary Warnock published its report.[20] The committee was given the task of establishing guidelines for any research or treatment of human infertility that involved handling embryos, and it is easy to feel that there was a underlying political motive to find a 'solution' that would enable research. Inevitably part of their time was spent coming to an opinion on the status of an embryo and the report set a benchmark for the legal status of a human embryo. To reach their decision they too studied the biology of fetal development that we have just reviewed.

At that time 'test-tube' babies were a recent reality. Louise Brown, the world's first baby resulting from fertilisation of egg by sperm in a laboratory, had been born in July 1978. However, to

20. Report of the Committee of Inquiry into Human Fertilisation and Embryology, Cmnd 9314.

improve on the very low success rate and make the technique available to a wider range of people, more information about embryonic development was needed. The pace of this discovery would be greatly accelerated if research could be carried out on human embryos.

Warnock's committee faced a dilemma. It has been a long-held belief that it is not ethical to carry out research on a human being, particularly if that research were to lead to the person's destruction. The Warnock report comments that extending this concept to cover the embryo would prohibit almost all research in this area. The argument is that 'the right to life is held to be the fundamental human right, and the taking of human life on this view is always abhorrent. To take the life of the innocent is an especial moral outrage.'[21]

Human subjects are often involved in clinical trials, but these are closely scrutinised by ethical committees whose task is to establish that there is a good chance that the experimental procedure or drug will benefit the person, and there is little risk that it will do active harm. Slow progress could be made by studying embryo growth in non-human animals, or by observing human embryos that are created in fertility treatment programmes with the express purpose of placing them in a womb and giving them the chance of life. But more rapid progress would occur if scientists could study human embryos and then destroy them. So, before permitting research on human embryos, a decision was needed as to whether the embryo is a full human being, and if not, when that status is achieved.

An additional concern involves consent. Any person who volunteers to become the subject of research must be informed of the risks involved and indicate that they have given their consent, normally by signing a consent form. Opponents of embryo research pointed out that an embryo could never give consent. The question returned, is an embryo a person?

21. Report of the Committee of Inquiry into Human Fertilisation and Embryology, Cmnd 9314, para. 11.11, p. 61.

The committee's conclusion, though not one that had unanimous support, was that the human embryo did not need to be afforded full human status before it was fourteen days old. It could therefore be a legitimate target of medical research up to that developmental age. The reason for this cut-off is that after fourteen days the primitive streak starts to develop, marking the beginning of individual development of the embryo. This is not a statement that after fourteen days they felt an embryo was definitely a person, but that before that time it was their opinion that the hollow ball of cells was definitely not a full human being.

However, the committee recognised that even over the first fourteen days of development the embryo is still human and as such has a sufficiently high status to mean that any such research should only be carried out in approved laboratories and only under licence. 'We recommend that the embryo of the human species should be afforded some protection in law,' states the report.[22]

Three members of the committee felt sufficiently concerned to write an expression of dissent that was included in the report.[23] They acknowledged that the question, *When does life begin?* cannot be answered in a simple fashion. They started by pointing out that eggs and sperm are cells which are very much alive, but that while they are human cells, no one would give them the status of a human being. The real issue is, *At what stage of development should the status of a person be accorded to an embryo of the human species?* This they say is a moral question that can be illuminated, but not answered, by scientific endeavour. Their response is that, once fertilisation has occurred, the embryo must be given a special status because it has the potential for becoming a human person.

22. Report of the Committee of Inquiry into Human Fertilisation and Embryology, Cmnd 9314, para. 11.17, p. 63.

23. The three members were Madeline Carriline, a social worker and former vice-chairman of British Agencies for Adoption and Fostering; John Marshall, the professor of clinical neurology at the Institute of Neurology, Queen Square, London; and Jean Walker, a psychiatric social worker and former student counsellor at Cambridge University.

While the science behind the committee's 'day-fourteen' decision has some justification, the legal situation regarding the issue of when a life starts is more confused. This brings us to the thorny issue of abortion. In the UK the limits have now been drawn at twenty-four weeks for most instances, but up to full term in situations where the growing baby is believed to have some severe physical abnormality.[24] The twenty-four-week cut-off was initially drawn up in the belief that prior to this stage of development a fetus could not survive if born. However, this is now less tenable, because neonatal baby units can keep babies alive from at least twenty-three weeks.

In reality, the age limits are now more determined by the limitations of screening and diagnostic techniques to spot fetal abnormalities at earlier ages, than by any notion of the status of the developing baby. In any case, the idea that a baby can survive alone even at term is poor, because, as any parent will tell you, without constant nurture for many years, no baby would survive. Which brings us back to Singer's argument that a newly born human baby is not fully human because he or she cannot survive if left unattended and is unable to reason for many months and years after birth.

## So where does this get us?

At this point you might think I have lost the plot. I started out looking to see what genetics tells us about what human life is and when it starts, and have finished by brushing up against the politics of abortion.

However, the method behind this particular piece of madness is to show that we are in danger of missing the obvious. Scientific observation can only describe our physical nature and, yes, that physical nature is a part of who we are. But that is not necessarily the whole story. Science is not very good at describing relationships, and

24. For the purposes of abortion, 'severe abnormality' has never been defined, though the Royal College of Obstetrics and Gynaecologists (RCOG) has produced a guidance report: 'Ultrasound Screening for Fetal Abnormalities', Report of the RCOG Working Party, 1997.

yet we found that the ability to form relationships is an important quality in establishing a person.

This debate clearly points to the danger of restricting any discussion of who we are, and when we started, to purely scientific terms of reference, as we have seen that science has so far shown itself incapable of producing any answers. If anything it seems to be adding more layers of complexity. While recognising the power of science, I can also see its limitations and find a need to seek other sources of reference.

Many spokespeople for science constantly argue that as a discipline it is value free, and to this extent I would agree with them. Science cannot say anything about the value we give to an observation. That can only come from some other discipline.

As I have said, my own source of reference that is external to science is the Bible and the Judeo-Christian concept of the uniqueness of humanity being founded on each one of us being made in the image of God. For me this speaks of the value of a human individual and the respect that that individual deserves. This places huge value on human life. It leaves me able to agree with the Warnock committee that the biological capability of a very early embryo is less than that of a newborn baby, and from that you could argue that it has less value.

But before you think I have written the embryo off, remember that the value given to a human being is so extreme, that marginally less is still a lot. An embryo even at day one is, after all, human and as such we need to give it respect. The dignity with which we should treat it is something we give to it, irrespective of the fact that it is incapable of demanding it. At the same time, however, I cannot see that it makes sense to call an early embryo a person. Prior to implantation it has not formed any relationships, and even immediately after implantation the relationship only develops over weeks and months. It also has no ability for self-awareness or cognitive thought.

The net result is that I do not see that pre-implantation embryos have the full status of human beings, but I do believe we should handle them with great respect. To my mind, the test we need to apply when considering whether any procedure is ethically appropriate would be to ask whether we are treating the embryo as a disposable commodity, or whether we are acknowledging that it is human, and therefore deserving of protection.

*Chapter 7*

# GENETICS AND PERSONALITY

Genetics may have a limited say over what it is to be human, but it is likely to have a greater influence over what it is to be you and me. In particular, it will have an influence over what is different between you and me.

Few people reach the end of their lives without at some point asking, *Who am I?*, *Why am I here?* or, *What's the purpose?* And there are any number of people touting their own particular answers, many of which come with some sort of underpinning moral foundation. The three major world religions, Judaism, Christianity and Islam, all point to a single God as their source of reference, and, while they have significant differences, at root these religions all teach that who we are is a product of our relationship with the God whom we worship. Other religions such as Buddhism teach that a person builds his or her own destiny by destroying greed, hatred and delusion – it is your job to shape your own personality.

A relatively recent arrival on the scene has been scientific reductionism, and even more recently genetic reductionism. The concept behind reductionism is to discover the answer to any question by breaking the issue down into its most basic units and studying them in detail. Genetic reductionism assumes that the most basic unit is the gene and that if you understand all the genes in a person's cells you will know how they work.

Genetic determinism takes the process one step further. This is the idea that analysing every gene, and knowing the consequence of every mutation, will enable us to build a complete picture of a person's physique, appearance and even their personality. Genes don't just make you tick, they determine who you are. Add an ounce of poetic hype and the genetic code becomes the 'book of life'.

Implicit in this is that a person's upbringing has little influence on them, because education or home environment cannot alter their genes. There is a huge degree of fatalism built into this thinking.

Sadly, what could be an interesting and even informative debate about the interplay between nature and nurture is all too often caricaturised as the religious or political dogmatists in the dark corner, pleading on behalf of 'nurture', and the scientific modernists in the light, piling up data that clearly establish 'nature' as the victor.

The issue can't be ignored, if only because the fight has a dark history, as the two philosophies turned into political strategies and fought for global domination through the late nineteenth and twentieth centuries. Francis Galton's 1869 book, *Hereditary Genius*, paved the way for the eugenics movement, which believed that ability was inborn and not acquired. This philosophy led to 25,000 Americans being sterilised to prevent them passing feeble-mindedness or criminality to future generations. In *Mein Kampf*, Adolf Hitler wrote, 'Whoever is not bodily and spiritually healthy and worthy shall not have the right to pass on his suffering in the body of his children.' Genetic determinism fitted well with Nazi ideology.

Conversely, nurture fitted well with communist thinking, which hoped to render all men and women equal by giving them identical environments. Marx maintained that altering the society in which people lived could change them. He believed that, once the revolution had propagated throughout an entire community, a new and better humankind would emerge. One consequence was the 'iron curtain' that stretched across continental Europe. Its purpose was to screen the socialist east from the capitalist west in order to allow the socialist experiment to run unhindered. A first step was to create a level playing field, so academics and anyone else with education were torn out of their ivory towers and 'purged', or at best given handleless brooms to sweep roads. Nurture was the critical issue, and no one deserved to have elitist treatment. The study of genetics was banned.

As we enter the twenty-first century, scientific capitalism has apparently triumphed, and, while at an international level the brutality of the fight may have diminished, the skirmishes are no less intense.

## Genetic intellect

So, while I would argue vehemently that we should treat all people with equal respect, we need to come to terms with Babel's finding that at a genetic level people are far from equal. Some people have mutations in their genes that make them good at fighting off particular diseases, while other people have mutations that mean they have increased susceptibility to cancer or early heart failure. As Babel's technologists are revealing more and more, we are beginning to see how the coding in the DNA that we receive from our parents may influence variations in traits as complex as intelligence. In saying this we enter hotly disputed territories.

In his book, *The Language of the Genes*, Steve Jones is anxious about the way that the debate about IQ and genetics has been conducted. He points out that it has been used as a cheap excuse for racist discrimination. He despises the way that differences in IQ tests between blacks and whites have been used to assert the genetic superiority of whites. He is also anxious about the political motivation behind many of the 'twins studies', in which people have examined pairs of identical twins who have been separated at birth, in an attempt to elucidate the relative contribution of nature (genes) and nurture. I share his concerns.

However, this leads him to conclude that 'much of the work on inherited differences in intellect between races is contemptible and most of the rest is wrong'.[1] He seems to be implying that there is no

1. Jones, S., *The Language of the Genes*, Flamingo, 1996, pp. 242–44.

good evidence that genes are involved in intelligence. But such a line of argument is in danger of ignoring the obvious. Brains are built following instructions encoded in DNA. As a geneticist Jones is more aware than many of the extent to which DNA is affected by mutations, and, as an ardent believer in evolution, he knows that those mutations can be detrimental or enhancing. It is reasonable, therefore, to suppose that this will have some influence over the ways in which people think. One, albeit controversial, study of 100 sets of twins and triplets reared apart claimed to show that about seventy per cent of variance in IQ was due to genetic variation.[2]

Surely Jones has missed the point. Genetic research is bound to show that genes have an influence over how well we can think, but the issue is what value we place on that discovery. To begin with, it is remarkably difficult to come to a real definition of what exactly we mean by intelligence. The current shorthand in Western industrialised countries is to apply a set of stylised tests that determine how well people perform a particular set of mental gymnastics – the intelligence quotient or IQ tests.[3]

2. Bouchard, T.J., Jr, Lykken, D.T., McGue, M., Segal, H.L., and Tellegen, A., 'Sources of Human Psychological Differences: The Minnesota Study of Twins Reared Apart', *Science* **250**, 1990, pp. 223–28.

3. IQ tests compare an individual with an expected norm for their particular age. We derive the result by using a test to assess the person's mental age and then dividing this by their chronological age. To make the figure easier to handle, the resulting value is multiplied by 100. Therefore, if an assessment reveals that a person's mental age is fifteen and they are fifteen years old, their IQ would be $15/15 \times 100 = 100$. So an IQ of 100 says that the person fits with the assumed idea of what is normal. An IQ of sixty-five or less means that they are in the bottom one per cent of mental capability (as assessed by the particular set of tests that was used), and an IQ of 135 or above puts them in the top one per cent. Three quarters of the population lie between eighty and 120.

The whole concept of IQ is therefore only as good as the test used to assess mental age. But there are numerous tests that can be used. The most commonly used sets are the Wechler tests that assess language skills and verbal reasoning, as well as the person's ability to construct objects and recognise shapes. The Stanford–Binet test was established by French-born Alfred Binet (1857–1911) who was director of physiological psychology at the Sorbonne in Paris from 1892. These tests aim to measure a person's scholastic ability. In the Goodenough–Harris test a child is asked to draw a picture of a man, and the score given depends on the complexity of the drawing.

To my mind, the problem comes with the tendency to equate a person's IQ with their value. There seems to be reasonable evidence that someone with a high IQ has an enhanced chance of succeeding in the capitalist system of wealth creation that is currently dominating developed and developing countries. But the danger comes when we say that someone with a high IQ is consequently of greater value than someone who has less mental agility.

We need to be careful, because we live in a society that has built gods in our own image, rather than the reverse. Let me explain. Those who are financially successful and powerful have set the goals such that financial success and power are the most sought-after aims in life – they are their gods. They genuinely believe that these gods are worthy of service and that generating wealth and power should be everyone else's aim. IQ tests identify the people who are most likely to achieve this great good. In these simplistic terms the tests sort out those whom we, as a society, should revere, from those whom we can ignore.

The issue we must never forget is whether wealth and power are the most important goals of a human existence. I would much prefer to live in a community that holds the forming and developing of strong relationships as the major goal. Going back to our criteria of being human, we can see that this society would enable us to develop and strengthen our humanity.

## Driven by genes

The extent to which our actions are determined by our genes is a hot topic. Look at the crisis that followed in the wake of the gay gene 'discovery'. When the link between a particular mutation and a tendency to live a homosexual lifestyle was initially published, people used the argument that if there is a gay gene, then no one can ever again question a gay lifestyle because the possessors of this mutation were made that way. They are simply living out their genetic inheritance – a clear case of arguing from a standpoint of genetic determinism.

It wasn't long before other people started drawing parallels between this and the court case in which a convicted criminal, Stephen Mobley, claimed that he was genetically inclined to be violent and therefore was personally innocent. In 1991 Mobley shot John Collins in the back of his head as Collins cowered on his knees behind the counter of the pizza parlour where he was working. No one denies that Mobley is the murderer, but his defence team points to the fact that his family has a history of violent and antisocial behaviour, thus quite possibly there was a genetic cause to his behaviour. They cited Dutch research which indicated that males with a defect in the gene that normally codes for monoamine oxidase A have histories of mental handicap, violence and impulsive behaviour. Monoamine oxidase A is an enzyme that controls the levels of chemical messengers within the brain, and the theory is that without working copies of this enzyme, the brain's function is disturbed.[4]

Soon the idea of a 'criminal gene' was out and about in public discussion. Thus genetic determinism was being claimed to be capable of giving a propensity to murder, and in this case murder is a feature that is universally condemned.

So, even if genetic determinism is shown to be very powerful, we are still left having to decide what we want to do with it. After all, genetics can give someone a predisposition to cancer, but we don't applaud cancer.

The idea of a genetic foundation for criminality has been around a long time, and was one of Galton's driving convictions. Writing in 1907 he claims:

*The ideal criminal has marked peculiarities of character: his conscience is almost deficient, his instincts are vicious, his power of self-control is very weak, and he usually detests continuous labour. The absence of self-control is due to an ungovernable temper, to passion, or to mere imbecility, and the*

4. Brunner, H.G., Nelen, M., Breakefield, X.O., Ropers, H.H., and Van Oost, B.A., 'Abnormal Behavior Associated with a Point Mutation in the Structural Gene for Monoamine Oxidase A', *Science* **262**, 1993, pp. 578–80.

*conditions that determine the particular descriptions of crime are the character of the instincts and of temptation.*

*The perpetuation of the criminal class by heredity is a question difficult to grapple with on many accounts… It is, however, easy to show that criminal nature tends to be inherited.*[5]

Galton was writing with passion, at a time when the physical basis of inheritance was yet to be discovered, but I think it is a safe assumption that he would have loved to work with the stream of genetic data that is currently available. The flaw with Galton's concept of genetically determined behaviour is that there are plenty of cases of identical twins who, while sharing a common genetic endowment, find that one has a condition such as schizophrenia, but the other is unaffected. Genetics cannot be the total culprit.

Nevertheless, there is a strong possibility that some people and companies will see a potential market. It will be all too tempting to pedal the notion of genetic determinism. We can already see genetic screening and potential genetic manipulation of embryos arriving in new Babel's market place, and these are making us reconsider these issues with a sense of urgency.

Foreseeing the possibility of people offering screening tests to look for potentially gay fetuses made the researchers place a warning in their paper. They maintained that it would be fundamentally unethical to use their research to 'assess or alter' such a 'normal variation in human behaviour'.[6] Their fear was that some people would start to follow the detection of the gene by abortion, or genetic therapies that could counter the influence of the gene. I'm particularly sad that the researchers' reaction to their own discovery gives credence in public debate to the notion of genetic determinism.

5. Galton, F., *Inquiry into Human Faculty and its Development*, 2nd edition, London: J.M. Dent & Sons, Ltd, 1907.

6. Hamer, D.H., Hu, S., Magnuson, V.L., Hu, N., and Pattatucci, M., 'A Linkage Between DNA Markers on the X Chromosome and Male Sexual Orientation', *Science* **261**, 1993, pp. 321–27.

Director of the Foundation of Genetic Education and Counseling in the USA, Joseph D. McInerney, sums up the debate thus: 'The debate about nature versus nurture is empty; the prevailing view is one of how nature and nurture contribute to the individuality of behaviour.'[7]

It seems inevitable that the next decade will see many companies offering gene tests that give risk factors for particular behavioural traits and that, driven by curiosity or fear, many people will make use of their services. The issue we will need to face in Babel is less about whether genetics has an influential role over a person, but more about how we value a person in the light of any genetic revelation. Which variations in human behaviour do we find acceptable, and which do we consider to be in some way unhealthy?

We may like or loathe what our genes have done in directing our physical development. But the reality is that we will have to choose to impose a separate, external reference to tell us whether we find that the messages encoded in our genes are acceptable or not. To believe that our genes have cast our personality in a genetic version of stone is genetic fatalism, which leaves no room for freedom of choice.

## The reasonable person

It would be easy to look at the Mobley trial and grin, saying, 'Well there go the "clever" lawyers again.' But the issue has serious implications. Civil and criminal law ask whether a person's conduct matches the community ideal of reasonable behaviour. The idea is to lead towards a unitary standard, but the effect is to create a diverse range of verdicts.

Already within our legal frameworks we have the notion that different standards are expected of different people. For example, the law holds children to a different set of standards from adults, deeming that they are not always responsible for their actions. In the

7. In 'The Growing Impact of the New Genetics on the Courts', *Judicature: Genes and Justice* **83** (3), 1999.

case of medical malpractice suits a specialist is expected to perform with greater ability than a junior colleague or a lay-person. In other situations physical impairment, such as blindness, is often taken into account when considering the reasonableness of a person's actions. In criminal law a person will be convicted of manslaughter rather than murder if the act was committed in the heat of passion. But, interestingly, according to legal expert Mark Rothstein 'the reasonable standard generally has not been adjusted for mental impairments or behavioral shortcomings'.[8]

Now season this 'reasonable-standard' debate with a little genetic uncertainty, stir and turn up the heat. And genetics will be brought into the courts simply because lawyers have the task of presenting before the court every conceivable reason why their client should not be found guilty, so it is inevitable that genetic predisposition is going to find its way into legal argument with increasing frequency. Philosopher Dan Brock presents a case for the defence: 'If a person's genetic structure is a principal cause of behaviour and that genetic structure is completely beyond the individual's control, can an individual justifiably be held responsible for the resultant behaviour?'[9] I would argue that this is premature, because we are yet to determine the extent to which genes rule behaviour. But Rothstein believes that 'it is virtually certain that parties in both criminal and civil cases will assert behavioral genetic arguments well before there is general support for such views in the scientific community'.[10] He further warns that 'legislative and judicial responses to new genetic discoveries will have a major effect on whether we are about to enter an unprecedented period of behavioral genetic determinism and,

8. Rothstein, M.A., 'The Impact of Behavioural Genetics on the Law and the Courts', *Judicature: Genes and Justice* **83** (3), 1999. Rothstein is the Cullen distinguished professor of law and director of the Health Law and Policy Institute at the University of Houston Law Center.

9. Brock, D., 'The Human Genome Project and Human Identity', *Houston Law Review* **29**, 1992, pp. 7–16.

10. Rothstein, *Judicature: Genes and Justice* **83** (3).

with it, social disruption, or the promised enlightened era of genetic marvels'.[11]

## Master or slave?

Before the true extent of any genetic involvement in behaviour has been fully established there has been a knee-jerk reaction by people asking whether we should use genetics to curb that behaviour. Writing in the *New Internationalist*, Professor Steven Rose from the UK's Open University challenges the idea that combining genetics and brain science cannot only explain, but also enable us to change our personalities: 'The question is whether such explanations are valid and useful or whether they merely exacerbate social distress while failing to provide meaningful scientific insights into the origins of the problems they seek to understand.'[12]

His gripe is that any simple quick-fix theory, such as saying that we are purely determined by our genes, or, for that matter, totally malleable to the influence of our environment, is bound to fall foul of reality. It will also cause us to misdirect our efforts at creating a better society. 'Such determinism serves to relocate social problems to the individual, thus "blaming the victim" rather than exploring the societal roots and determinants of the issues that concern us,' he says. Rose's argument is that violence is no longer explained in terms of inner-city squalor, unemployment, the wealth–poverty divide and resulting loss of hope, but rather is presented as a problem that comes from having 'naturally' violent people around. This is clearly the view of the would-be cloner, Richard Seed, who believes that all of inner-city deprivation results from the people living there having bad genes. 'Solve the genes – solve the problem,' is his concept of a solution.

For all of our lip-service about wanting to create an open society that is tolerant of all peoples, we find that the consequence of concentrating on maximising people's genetic potential is a tendency

11. Rothstein, *Judicature: Genes and Justice* **83** (3).

12. Rose, S., 'The Genetics of Blame', *The New Internationalist*, April 1998.

to fund programmes that seek to alter individuals, rather than attempt to sort out society. In the new Babel we could find ourselves rebuilding individuals so that they fit comfortably into our idealised well-ordered society, rather than asking if there are aspects of society that should be remoulded instead.

## Full circle

So we return to the question of, *Who am I?* We've seen that genetics sheds light on my physical make-up and that physique affects my capabilities. I am influenced by my genetic endowment, but it doesn't define my personality.

This sense of freedom from fatalism is very important. All of the declarations on human rights assert that a person must be allowed to live their own life, and not be dictated to by others. I believe that this is also an essential ingredient of the message wrapped up in the Bible, in that God formed human beings with the intention of having a relationship with them. If the biological structure used to embody that humanity dictated the nature of the person, the result would have been a dictatorship in which people would have been automatons. Instead God made us free – free to disobey him, to ignore his guidelines, or even to deny his existence.

All this is great, but to this I add that we can also form relationships that draw on our notion of our interdependence. We can even extend that relationship-forming ability to encounter the God who made us. Our task is to ensure that these relationships honour each human individual and build a society that holds human life in high regard.

## Chapter 8

# BABIES BY DESIGN

In an age when mass-production has given us prosperity and pushed living standards to unprecedented heights, we have seen the emergence of the 'designer label' – the backlash against mass-produced uniformity. The genesis of mass-production is often linked to Henry Ford and his famous statement that you could have his new Model T Ford in any colour you wanted, as long as you asked for black. To produce cars at a price that a 'working man' could afford, he had established a streamlined factory with each worker performing specific tasks. The notions of efficiency and uniformity were born.

But then, with the prosperity, came the demand for choice. The tail-end of the 1900s was marked by increasingly vocal calls for personal freedom. Living my life in the way that I want to without reference to anyone else or any other system is supposed to be the highest goal of Western society. The restrictive cloak of modernity, with its constraining idea that science and rationality will always show us the best way to do things, has been swept away by what some philosophers call postmodernity. In reality, postmodernity describes an absence rather than a presence – there are no rules, no guiding principles. Except, of course, the golden rule that there are no rules or guiding principles.

The fashion industry loves it. No longer is everyone happy to wear jeans made by a single manufacturer. Instead people want 'designer jeans', designed, so the advertisements claim, by their favourite celebrity. The more exclusive the brand, the higher the price and the greater the feeling of success and status that an owner achieves by strutting around in them.

New computer-controlled technologies, which are the throbbing heart of mass-production, allow for a single machine to switch design at minimal cost, so much so that some designers in the car industry claim that new models could arrive in the showrooms every few months, satisfying ever-changing demands.

The free market is the name of the game, and the game is set up to look as if the consumer is the driving influence, and we like to think that it operates this way. If someone wants to buy, then someone else will soon set up shop ready and waiting to sell. But more often we see the provider in the driving seat. A new technology or product is dreamed up and the advertiser's task is to draw it to our attention. Often this involves turning luxuries into necessities. How could you ever live, they ask, without a car? – a dishwasher? – two cars? – electric windows? – a mobile phone? – the internet? – perfect health? The answer is, of course, that plenty of people did live without them, and millions still do.

Many wonderful inventions have fallen by the wayside, not because they didn't work or were not useful, but just because they failed to catch the public's attention. Conversely a few useless inventions have been marketed so well that everyone has bought them.

Now babies are entering the consumer market, and the potential is vast. To start with there is the whole process of producing babies, and, in the developed world, one-in-six couples have difficulty conceiving and giving birth to a baby of their own. That's a lot of people and many of them are genuinely desperate to fulfil their desire to become parents. A great potential market. On top of this, many other couples find that their genetic make-up is such that any offspring they do have stand a high risk of some serious, sometimes life-threatening, disease. Another market.

Then there are people who, through ideology or as a result of wanting to fulfil personal desires, would like to redefine the nature of families, and see new technologies as giving them the possibility of fulfilling their dreams. There are many examples that spring to mind and I'll list a few. Quoted in the *Sunday Times*, 14 June 1998, lawyer Karen Synesiou explained her move from the UK to work for a Californian agency that supplies human eggs for a new fertility treatment. This new treatment 'rejuvenates' eggs from older women by taking much of the cell contents from a young woman's egg and injecting it into the older woman's egg. It is the reason for her move that stopped me in my tracks: 'I am interested in redefining the family, which is why I came to work here. This is exciting treatment for a specific group of suitable parents. It is the next stage from simply using donor eggs.'

Add to this the single women and lesbian couples who would like a baby without having a relationship with a man. In this category we could include people like Diane Blood who famously fought for the right to have the opportunity of trying for a baby fathered by her dead husband's sperm; baby Liam was born on 10 December 1998. Furthermore, in December 1999, at the age of sixty, Natasha and Barry Smith started their fight for the right to use sperm from their son Lance to father grandchildren. Lance was killed in a car crash and his girlfriend of ten years did not want to use his sperm, so Natasha and Barry also had the task of searching for a surrogate mother. Yet more markets.

And we mustn't forget the much-talked-of enhanced-performance, or 'designer-baby' market where parents could potentially choose to have children with or without certain physical or maybe even social attributes. Parents spend vast fortunes on private education and coaching to help their children win, be it to win at the exam table or the sports field, so why not spend a little on giving the child any genetic advantage that is technologically possible?

## Assisted consumerism

Since the late 1980s, developments in procedures that can increase the chance of a woman getting pregnant have led to thousands of babies being born who would otherwise not have existed. The more successful the treatments become, the more people sign up for them, and with more people to practise on, the treatments themselves have become even more successful. In the UK, the most proficient centres now claim a 'take-home-baby rate' of between twenty-five and thirty per cent, with an average across the country of somewhere around seventeen per cent. This is comparable to the estimate of the success rate for fully fertile couples, where in any given month some twenty per cent of couples having regular unprotected intercourse can expect the woman to become pregnant.

In the USA, some centres now claim a fifty per cent success rate. This higher rate is largely because in the USA there is no restriction to the number of embryos that can be placed in the woman's womb at a time. In the UK the HFEA places a limit of three embryos in order to prevent high-number multiple pregnancies, and there are calls for this number to be reduced to two. In the USA, clinics routinely place six or seven embryos in the womb to increase the chance of implantation, but also increase the risk of multiple pregnancies. Their 'solution' is to offer selective reduction – where some of the developing embryos are selectively killed by lethal injection, thereby reducing the number to a desired level. The HFEA views selective reduction as dangerous and ethically suspect although it has occasionally been carried out in the UK. The technique is dangerous, because selective reduction can trigger a full-scale miscarriage of all embryos.

At first sight this increased success rate is great, but it has consequences. As happy smiling babies appear on news programmes and documentaries, people who have more marginal fertility needs start to become anxious earlier and consider turning more rapidly to the new technologies. Many couples fit into a classification of being sub-fertile. They are not incapable of having children without assistance, but it might just take a bit longer than for other couples. Rather than waiting two or three years before turning for help, it is now common for couples to approach their doctors after only a few months of unprotected intercourse, anxious that they are infertile.

An American survey suggested that concern about fertility problems has risen,[1] despite the fact that the actual age-adjusted incidence of impaired fertility remained stable.[2]

The more fundamental change in attitude, which has coincided with this increased success, has been the realisation that we can influence our own reproduction. True, the first move in this direction came with the advent of reasonably proficient contraception, which gave women, in particular, more control over the number of children they had. But as soon as you use any method to influence the size of your family, be it some form of 'natural family planning' as advocated by the Roman Catholic Church, or some chemically or physically induced method, you have become involved in the decision to create a new life.

Theologians refer to our involvement in the creation of new life as procreation. They acknowledge human beings' part, but hold that their role is to initiate, or trigger, a process that in the world order which God created results in a new human life. God set up the systems and gave us the task of using them. The Genesis narrative in the Bible tells us that God created human beings with the ability to 'Be fruitful and increase in number; fill the earth and subdue it.'[3] 'Parents procreate by acting on behalf of the creator to create offspring,' says philosophical theologian J.H. Olthuis.[4] He claims

1. Chandra, A., and Stephen, E.A., 'Impaired Fecundity in the United States: 1982–85', *Family Planning Perspectives* **30**, 1998, pp. 34–42.

2 In 1999 E.R. Te Velde and B.J. Cohlen published a letter drawing attention to this issue, and in part blamed the increased level of fear on the level of advertising and publicity given to the fertility industry: 'The Management of Infertility', *The New England Journal of Medicine* **340**, 1999, pp. 224–25.

3. The statement in Genesis 1:28 was given to humankind on the 'sixth day of creation' and a similar statement is found in Genesis 9:1 when God blesses Noah as he leaves the ark at the end of the flood. It is noteworthy that on both occasions the world is empty and needs populating. Theologians argue over whether these are commands, or blessings – whether they are duties to be performed, or privileges to be enjoyed where possible. However, the prophet Isaiah points out that the Lord 'did not create [the world] to be empty, but formed it to be inhabited' (Isaiah 45:18).

4. In *New Dictionary of Christian Ethics and Pastoral Theology*, Inter-Varsity Press, 1995, p. 691.

that procreation, in the fullest sense of the word, also includes the requirement that parents care for and nurture any resulting children.

The issue that the new Babel forces onto the agenda is the extent to which we are allowed to be involved in, or alter, the natural processes of procreation, and/or its products. In the language of the news headlines, when do we start to 'play God'? Translated more thoughtfully, what are the limits of responsible human action?

At the moment great emphasis is placed on the desire to give people autonomy. This is often taken as the right to do what they want. The idea is that everyone should be able to make up their own mind as to what they think is, or is not, allowable. This would suggest that there are no definable limits applicable to everyone, just boundaries that individuals set for themselves. There is, however, a fine line between this and anarchy, where the actions are autonomous, but there is no concern about the effect they may have on another person. The reality of the situation is that we live in communities where one person's action often impinges on another's freedom. In addition, in the medical domain, one person's wishes will often require another person to supply the solution. If treatment is demanded, then this encroaches on the provider's autonomy. For autonomy to have credibility it needs to be seen as the right to act within a framework of responsibility.

## Responsible reproduction

So what does it mean to act responsibly at the interface of reproduction and genetic technologies?

When in 1978 Louise Brown was born, the world was shocked. Louise was the first baby born following fertilisation outside the body, the first 'test-tube baby'. Since then the process has become unsurprising. One consequence is that childless women not only feel they would like a baby, they increasingly voice the opinion that they have the right to have a baby. In the UK, this right extends to the belief that the NHS has a duty to help them in this quest.

While this duel of rights and duties is played out, the baby is in danger of becoming marginalised. One chain of thought is that this marginalisation is quite justified because, at the point when treatment is being considered, the baby doesn't exist. The only people present are the would-be parents and so it is their concerns alone that need satisfying. This at times runs into conflict with the HFEA, which demands that, for a reproductive technology to be used responsibly, the welfare of any children created in fertility programmes must always be taken into consideration.

As we saw with cloning, the market-driven culture, if left unrestrained, will have a tendency to relegate babies to the status of a commodity. It is a foundational principle of our culture that 'all human beings are born free and equal in dignity and rights'.[5] No one has the right to treat anyone else as a commodity that they own. For this reason, no declaration of human rights states that a woman (or couple) has the right to have a child of their own. Instead our declarations and treaties uphold the rights of a couple to desire to have children. Article 16 of the United Nations' Universal Declaration of Human Rights says that every adult has the right to marry and to found a family and that the 'family is the natural and fundamental group unit of society'. The European Declaration of Human Rights also asserts the right of a person to have a family, and the United Nations' 1969 Declaration on Social Progress and Development says in Article 4 that 'Parents have the exclusive right to determine freely and responsibly the number and spacing of their children.'

However, all this falls short of giving anyone the right to bear their own children. To start with, this would be impossible to achieve, but more fundamentally this would be treating the child as a commodity that can be acquired.

Having said that, we could interpret some other social changes as signs of growing commodification. A couple spots a patch in their lives or careers when it would be convenient to have a baby, and they

5. Article 1 of the Universal Declaration of Human Rights, established by the General Assembly of the United Nations on 10 December 1948.

go for it. In the back of their minds is the thought that if it doesn't happen naturally, don't worry because, after all, we have the technology. We can have a baby when we want. We are successful and capable and have had everything else when we wanted it, so why not a baby? These thoughts are backed up by media stories of advances in the area of fertility. When the HFEA announced in January 2000 that it would permit women to use eggs that have been removed and frozen earlier in their life, the main interest in the press became whether this would be used by people who wanted to extend their career before pausing to have children.

If a picture is worth a thousand words, a photo of a smiling 'infertile' mother with a newborn baby held snugly in her arms is worth millions. The UK's most famous fertility specialist, Robert Winston, enjoys having his picture taken in front of the pin board in his London office bearing the photos of hundreds of babies that have come from the work of his clinic. It's an impressive sight. But the harsh reality is that, even with the incredible changes in reproductive medicine seen in the last couple of decades, many couples try for years and decades without ever receiving their longed-for child. Even so, the thought is firmly in the public's mind that we have a right to have children whenever we want them.

A responsible use of our autonomy will show that we have the right to try for a baby whenever we want, but that is not the same as claiming the right to a baby. Slavery was abolished because we recognised that one person could not use another to fulfil their needs, and we need to be cautious before responding to the heart-rending pleas of couples who say that they need to have a child to fulfil their aspirations. I'm not saying that we don't respond, just that we need to act responsibly.

Our society has grown used to the argument that the woman has the right to choose the fate of her unborn child and have an abortion if the developing baby is going to cause severe difficulties. Without rehearsing the arguments for and against this choice, we can see that this too causes us to see a baby as a commodity, one that we may or may not want to allow to encroach on our life. The woman is being given the right to decide the fate of the child; its life is in her hands as if she owns it. It's an awesome responsibility.

Against this background it is easy to see how we can slip gently into the mindset that, wherever possible, we have the right to choose healthy children.

## Generating health

While many, if not most, people feel at best distinctly uneasy towards the ideas of in some way designing offspring, the whole area of debate becomes more complex when you start to consider genetic disease.

A couple of years ago I wrote an article about a nine-year-old boy who suffers from a genetic disorder called epidermolysis bullosa. It is a distressing skin condition that causes skin layers and internal body linings to separate and blister. His skin is incredibly delicate. The slightest knock or rub can cause long-lasting damage and increasing disability and he needs painkilling morphine to help get through his daily bath. With the help of a full-time carer, he attends a mainstream school and although he is unable to run or walk very well he joins in as best he can.

Tay Sachs is another often-quoted genetic disease with a cruel outcome. Children affected by this disease develop normally for the first six months of their lives and then problems start. A fatty substance that has been accumulating in the child's brain starts to make him or her blind, triggers seizures and paralysis, and leads to dementia. Most children die before they reach their fourth birthday. The disease is concentrated among the Ashkenazi Jews, who share a common ancestry in Eastern Europe. Within this community about one person in twenty-five carries a single copy of the mutation, a concentration that is about 100 times greater than in any other ethnic group. If two carriers marry, any of their children has a one-in-two risk of being a carrier and a one-in-four risk of having the disease.

The current wisdom is that parents who know they are at risk of giving birth to babies with a genetic disease should be offered genetic counselling. Ideally this counselling takes place before the woman is pregnant, when there is time to think more clearly. Conventionally, some people who believe they are at high risk of having severely ill children have chosen not to have any children or to look into the possibility of adopting or fostering.

If the woman only starts to consider the options when she discovers that she is pregnant, the choices available are stark. She can decide to continue with the pregnancy and 'let nature take its course', or she could have a test to see if the developing baby has genes bearing the disease-causing mutation. This in the UK would then give the woman the option of aborting the baby. The tests require a sample of cells to be taken from the placenta or amniotic fluid, and one problem with this is that the mechanisms used to get these samples can trigger a miscarriage. Chorionic villus sampling (CVS), which can be carried out when the fetus is nine weeks old,[6] induces miscarriages in one-in-fifty people, while the alternative of amniocentesis, which has to wait until fourteen to eighteen weeks have passed, has a miscarriage rate of about one in 100.

Cell samples collected by these procedures can then be analysed to see whether the critical genetic mutations are present, indicating whether the fetus has escaped, or whether he or she is likely to suffer from the disease.

So, with CVS, the woman is asked to balance the one-in-fifty chance of losing the baby with a comparable risk of the child having some abnormality. I can't think of any other medical test that is allowed that carries with it a one-in-fifty chance of killing the person being tested. And, let's face it, many of the tests can only be performed well after the nine-week point when all the organs are in place. I'm therefore surprised by the relatively relaxed attitude with which the healthcare profession embarks on providing the test, and

6. Medics date pregnancies from the time of the period that precedes fertilisation. This occurs an average of two weeks before the egg and sperm meet, so, confusingly, an embryo is only nine weeks old when the woman is said to be the eleventh week of her pregnancy.

the relatively relaxed way that people approach the test. These tests are often carried out when there is a theoretical risk of one in 200, sometimes one in 400, of the child having an abnormality. In this case, the most likely outcome is going to be finding a healthy baby; the second most likely outcome is triggering the miscarriage of a healthy baby and the most unlikely outcome is the detection of a baby carrying an undesirable genetic mutation. Presumably the only reason why someone would expose themselves to this level of risk is that they consider the birth of a child with the particular disease to be extremely undesirable. Or that the mid-term fetus, sometimes even at an age when it would survive in an incubator, is not yet a person.

## Quality control

The need for responsible action is growing as the potential scope of consumerism is being expanded by the arrival of new genetic knowledge. Not only do we want a baby, but we want a good one – one that will require low levels of maintenance and be successful because he or she will be better at performing various tasks than his or her peers. An overarching requirement is likely to be that the person will rapidly be independent, especially financially independent.

This brings the nightmare spectre into view of the ultimate status symbol – the designer baby.

The people who are often placed at the forefront of debate are those who find that their genetic make-up includes damaging genetic mutations that they would rather not pass to their children. But in the background are other people with less extreme demands. There are those who are keen to maximise their chance of having a baby of a particular sex for social reasons – for example a boy baby because they carry higher social status in the country they live in, or a girl baby, because the parents already have a number of boys. Others would like to 'select' for good looks or high potential for success.

To prove how far this sort of supply-and-demand process has already reached with currently available technology, there are now internet web sites as well as conventionally operating agencies that allow you to select human sperm and eggs to use in fertility treatment based on a variety of criteria. Most agencies allow you to select from donors that share your hair colour and other physical attributes. But the boundaries of acceptability are now being pushed so that you can also choose sperm or eggs from people who have a good track record for intelligence, good looks, artistic ability or sporting success.

The idea of artificially transferring sperm into the vagina is not new, and the first reported case of artificial insemination was in animals in 1785 when Italian churchman Abbé Lazarro Spallanzini injected sperm from a dog into a bitch's vagina – sixty-two days later three puppies were born. The Scottish physiologist and surgeon John Hunter (1728–93) is credited with performing the first human artificial insemination, using sperm from the woman's husband, and in 1866 J. Marion Sims performed the first artificial insemination in the United States, again using the husband's sperm.

Since then, things have moved on and sperm banks have been in existence around the world for decades. No longer are couples restricted to using their own sperm, but they can shop around. In the market place, for example, are banks that are set up to provide sperm specifically from high-achieving males. The most famous of these so-called genius sperm banks, the Repository for Germinal Choice in Escondido, California, USA, which stocked samples from Nobel prize winners, has run out of cash and closed. But there are other organisations and individuals ready to help, many using the internet to advertise their services.[7]

Some agencies charge nominal fees simply to cover running costs; others are downright commercial. One web site allows members to bid in an auction for eggs and sperm produced by glamour models.[8] The owner of the site, fashion photographer Ron

---

7. http://www.geniusspermbank.com catalogues extensive information about sperm donors' scientific discoveries, inventions, published papers and patents, school records, music and artistic abilities, athletic abilities, as well as the usual race and appearance information.

8. The site's address is http://ronsangels.com and it was launched in October 1999.

Harris, defends it by saying, 'We bid for everything else in this society – why not eggs?' After all, 'What mother wants an ugly child?'[9] Harris anticipates that eggs will sell for 15,000 to 150,000 dollars and sperm for 10,000 to 50,000 dollars and plans to add a twenty per cent charge to the bid price. The announcement that this site had been launched prompted Robert Stillman, medical director of Grove Fertility Center in Rockville, Maryland, to say, 'This is deplorable, unethical and speaks only to the basest of human desires.' But in America it breaks no laws.

Sperm banks have the 'advantage' of being able to provide a very low-tech service. Send them the fee and your address and they post you a vial and instructions. A turkey baster or syringe is all that a woman needs to place the sperm in her vagina. Many ask no questions about the recipient. Follow the DIY instructions and a fertile female stands a reasonable chance of getting pregnant. While most participants would not like to acknowledge it, influencing their babies involves making eugenic choices. The very existence of sperm banks with deposits listed by academic, financial, artistic or sporting success shows that some people are already making choices about the nature of the child they would like to bring into the world.

You could dismiss this as a peripheral issue, because relative to the millions of babies born around the world each year, the number of people taking these choices is small, and in countries with reasonable levels of supervision of the fertility industry, there are strict guidelines that need to be followed. In the USA, however, where individual freedom is given ultimate status, there are few if any restrictions over what a private individual may do if the process is financed by their own money. A New York-based infertility clinic, which has its offices among the fashion shops on Madison Avenue, specialises in creating embryos that satisfy as much as possible the potential parents' demands.[10] Lee Silver comments that, in American

9. Quoted in Horovitz, B., 'Selling Beautiful Babies', *USA Today*, 25 October 1999.

10. An interview given by the head of the clinic, Dr Mark Sauer, was broadcast as part of the 'Perfect Babies' series on Channel 5 television in January 1999.

culture, there is no reason for restricting the growth of this market: 'In a society that values individual freedom above all else, it is hard to find any legitimate basis for restricting the use of reprogenetics.'[11]

It's worth restating that, as we saw in the previous chapter, we are more than our genes, and that just because you get eggs or sperm from a winner, there is no guarantee that the characteristics you hoped to choose will be passed on to the new individual. The agencies exist partly because of a level of ignorance among clients, and partly because people think that it's worth a try: 'If you are going to use donated eggs or sperm then at least get the best available.' The level of inaccuracy intrinsic to the process could even allow you to turn a blind eye to any ethical considerations because it probably won't work in any case.

## Testing before implantation

The techniques offered in the new Babel introduce a new level of precision. While we are still a long way from being able to assess individual sperm and eggs without destroying them, we can make considerable judgements about early embryos. Pre-implantation genetic diagnosis (PGD) – where a single cell is plucked off a three-day-old embryo, using an incredibly fine glass tube, and its genes analysed – will give a much stronger indication about the nature of the individual.

In 1990 the first babies were born after having been the subjects of PGD. They were twin girls. The technique had been used to identify the sex of the embryos, as males could have been affected by a genetic 'mental retardation' caused by a defective gene on the X chromosome.[12] While this was a new process, it was fairly crude in that it was just detecting whether an embryo contained the Y chromosome; in other words, was it male? Since then the group,

11. Silver, *Remaking Eden*, p. 9.

12. The pregnancy was announced in a paper: Handyside, A.H., Kontogianni, E.H., Hardy, K., and Winston, R.M., 'Pregnancies from Biopsied Human Pre-implantation Embryos Sexed by Y-Specific DNA Amplification', *Nature* **344**, 1990, pp. 768–70.

which works at Hammersmith Hospital in London, has gone on to refine the process so that it can look for individual gene mutations. This led in 1992 to the birth of girl who was known to be free from the risk of having cystic fibrosis.[13] Both of her parents were carriers, meaning that in a normal situation any child would have a one-in-four risk of having the disease. In theory, this now means that any condition known to be caused by a mutation in a single gene can be detected in developing embryos.

By 1999, only four fertility-treatment centres in the UK were licensed to carry out PGD, and around twenty babies had been born following such tests. In the USA, testing is more widespread and estimates suggest that already 200 children have been born after PGD gave them a clean bill of health, or at least showed that they were free from the risk of a particular disease.[14]

As the human genome project reveals more details about the location and function of different genes, we will be able to make increasingly accurate assessments about the person's potential health and abilities.

It will even be possible to look for combinations of gene mutations that could indicate the likelihood of particular traits in the individual, although this will be limited by our poor understanding of how genes work together. Once again, the technology to detect gene mutations is running ahead of our understanding about what these mutations mean, so would-be parents are likely to be handed the responsibility of making decisions using very imprecise information.

We can see how such multi-gene information could be used by looking at a research project underway at University College London, which is headed by Professor David Hopkinson at the Galton Laboratory.[15] In this project, volunteers come and have their

---

13. Handyside, A.H., Lesko, J.G., Tarín, J.J., Winston, R.M., and Hughes, M.R., 'Birth of a Normal Girl After *in vitro* Fertilization and Pre-implantation Diagnostic Testing for Cystic Fibrosis', *The New England Journal of Medicine* **327**, 1992, pp. 905–909.

14. Boyce, N., 'Designing a Dilemma', *New Scientist*, 11 December 1999, pp. 18–19.

15. Named after the father of eugenics.

faces scanned by a computer that analyses the data using a sophisticated three-dimensional-imaging programme. By taking a blood sample or mouth swab from the volunteer, the researchers can then compare the face shape with the detailed spelling of several genes. The researchers hope to identify the genes that control our appearance and that give members of a family a recognisably familiar set of facial features. 'This research on normal variation will have benefits, in the long-term, for the understanding of abnormal facial development, its prevention and treatment,' says a letter written to encourage people to join in. The researchers believe that this knowledge may lead to the point at which a police forensics team will be able to build a 'photofit' of the face of a suspect, using genetic information found at a crime scene. Indeed, the UK's Forensic Science Service funds some of the work. If this sort of detail is realised, then what is to stop prospective parents from using methods like PGD to check the facial appearance of any potential offspring? This research group has spent the last few years trying to understand the structural basis of beauty. So, if we ever got to the position of being able to manipulate the genetic code in an embryo – and that is a big if – we might conceivably be able to sculpt the face shape of our desire. It's a wild idea, and it's not going to happen in the near future, but the potential may be there for future generations.

Talking of the use of PGD, the director of the UK's Genetic Interest Group, Alistair Kent, says that parents should be allowed to choose to have children who are free of specific genetic diseases: 'The people who really need to be heard are those for whom the technique of PGD offers hope of a baby who does not have a serious, life-threatening disease. They are the ones who know what the issues really are, because they know what life with the condition is like from their own experience or from that of another family member.'[16]

Commentator on all things genetic, Dave King believes that

16. Quoted on *BBC Online*, 'Head to Head: Choosing Life?', 16 November 1999.

any PGD allowed should be provided on the same charter as the NHS, in other words, that it should be 'free to all at the point of use'. To force people to pay for this service will, he says, create a two-tier society. One that can afford to be free of certain genetic ailments, and the other that has no option but to live with the genes they inherit by chance.

Joy Delhanty, professor of human genetics at University College London, defends the option of offering PGD to couples who are at risk of having children who are genetically susceptible to colon cancer: 'What we are aiming to do is to give these parents the option of starting a pregnancy knowing it will not have that faulty gene.'[17] If we are not careful we could soon create a situation where the parent, rather than the child, is the primary focus of attention.

The *in vitro* fertilisation pioneer Dr Robert Edwards puts it more forcefully and controversially. He moves the focus of argument from one that suggests parents should be offered the choice, to one where taking this 'choice' should be obligatory: 'Soon it will be a sin for parents to have a child which carries the heavy burden of genetic disease. We are entering a world where we have to consider the quality of our children.'[18] For anyone anxious that the new genetics of Babel could rekindle eugenic sentiments within our community, this sort of statement must send cold shivers down the spine and sound an urgent alarm.

Speaking to the BBC, Dr Richard Nicholson, editor of the *Bulletin of Medical Ethics*, warned that PGD was fraught with ethical difficulties:

*We are now moving rapidly into an age of saying there are lives that are not worth living, and we either prevent them by abortion if they are discovered antenatally, or we now are moving into the hi-tech way of pre-conceptual prevention. People hate to talk about the Nazification of medicine, but this is actually what is happening. It took only twenty-five years in Germany to*

17. Quoted on *BBC Online*, 'Warning Over "Nazi" Genetic Screening', 9 August 1999.
18. Quoted in *The Sunday Times*, 4 July 1999.

*go from individual doctors saying there are certain lives not worth living, to having mass euthanasia programmes. We have got to look very carefully to the way we are gradually progressing to preventing people with disease, rather than preventing disease.*[19]

Charged with overseeing this minefield, the chairman of the HFEA, Ruth Deech, gave a little reassurance when she said that 'The HFEA decided it would be unacceptable to allow PGD to be used to test for any social, physical or psychological characteristics, or any other conditions that are not associated with serious, often life-threatening, medical disorders.'[20] The problem that the HFEA will find is deciding and defining what constitutes a serious medical disorder.

And what of the effect that this may have on the children created? The Wellcome Trust, one of the largest funders of biomedical research in the UK, has produced a video play, whose intention is to stimulate discussion. Spanning three decades, the play depicts a sixteen-year-old who, in the year 2028, discovers that his ability to play tennis is due in part to his father's deliberate choice of an embryo with athletic potential. When the son discovers this he is furious, claiming that his father has made him to fulfil his desires, leaving the son with no sense of achievement or independence.

Before we get carried away with the possibilities of PGD, we should pause to check that it is safe. There are question marks over the reliability of the test. In 1996, one set of researchers found that it was only able to detect seventy-three per cent of embryos that had a known mutation in the gene associated with cystic fibrosis.[21] While individual tests will improve, this shows that such tests are never likely to be able to give 100 per cent certainty. Part of this lack of

---

19. Quoted on *BBC Online*, 'Warning Over "Nazi" Genetic Screening', 9 August 1999.

20. Quoted on *BBC Online*, 'Gene Screening Debate Goes Public', 16 November 1999.

21. Ao, A., Ray, P., Harper, J., Lesko, J., Paraschos, T., Atkinson, G., Soussis, I., Taylor, D., Handyside, A., Hughes, M., and Winston, R.M., 'Clinical Experience with Pre-implantation Genetic Diagnosis of Cystic Fibrosis (delta F508)', *Prenatal Diagnosis* **16**, 1996, pp. 137–42.

precision occurs because the mutations in genes are prone to change when a cell is taken out and tested. This 'allele-specific drop-out' appears to introduce errors in the test in between ten and fourteen per cent of tests.[22] There is also some indication that, after having a cell removed, the embryos produce less human chorionic gonadotrophin, the hormone that says, 'Hi, Mum. I'm here. Don't have a period or I'll get washed away.'[23] Presumably something has been disturbed, so is there any long-term effect caused by pulling a cell off an early embryo? Only time will tell. Currently there have been too few babies born following the use of this technique to make any proper assessment, and those born have not yet reached adulthood.

## Paying the piper

The difficulty with all of this is that we are providing a health service that operates not by making people better, but by removing anyone who stands a high chance of being ill.

In relation to this area, it's interesting to compare public opinion with reality. A Mori poll of 2,000 people conducted in 1999 found that almost one third of women said they would consider aborting a child if it was found to be affected by a severe inherited disease.[24] In a report produced by the UK's Royal College of Obstetricians and Gynaecologists (RCOG), the reality is more severe: 'Once a serious abnormality, such as Down's syndrome or anencephaly, has been identified, evidence shows that parents will elect to terminate the pregnancy in eighty to ninety per cent of cases.'[25]

22. Rechitsky, S., Freidine, M., Verlinsky, Y., and Strom, C.M., 'Allele Drop-out in Sequential PCR and FISH Analysis of Single Cells (Cell Recycling)', *Journal of Assisted Reproduction and Genetics* **13**, 1996, pp. 115–24.

23. Dokras, A., Sargent, I.L., Gardner, R.L., and Barlow, D.H., 'Human Trophectoderm Biopsy and Secretion of Chorionic Gonadotrophin', *Human Reproduction* **6**, 1991, pp. 1453–59.

24. The opinion poll was commissioned by the UK-based medical research charity Action Research, as part of a fund- and awareness-raising campaign.

25. 'Ultrasound Screening for Fetal Abnormalities', Report of the RCOG, October 1997, para. 2.2.

The argument for giving people screening and diagnostic tests is that these tests simply hand the person information without any sense of bias or coercion. However, this doesn't bear thoughtful criticism. After all, why would a health system that is strapped for cash spend its resources giving you information if the system didn't expect you to act on it? And here we discover a conflict of interest in the views and desires of healthcare policy-makers, genetic counsellors and the public. The policy-makers are interested in populations, the counsellors in information and the individual person, the client, wants to know what to do and to be supported.

Healthcare policy-makers talk in terms of cost–benefit analysis. How much do they have to spend to achieve a particular beneficial outcome? It's easy to say, but it is almost impossible to compute. To start with, what do we mean by cost, and, for that matter, what do we mean by benefit? For screening and diagnosis the costs include some items of equipment, training staff, the chemical reagents, the time for performing each test and the cost of any subsequent procedure that might result from the information. Benefit is often calculated in terms of trying to assess how much has been saved by doing the test, in other words, what costs would have been incurred had the test not been performed. In the case of antenatal testing these costs boil down to the extra time and money that will be needed to look after someone born with the given condition. This saving is a major component of the benefit, but to that some people add the notion that it is beneficial in itself to avoid passing faulty genes on to the next generation.

Adding the numbers together is not easy, and so there is wide discrepancy in the estimates. However, all calculations show that the costs are appreciable: estimates for screening the population to look for fetuses with cystic fibrosis put the cost per fetus detected at between £40,000 and £143,000, and detecting Down's syndrome costs between £22,000 and £36,000 per individual found to be affected.

The RCOG justifies these costs, saying that the long-term cost implications of subsequent treatment, or, more specifically, the long-term costs of caring for a baby born with these conditions, are 'potentially very high, especially if the baby survives for any length of time. Avoidance of these costs can be used to justify the relatively high costs of screening.'[26]

The policy-makers are aware that supplying expensive antenatal screening tests can only be justified on the basis that it may help to reduce the costs of caring for people with diseases. The RCOG is far from alone. A report prepared for the Health Technology Assessment Programme funded by the NHS states,

*The aim of genetic screening for CF is to reduce the birth prevalence of the disorder. This is principally achieved by identifying carrier couples who can have prenatal diagnosis and selective termination of pregnancy. Other options are to: avoid pregnancy; change partners; have artificial insemination using donor sperm or egg; and have pre-implantation diagnosis to select unaffected [embryos].*[27]

I find this statement alarming. Not only is it clearly stating the aim to shape future generations, but it is also suggesting that current generations are moulded as well, changing partners being one of their suggested courses of action.

In making this suggestion they are following the lead set by the Ashkenazi Jews. Realising that Tay Sachs was prevalent in their tightly knit society, Rabbi Ekstein founded *Dor Yeshorim*, the Association for an Upright Generation. Having had four children die of Tay Sachs he is very aware of its severity. Teenagers in the community are tested to see if they are carriers of the Tay Sachs mutation. The test is carried out years before they are considering marriage and the result of the test stored away in a numerically ordered database. No one knows their own result and the theory is that they consequently don't worry about what it revealed.

26. 'Ultrasound Screening for Fetal Abnormalities', para. 7.17.

27. Murray, J., Cuckle, H., Taylor, G., Littlewood, J., and Hewison, J., 'Screening for Cystic Fibrosis', *Health Technology Assessment* **3**, 1999, p. 8.

When some years later two people consider marrying, their two numbers are submitted to the database and if they are both carriers then they are recommended to find other marriage partners. The idea is that the whole process is anonymous and that people do not know their status, but once a couple is advised that marriage would be unwise they both know that they are carriers – and so too, presumably, would the surrounding community.

In theory the test is taken voluntarily. If it were compulsory it would be a gross infringement of the individual's rights. However, as the aim is to prevent two carriers marrying, it seems to me that it would be difficult for any member of the community to find a partner without having submitted to the test.

This bold programme gives the illusion of freeing this group of people from one particular disease. I say, 'illusion', because the genetic mutation is still at large and will remain so. It does, however, work in this part of the Jewish community because arranged marriages are part of the social scene. In addition, marriage is seen as an institution that unites families as much as it unites individuals and so the whole family feels that it has a personal stake in seeking a healthy outcome.

The need to keep population-shaping agendas far away from medicine is fully understood by genetic counsellors as they are constantly at the sharp end of the eugenics debate. They see counselling 'as a communication process that deals with the human problems associated with the occurrence, or risk of occurrence, of a genetic disorder in a family'.[28] The goal is to help people understand their medical situation and the way that inheritance influences them. Then they can be shown their options, and helped to make the most appropriate decisions in the light of their own situation. Finally, any affected family member can be helped to live the fullest possible life. In a paper published in the *Journal of Medical Genetics*, Susan Michie and her colleagues point out that 'We

28. Fraser, F.C., 'Genetic Counselling', *American Journal of Human Genetics* **26**, 1974, pp. 636–59.

know little, however, about the extent to which this coincides with what actually occurs in genetic counselling or with what patients want from genetic counselling.'[29]

Genetic counsellors would much prefer to see people before a pregnancy starts, when the options could at that point include deciding not to have children of their own, sperm or egg donation to avoid passing on the disease-causing genes or *in vitro* fertilisation coupled with PGD. As the Babel tower grows, genetic counsellors will be in an increasingly powerful position to give accurate information about specific genetic diseases. In addition, the increased precision of tests will mean that individuals can be told more about their circumstances and the sort of limitations that any affected child may expect.

All this is fine, but if genetic counsellors are not going to assume the role of the shapers of future humanity they need to give information, not advice. However, I don't really believe this is possible, and when surveyed few, if any, believe it is either. In one study all of the counsellors said that they gave an element of directive advice in the way they handed over information. This could be in terms of straightforward comments, or selectively reinforcing comments made by the client. Intriguingly, only half of the counsellees felt that they had been steered by the counsellor.[30] The study also found that counsellors were more directive in their style when talking with people whom they rated as having low socio-economic statuses than they were when talking to people whom they felt were more highly educated.

So policy-makers are trying to create healthy populations, and genetic counsellors to provide unbiased information, but what do the end-users of the service want? A survey of purchasers, counsellors and clients points to a disquieting discrepancy by

29. Michie, S., Theresa, M., and Bobrow, M., 'Genetic Counselling: The Psychological Impact of Meeting Parents' Expectations', *Journal of Medical Genetics* **34**, 1996, pp. 237–41.

30. Michie, S., Bron, F., Bobrow, M., and Marteau, T., 'Non-directiveness in Genetic Counselling: An Empirical Study', *American Journal of Human Genetics* **60**, 1997, pp. 40–47.

quoting a public-health doctor[31] – one of the key policy-makers: 'The highest consensus was that genetic counselling should provide support: the highest proportion gave this in each group except for the public-health doctors. This is worrying because public-health doctors have considerable influence on purchasing decisions and yet were obviously out of tune with all other groups.'[32]

## A listening ear

In all the clamour of people making claims and cures it would be easy to forget to listen to those who are really most directly affected by Babel: those who have some form of disability. Various support groups are now in existence, run by people with disabilities for people with disabilities. They point out that the focus of these groups is often very different from those set up by parents of people with disabilities.

One such group is the British Council of Disabled People (BCODP). This is an umbrella organisation for many groups controlled by disabled people and it is anxious that Babel's technology may remove what social status they have at the moment. 'Many of us feel under threat... by the publicly touted, high-profile "promises" of the genetics revolution, a revolution which seems set on making sure the people like us are never born,' says Dr Bill Albert, who is chair of the International Committee of the BCODP. In a discussion document on genetic technology the BCODP says, 'As disabled people we know that our lives have a value equal to anyone's. We know that, although our impairments may cause us pain or discomfort, what really disables us as members of society is a socio-cultural system which does not recognise our right to genuinely equal treatment.'[33] And there is also a more positive message:

31. Public-health doctors are the unsung heroes of the UK's health system. They are involved in strategic planning and in preventing outbreaks of disease.

32. Michie, S., Allanson, A., Armstrong, D., Weinman, J., Bobrow, M., and Marteau, T., 'Objectives of Genetic Counselling: Differing Views of Purchasers, Providers and Users', *Journal of Public Health Medicine* **20**, 1998, pp. 404–408.

33. 'The New Genetics and Disabled People: A Discussion Document'. Available from the British Council of Disabled People, http://www.bcodp.org.uk/general/genetics.

*We affirm that our lives are not only of equal importance to anyone's but also that as disabled people we offer much that is positive to society, not least by demonstrating the inherent value of life itself. This is a vital corrective to the heartless utilitarianism underlying much of the new genetics, which posits a 'less messy' society free from the inconvenience of disabled people.*

Their fear is that by concentrating on genetic testing and techniques that prevent people with genetic disability ever being born, we are establishing a principle that disability is so bad it should be banished – at any cost. It is all too easy to join the WHO in claiming a desire to see all people free of any physical, mental and social disease or infirmity.[34] But there are a few harsh realities. To start with, no amount of technological intervention is going to prevent people being born with genetic diseases. The BCODP points to the impossibility of ridding society of disability, saying that eighty per cent of disabled people are not born with their impairment, but acquire it later in life, and no one is going to stop people having accidents.

People with disabilities need assistance not charity, inclusion rather than patronisation and care instead of eradication as the primary aim of medical intervention. 'Would it not be preferable to live in a society which did not strive for some sort of unobtainable, and probably undesirable, genetic perfection but instead sought to preserve diversity and enhance standards of human decency?' asks the BCODP.

People involved in supplying and developing techniques like PGD argue passionately that they have no intention of offending people who already have an impairment; they would just like to see if there is a way of preventing that impairment affecting anyone else. To me, this seems reasonable – but is it really possible?

UK abortion law enshrines the right of a woman to make certain decisions about the life of any developing baby. However, if

34. Remember the WHO definition of health? 'Heath is a state of complete physical, mental and social well-being, and not merely the absence of disease or infirmity.'

the woman is going to have genuine choice, then society needs to be ready and waiting to give every assistance and support to her and her child. At the moment we seem to be saying to people, 'It's your choice, and you have to live with the consequences.' For many this offers no choice at all.

## Hype and hypotheses

So where does this leave us? Steve Jones enjoys using the quip that genes are spelt using a four-letter code, 'H, Y, P and E', and there is a lot of truth in that. The task is to sort out the hype from the reasonable hypotheses. It is all too easy to dismiss every potentially unsavoury application of genetic technology as another piece of hype, because all this does is raise a smokescreen that prevents sensible debate.

The history of fertility treatments shows that there is a powerful drive to make anything that is attainable available. Some say that for this reason we should forget any attempt at regulating or restricting the use of techniques, because any such actions will be futile.

*Chapter 9*

# INFORMATION WARS

'All information is imperfect. We have to treat it with humility.' Thus wrote Jacob Bronowski in his book, *The Ascent of Man*,[1] and anyone charged with the responsibility of handling genetic information would do well to remember it.

Part of the 'genohype' has been generated by scientists and journalists as they discuss the potential of the new Babel. It arises from the mistaken notion that we have somehow reached the point of absolute knowledge – that we have the ultimate level of information. 'In the popular imagination, genes are thought to contain the code to an individual's fate, and the idea that someone might crack our personal code and use it against us is unsettling,' writes the president of the California Healthcare Institute in La Jolla, David Gollaher.[2]

Remember the genohype that surrounded the announcement in December 1999 that genetic sequencers at the Sanger Centre in Cambridge, UK, had determined the complete sequence of human chromosome 22.[3]

In almost every situation we will look at in this chapter, Babel is at a stage when it gives us a little information and allows us to

1. Bronowski, J., *The Ascent of Man*, BBC Publications, 1973.

2. 'The Paradox of Genetic Privacy', *New York Times*, 7 January 1998.

3. Dunham, I., and 217 other co-authors, 'The DNA Sequence of Human Chromosome 22', *Nature* **402**, 1999, pp. 489–95. See chapter 3.

make some tentative statements about what that information may mean. Believing that the information is more definite or powerful than it really is stands a high chance of hurting those affected by it.

The other issue that will recur is that of confidentiality – who needs to know the result of a test? For example, if you know that you have a genetic predisposition to have a disease, should you tell your relatives? They are also at risk as they come from a common line of descent. If they don't want to know about future gremlins, then you are forcing information into their lives without their consent. The ultimate complexity of this nature would be an identical twin having a genetic test, while the other twin wanted to carry on life in blissful ignorance.

Genetic counsellor Caroline Berry paints a picture of another awkward dilemma: a young woman with a brother who has muscular dystrophy is pregnant and wants to know whether she is a carrier for the disease and therefore find out whether there is a possibility that the developing child is affected by the disease. To do an accurate test geneticists will need to know the exact mutation that her brother carries. However, she may not want her brother to know of her pregnancy, or that she is worried about having a child with his disorder. Should the geneticist obtain the man's mutation result without his consent? If approached, does the brother have a duty to disclose information about himself? These questions are not easy to answer.

In fact, sharing genetic information between family members can have potentially unforeseen consequences. One study found that in a family where most members had a genetic predisposition to get Huntingdon's disease, those members who didn't carry the faulty gene were rejected. The 'healthy' members no longer possessed one of the key bonds that held the family together.[4]

In most situations, however, there are few problems in

4. Tibben, A., Vlis, M., Niermeijer, M.F., Kamp, J.J., Roos, R.A., Rooijmans, H.G., Frets, P.G., and Verhage, F., 'Testing for Huntington's Disease with Support for All Parties', [letter], *The Lancet* **335**, 1990, p. 553.

disclosing genetic information within families, but the risks and complications must not be overlooked.

## Insurance

One of the areas where it is easy to see how quickly individuals could get hurt is insurance, where groups of people pool resources so that any one of them can draw on the money at times of unexpected loss or damage. There are two models for pooling financial risk: solidarity and mutuality. In a solidarity system, every member of a society is required to pay into a central fund, usually with some measure being taken of his or her ability to pay. Effectively this is a tax scheme, much like the UK's Social Security system and NHS. When a person is in need, they can then draw from the scheme. Everyone contributes according to their resources and receives according to their needs.

Over the last few decades, Western governments have progressively moved provision towards a mutuality model of insurance. The idea has been to encourage everyone to make provision for his or her own needs. In this model people volunteer to pay into the pooled fund, with the level of their contribution set after an assessment of the likelihood of their needing help. Contributions are said to be 'equitable', not because everyone contributes the same amount, but because people at an equal risk pay an equal contribution. The greater your risk of being ill, the more you will be charged for a policy. If you are thought to be at a very high risk, you may be denied insurance altogether.

The standard practice in insurance companies is to set their assessment systems so that ninety-five per cent of people qualify for standard levels of insurance, three per cent are asked to pay elevated premiums and the final two per cent are refused cover.

Mutual insurance can only operate if information is shared equally between the insurer and the applicant. To establish how much money the insurance company needs to have in its coffers to be certain of meeting all claims, the company needs to have a reasonable assessment of the level of risk it has taken on. With car insurance they do this by taking into consideration elements like the age of the driver, their sex, the type of car they are planning on driving and where they plan to leave it overnight. If you make a lot of claims on your insurance, your premium will rise; if you take care and avoid claiming then you are awarded a 'no-claims bonus', and your premium falls.

This seems reasonable enough, but the effects of this sort of process are more complex when the insurance is taken out to protect against something that is related to the person's health. The risk of an individual developing some illness will be affected by their age, sex, employment, where they live, previous history of personal illness and their genetic endowment. For pretty much as long as life insurance has been around, insurers have used evidence of disease running in the applicant's family to help assess their personal risk. It's the same basic concept that geneticists used to start tracking down the genetic principles underlying the risk of some diseases like cystic fibrosis and breast cancer.

An example of the sort of anxiety that this can cause is seen in the American Ashkenazi Jewish population. Recent studies have shown that they have a high prevalence of genetic mutations that increase the risk of breast, ovarian and colon cancers. There is already a fear that 'anyone with a Jewish-sounding name could face discrimination in insurance and employment as companies struggle to keep down healthcare costs'.[5]

This sort of discrimination is not just a fear for the future. A research project which surveyed 7,000 members of support groups for families with genetic disorders found that thirty-three per cent of families had problems when applying for life insurance, compared with five per cent of the general public.[6] In addition, thirteen per cent of people who were carriers of recessive or sex-linked disorders that would not affect their insurance risk experienced problems obtaining life insurance. Remember that carriers of a disorder will have no

5. Lehrman, S., 'Jewish Leaders Seek Genetic Guidelines', *Nature* **389**, 1997, p. 322.

6. Low, L., King, S., and Wilkie, T., 'Genetic Discrimination in Life Insurance: Empirical Evidence from a Cross-Sectional Survey of Genetic Support Groups in the United Kingdom', *British Medical Journal* **317**, 1998, pp. 1632–35.

symptoms of the disease themselves; in some cases they may even benefit from the genetic mutation. The researchers point out that such findings raise questions about the insurers' ability to interpret genetic information accurately. Certainly some people questioned felt that they had faced 'unjustified genetic discrimination'.

But now insurance companies are worried that people will start using genetic information against them. The fear is that people will have a test, find that they are at an increased risk from a particular disease and, as a result of this new-found knowledge, take out a large policy at a standard premium without declaring the test result to the insurers. It's a process that insurers call 'anti-selection'. If this happened too often, the company would start to run out of money and would have to increase the level of contribution from the standard-risk customers. These people would look elsewhere, or decide that insurance was too expensive and shoulder the risk themselves, leaving the company with just the high-risk clients. That, says the industry, is unsustainable

A more subtle form of selection might be unavoidable though. People who take tests and find that they are not at a high risk of developing the illnesses they were worried about might decide not to take out any insurance. This would bias the market, with only the higher risk individuals seeking cover. Taking out a mutual insurance policy is a voluntary action – you can't force someone who considers his or her risk to be low to buy one. Alternatively companies could engage in 'cherry-picking', offering lower premiums for genetically 'clean' individuals, whom they deem to be at lower risk. This would again bias the market, leaving the general insurer with the task of taking on a statistically less healthy set of clients.

However, the client's side is just as worrying. If you have a genetic test that indicates an increased level of risk, you could find yourself in the position of being unable to get standard-rate cover, or for that matter cover at any cost. A consequence of this is that people who could benefit medically from the information that a test would give decide against it to avoid this discrimination. A National Opinion Poll survey conducted for the Genetics Forum found that three out of ten people would not take a genetic test if they knew they were going to have to disclose the results.[7]

Speaking in the White House in July 1997, President Clinton made an outspoken attack on the idea that genetic tests should be used as a basis of assessing insurance risk. He was concerned that this would prevent people having tests that could be medically useful: 'Now this kind of discrimination is – really it's more than wrong, it's a life-threatening abuse of a potentially life-saving discovery… Americans should never have to choose between saving their health insurance and taking tests that could save their lives.'[8]

American politicians aren't alone in calling for restraint. Legislation in Austria, Belgium, Denmark and Norway prohibits the use of genetic information by the insurance industry, and Australia, France and the Netherlands have voluntary restrictive arrangements with the industry.

And many scientists agree. At HUGO's second international genome summit in Canberra, Australia, in 1996, David Cox, of the Stanford School of Medicine, California, said, 'Protection against discrimination should prevail over conflicting societal values. Such protection must be mandated by law.'

In December 1997 the Association of British Insurers (ABI) rejected a UK government advisory commission recommendation that there should be a moratorium on the use of genetic testing in assessing insurance premiums for at least two years. The HGAC based this on the decision that 'it is unlikely that actuarially important genetic predictions of common causes of adult death will be available and validated, for some time to come. This is because information linking genetics and multifactorial disease is at too early a stage to make sound assessments of added risk.'[9] They also pointed out that the European Convention on Human Rights and Biomedicine prohibits, under Article 11, any form of discrimination against a person on the grounds

7. Genetics Forum opinion poll, published in *Spice of Life*, issue 5, vol. 5, April 1997.

8. Speaking in the East Room of the White House on the afternoon of 14 July 1997.

9. 'The Implications of Genetic Testing for Insurance', Report prepared by the HGAC, December 1997, para. 6.2.

of his or her genetic heritage. This is echoed on the other side of the Atlantic, where at least twenty-two states have legislation against genetic discrimination and, at the federal level, the Health Insurance Portability and Accountability Act 1996, and the Americans and Disabilities Act both prohibit some forms of genetic discrimination.

President Clinton again: 'It is also clear that it is wrong for insurance companies to use genetic information to deny coverage. It's happened before. It happened in the 1970s with some African Americans who carried sickle-cell anaemia. And it can happen in other ways.'[10]

Despite this the ABI initially insisted on allowing its member companies to use information from tests relating to seven different diseases, namely Huntington's disease, familial adenomatous polyposis, myotonic dystrophy, Alzheimer's disease, multiple endocrine neoplasia, hereditary motor and sensory neuropathy and hereditary breast and ovarian cancer. This decision was spelt out in the August 1999 update of the ABI's code of practice.

Along with the disincentive to seek genetic advice, there are two further issues. First is the nature of discrimination implicit in this decision, and secondly, is the problem that the decision to allow some of these tests is based on poor scientific evidence.

In a written response to the insurance industry, the UK's Alzheimer's Disease Society said that 'The Government's decision to endorse the ABI Code of Practice legitimises discrimination. People with Alzheimer's disease and their carers already experience high levels of social stigma. This action can only make an individual and their family further excluded from society.'[11] Intriguingly, the insurance industry recognises that it does have a duty to society in that it has decided that genetic information should not be used in assessing requests for life insurance to cover mortgages up to the value of £100,000. The rationale is that having a house, and therefore a mortgage, is recognised as a social norm in the UK, and no one should be prevented from

10. Speaking in the White House on 14 July 1997.

11. *The Use of Genetic Tests for Alzheimer's Disease by the Insurance Industry*, Alzheimer's Disease Society, January 1999.

ownership on the grounds of his or her genetic constitution. The limit of £100,000 assumes that you can buy a house for that sort of sum of money, though in reality you would be restricted as to where you could live in the UK if you only had £100,000 to go shopping with.

However, the insurance industry has always operated by discriminating against five per cent of the population. Genetic testing could cause it to increase that percentage. In the foreseeable future people could have information on the state of hundreds, maybe even thousands, of their genes. Most probably everyone will find that some of the information indicates an increased risk of particular diseases. If the insurance industry discriminates against them all, it will soon have no clients.

In time this could even things out, because once we are all discriminated against we will be back on a level playing field and the insurers will be able to relax again. Genetic information will then become valuable to healthcare planners as they try to apportion funds to meet specific demands, because they want to know exactly which diseases are going to show up. But it will be of less use to the insurers, who basically want to know whether a person will be well or sick, while the exact nature of the illness is not of so much interest.

Then came a March 2001 publication of a House of Commons Science and Technology Committee report entitled 'Genetics and Insurance'. It roundly condemned the current practices of the insurance industry: 'The insurance industry has failed to give clear and straightforward information about its policy on the use of genetic test results to the public, and appears to be uncertain itself about what exactly its policy is.'[12] The report also noted that four of the seven tests that it had initially sanctioned for use had now been withdrawn. The tests still allowed look for genes that could predispose a person to be affected by Huntington's chorea, early-onset familial Alzheimer's disease and hereditary breast and ovarian cancer. 'The ABI's decision that four of the tests it recommended insurers use three years ago are now no longer relevant or reliable casts the gravest possible doubts on the validity of the

12. House of Commons Science and Technology Committee report, para. 29.

tests not explicitly approved by the GAIC, being currently used by insurers. Insurers have given the test results a predictive significance that cannot, at present, be justified,' said the report (para. 33).

The report also concluded: 'If the choice has to be made between exposing insurance companies to a small degree of short-term risk, and increasing the stigma and discrimination many of these sufferers feel, then the choice for Government, and our society, is clear' (para. 76).

By May the insurance companies had bowed to pressure and introduced a two-year moratorium on the use of genetic test data for life-insurance policies of less than £300,000. It was a slight climb down, but even then had a note of defiance, as the Government's Human Genetics Commission had called for the limit to be set at £500,000.

The saddest thing about this whole debate is that it is based on a good dose of genohype. The evidence of a causal link between the gene mutations and the diseases is not conclusive, and the insurers give the appearance of acting as if they believe in an extreme form of biological determinism.

The saddest thing about this whole debate is that it is based on a good dose of genohype. The evidence of a causal link between the gene mutations and the diseases is not conclusive, and the insurers are acting as if they believe in an extreme form of biological determinism. According to the ABI's own data, only half of the people found with the relevant gene mutation will have developed Huntington's disease by the age of fifty, and less than one-in-four people with the Alzheimer's mutations will have succumbed by the same age. On top of this, the Alzheimer's Disease Society points out that of the forty-seven different mutations to the PS1 and PS2 genes that the insurance industry is now allowing itself to include in assessments, thirty-five are extremely rare. This means that testing for the presence of these mutations will be useless for providing a diagnostic test. In addition, they say that fewer than 3,000 of the 17,000 people with early-onset dementia in the UK will have one of the three gene mutations identified by the ABI.

As if this were not enough, the Alzheimer's Disease Society also claims that the ABI fails to establish the difference between early-onset Alzheimer's disease, for which there is some genetic link, and late-onset disease, which is still more elusive. Only one per cent of people with Alzheimer's disease have the early-onset version.

When you ask them, representatives of the insurance industry are keen to stress that family history is still the strongest guide to a person's individual health risk. They also stress that genetic testing had allowed some clients to achieve lower insurance premiums. The cases they refer to are ones where the applicant's family has a history of a particular disease, but the test indicates that the individual has not personally inherited the faulty gene. While this might seem laudable at first sight, it could force people who have a family history of disease to play Russian roulette – either take a high premium based on the family history, or have a gene test, the result of which could either put them in the clear, or leave them uninsurable.

America is seen as an example of the costs and inequality that result from a system of provision which relies heavily on mutual insurance schemes. As genetic testing begins to give more accurate diagnoses, groups of people are likely to find themselves increasingly cut off from this protection.

The alternative to this discrimination is to head for solidarity-based systems, and there are signs of movement in this direction. In Australia, life insurance is compulsory in certain retirement plans and the Institute of Actuaries of Australia states that insurers 'may not seek medical information and members of the plan do not have to disclose [medical or genetic] test results'. British insurers are effectively doing this with their mortgage cover for less than £100,000, and in France there is an agreement between the Federation of French Insurers and the Ministries of Trade and Health to provide mortgage insurance to people infected with HIV.[13] It strikes me that the NHS had it right when it pooled the risk of ill health across the whole population of the UK, funding itself by compulsory donations from all employed people and providing for all needy people.

13. Reported in Pokorski, R., 'A Test for the Insurance Industry', *Nature* **391**, 1998, pp. 835–36. Robert Pokorski works at the Cologne Life Reinsurance Company, Connecticut, USA.

## Employment

The other area of concern regarding potential genetic discrimination is employment. In Western societies, part of the task of caring for people is passed to the employer in that they are bound to make at least some contribution towards an employee while he or she is sick. In addition to this, having employees off work is costly because the organisation will lose efficiency. Employers therefore often ask for medical reports before taking someone on.

Disabled groups are quick to point out that their members have great difficulty getting jobs, and are anxious that genetic testing could broaden the scope of the discrimination. People who are seen to be at a high genetic risk from diseases could discover that it is very difficult to find paid employment. Should the employee be protected from discrimination by having legal rights not to disclose the genetic information, or should the employer be protected from taking on someone who may be frequently away from work by forcing disclosure?

Certainly, Bill Clinton has a clear opinion. In February 2000 he signed a bill that bars federal agencies from discriminating against their employees on the basis of genetic tests. 'We must protect our citizens' privacy – the bulwark of personal liberty, the safeguard of individual creativity,'[14] he stated. The bill prohibits federal employers from requiring or requesting genetic tests as a condition of being hired or receiving benefits. Clinton is also actively supporting bills that intend to prohibit all employers from refusing to hire people on the basis of an adverse genetic finding. Interestingly, sharing the stage with the president was Francis Collins, the director of the National Human Genome Research Institute, the US body charged with the task of unravelling the human genetic code, who is also anxious to prevent genetic information from being used unwisely.

There is also anxiety that employers will look for tests that show a person to be less likely to suffer from particular work-related diseases than people who appear to be 'genetically unhealthy', and

14. Quoted in 'Clinton Bans DNA Job Tests', *BBC News Online*, 8 February 2000.

employ these people instead of cleaning up their working conditions. Even Clinton's bill allows for genetic information to be disclosed to ensure workplace health and safety.

A 1999 report by the HGAC stated that thus far, with the exception of the Ministry of Defence, no UK employers were using genetic test results when they decided who to employ.[15] The report concludes, 'It will take major developments both in our understanding of common diseases and in genetic testing itself before genetic testing becomes a serious issue for employment practice.'[16] However, we need to remember that the experience of the insurance industry is that business leaders seem to be more convinced about the predictive capability of genetic tests, than do many of the scientists who are developing the technology.

In the same document, the commission recognises that technology may change, but stresses that, even so, it would 'not be acceptable for genetic test results to exclude people from employment or advancement on the grounds that they have a predisposition to future ill health'.[17] However, this does not mean they would like to see it removed from the employment market: 'We note that there are situations where it might be appropriate for genetic test results to be used in employment.'[18] This is where the test reveals that the person could put themselves or other employees at risk.

It is in this context that the Ministry of Defence checks all aircrew for sickle-cell anaemia. Individuals with the disease, or even those who are simply carriers (i.e. they have one faulty gene and one healthy one) may be less able to cope with the low-oxygen environments experienced at high altitudes.

In more mundane environments we already use this type of medical information, albeit derived from conventional, as opposed

15. 'The Implications of Genetic Testing for Employment', Report by the HGAC, chaired by Baroness O'Neill, 1999.

16. 'The Implications of Genetic Testing for Employment', para. 3.5.

17. 'The Implications of Genetic Testing for Employment', para. 3.12.

18. 'The Implications of Genetic Testing for Employment', para. 3.14.

to genetic, tests. For example, heavy-lorry drivers are banned from working if they have some form of diabetes that could cause them to black out in the cab, and airline pilots are required to have good health and excellent vision.

We need to recognise that everyone is different and these differences make us better suited to various forms of employment. Genetic testing could help people find suitable jobs, and could allow employers to tailor working conditions to fit individual employees. Or the tests could lead to employers simply setting up the cheapest working environment, and then finding the people who are genetically most likely to be able to cope with it. It strikes me that we will need some carefully composed legislation to promote the former.

As with insurance, we may also want to question the move to make individuals responsible for their own security. In insurance, the problem is that the most vulnerable members of society become the least capable of finding financial security. In employment, any employer with a social conscience will be disadvantaged by accepting the responsibility of caring for people who have the risk of returning low levels of productivity. Anti-discrimination legislation may help, but an agreement to supply a stronger government-funded safety net would make employers less anxious and reduce the need for the legislation. Without this, there will always be a battle between employers demanding disclosure and employees pleading for privacy.

## Forensics

'It is better that ten guilty persons escape than one innocent suffer,' said William Blackstone in his famed exposition of the structure of English law, *Commentaries on the Laws of England*.[19] A part of the outworking of this is the assertion that a defendant is innocent unless proven guilty. The task of any investigating and prosecuting authority is to provide hard evidence of guilt. Genetic technology brings with it the hope of a new and powerful way of pointing the finger of blame at individuals, with such compelling force that no further evidence is required.

19. *Commentaries on the Laws of England*, vol. 4, chap. 27 (1765–69).

In ancient Babylon, the land of Babel, fingerprints were used on clay tablets for business transactions, but it wasn't until 1856 that a chance observation led the way to their use in fighting crime. Chief magistrate of the Hooghly district of Jungipoor, India, Sir William Herschel, started getting people to make an imprint of their hand or fingers on the backs of contracts that they had signed. The initial idea was that the personal physical contact with the document would instil a greater concept of ownership and responsibility. It wasn't long, though, before he began to see that each print was unique to the individual and permanent throughout the individual's life. A letter to *Nature* in 1880 by Henry Faulds[20] suggested that fingerprints could be used as a practical means of identification, and in Mark Twain's book of 1883, *Life on the Mississippi*, a murderer is identified by the use of fingerprints.

In 1892 Francis Galton published a practical guide to differences in people's fingerprints, laying the ground for their use in future criminal investigations. The book, called simply *Fingerprints*, established a system of classification for prints, Galton's Details, which underpins the systems that are still used today. His initial aim was to find a link between the style of print and an individual's intelligence – an aim that was not to succeed, but he did come to the conclusion that the chance of any two people sharing a common print was one in sixty-four billion. In 1901 fingerprints were deemed to be acceptable for criminal identification in England and Wales, and 1902 saw their first systematic use in the USA by the New York Civil Service Commission. In 1911 Thomas Jennings became the first person in the USA to be convicted on the basis of fingerprint evidence. It appears that Jennings had murdered someone called Charles Hiller while committing a burglary.

So, over the last century, fingerprinting became the forensic service's gold standard of proof. It's not surprising then that when a genetic method of identifying individuals was dreamed up, it acquired the title of 'genetic fingerprinting'. In the same way that a fingerprint bears no resemblance to a portrait of the person, the DNA fingerprint is not a record of the person's genes. In chapter 3 we saw that genetic

20. Published in *Nature*, 28 October 1880.

fingerprinting makes use of apparently non-message-carrying regions of DNA that are sandwiched between functioning genes. The number and length of these regions turns out to be so variable between individuals that they can be used as a genetic name tag.[21]

Add to this the power of new-generation machines to analyse the DNA from individual cells, and forensics has a new weapon. A single piece of dandruff, a spot of blood or an individual hair is all that is needed to generate a genetic profile. Crimes involving sexual assault and rape often leave traces of the assailant's semen, which is a superb source of genetic material. When previously a criminal might have felt safe by simply donning gloves to prevent leaving any incriminating impressions or prints, now he or she would need to wrap up in a perfectly clean, totally covering boiler suit.

The advent of genetic forensics has allowed police forces to take a new look at old cases. In September 1999, 'professional thief' Edgar Chambers was convicted at Nottingham Crown Court of a burglary that had been committed two years earlier. Chambers had taken a sip from a carton of orange juice and the police matched his DNA fingerprint to that of saliva found on the carton. When Peter Hastings polished his shoes after stabbing his girlfriend, Jean Bellis, to death in her home in Birmingham, UK, he was unaware that he was preserving DNA evidence of the crime. Blood on his shoes was locked in by the polish, and six years later DNA analysis showed that there was a very strong possibility that this blood came from Bellis. Hastings was subsequently found guilty.

The power of this technique has not been lost on the UK government, which in 1995 established a database of DNA profiles of convicted criminals.[22] Once a person's DNA fingerprint has been loaded into the National DNA Database, the database can rapidly search for a match with any forensic sample found at the scene of any other unsolved crime. By the end of 1999, this database contained 700,000 records, making it the largest in the world. Home Secretary

21. It's sometimes referred to as the person's genetic bar code.

22. Established under the Criminal Justice Public Order Act 1994.

Jack Straw claimed that 'a single hair left in a stolen car is enough to identify the thief'.[23] He believes that Britain is 'on the threshold of some of the most exciting changes to police technology in decades'.[24]

As the new millennium dawned, the database had already been used to identify suspects in sixty-eight cases of murder or manslaughter, 253 rapes and 212 cases of serious robbery. In addition it had pointed the finger of blame at people suspected of carrying out 12,016 domestic burglaries, and 11,635 commercial break-ins. 'The deterrent value of having a convicted criminal's DNA profile stored on the database should not be forgotten,' says Ben Gunn, chief constable of Cambridgeshire Constabulary and Association of Chief Police Officers' spokesman on forensic science.

For law-abiding citizens this at first sight seems great. However, as with every powerful technique, there are drawbacks if you believe they are perfect. Expert in forensic science Ian Shaw points out that, although DNA tests are increasingly sophisticated, the results are never 100 per cent certain. This, he says, is why forensic experts talk about the probability that a sample came from a defendant, rather than simply answering 'yes' or 'no' when acting as expert witnesses in court. Great care is needed if juries are not going to be forced to come to particular verdicts on the basis of a single piece of genetic evidence, because to a lay audience large probabilities can often sound like certainties. 'The problem is that we will never really know how many people we've locked in prison with DNA matches who are not guilty,' says Shaw.[25]

There is a general consensus that once someone has been found guilty of a crime they forfeit their right to certain freedoms. Placing someone in prison is the most obvious example, but a less severe sanction is to give the person a criminal record. Your details are carefully stored away so that you can be more readily traced should you offend again. With DNA fingerprints now being part of that record, there has

23. Quoted in 'DNA Testing Expanded', *BBC News Online*, 29 November 1999.

24. Quoted in 'Plans for Vast DNA Library to Fight Crime', *Electronic Telegraph*, 31 July 1999.

25. Quotations from Professor Shaw of the University of Central Lancashire were reported in 'DNA = Do Not Assume?' *BBC News Online*, 29 November 1999.

been a renewed discussion about the level of crime that should warrant a permanent record. Should shoplifting or petty vandalism be enough?

Life becomes even more complex when police forces start to take DNA samples from entire populations in order to trap a wanted person. In 1995, 31-year-old James McIlroy was convicted of three charges of rape, each being committed in Derby. In each assault he had covered his face with a sweatshirt hood, so his victims were unable to provide any identifying evidence. After consultant forensic psychologist Paul Britton drew up a psychological profile of the rapist, police asked all men aged eighteen to thirty-five who lived on the Austin housing estate in the city's Sinfin area, where most of the attacks had occurred, to come forward and provide DNA samples. Of the 150 samples given, only McIlroy's matched DNA found in semen samples taken from some of his victims.

While it is exciting to see dangerous people being caught and prevented from injuring even more people, we need to ensure that this is not done at the expense of civil liberties. Asking a whole population to step forward and provide a DNA sample is getting dangerously close to asking people to prove their innocence – a radical departure from the original ethos of 'innocent until proven guilty'. To start with, many people fear that refusing to give a sample to the police would place them under suspicion.

So far, each time the police have asked for public help there has been general acceptance. By July 1999 there had been 120 mass screenings in England and Wales, gathering an average of 4,000 samples at each. The level of public support has partly been given because of the assurance that after the case has been solved all records will be destroyed, but it appears that this reassurance might be about to be lost.

In a high-profile speech, Prime Minister Tony Blair set out the UK government's desire to extend the scope of the nation's DNA database. 'More testing will help solve more crimes and catch more criminals,' he said when visiting a police station in Kent.[26] He

---

26. Quoted in 'Make All Suspects Give DNA, Says Blair', *Electronic Telegraph*, 29 November 1999.

announced plans that any samples taken and analysed in mass-screening programmes would be logged on to a new database. Individuals would have the right to ask for the data to be destroyed, but the existence of the database will become a source of anxiety. In addition, anyone arrested and taken to a police station under the suspicion that they may have committed all but a minor offence would be compelled to give a sample for DNA testing. Under current legislation, this record would have to be destroyed if the person was not found guilty of the offence which led to the arrest, but Blair proposed that this information should now be stored indefinitely.

John Wadham, director of the civil rights group Liberty, is strongly opposed to the idea that the police could keep DNA records of innocent people, and believes that such a move would promote a backlash, with fewer people being willing to cooperate with the police. John Scott of the Scottish Human Rights Centre said that, while DNA testing obviously had some value, 'the powers the police are exercising should only be used in relation to very serious offenders and only in a situation where the police can justify it'.[27] Civil liberty expert Derek Ogg, QC, is also dubious about the right to force suspects to provide samples for DNA analysis, believing that if suspects have the right to remain silent after being arrested, they should have a right not to provide a sample.[28]

The Home Office states that its reason for wanting to create this database of innocent people is to save time, money and inconvenience. With DNA-fingerprint samples costing about £40 each to process, each mass screening will have cost in the order of £160,000. However, it strikes me that protecting civil liberties is worth a lot of time and money, even if that is inconvenient.

I am also worried that we will achieve a new set of errors with an outcome similar to Heisenberg's uncertainty principle, in that the more closely you observe a system, the less useful the data may

27. Quoted in 'Automatic DNA Tests "Cut Crime"', *BBC News Online*, 27 July 1999.

28. 'Automatic DNA Tests "Cut Crime"'.

become.[29] DNA fingerprinting gives you the ability to take a single cell and speculate on its original owner. However, once you have to resort to using microscopic fragments you must introduce worrying errors. Each time you brush against someone on a street, use public transport, or go to the theatre, you will exchange the odd hair or flake of skin. There is nothing to stop innocent people's DNA showing up at crime scenes, and it would be very easy for someone to deliberately plant genetic 'evidence' at a scene in order to frame another individual.

The first safeguard against this is if a DNA fingerprint is only used as additional data, and not as the sole, or even the most important, piece of evidence.

The second safeguard is that everyone involved in a court case understands the value of genetic evidence. The complexities of this were first raised in the UK's Court of Appeal in December 1993, where Andrew Deen was appealing against his conviction for rape. Peter Donnelly, a professor of statistics at Queen Mary and Westfield College, London, told a story. He asked the judges to imagine playing a game of poker with a person whom you assumed would not cheat, say, the archbishop of Canterbury. If the archbishop dealt a royal flush on the first hand, would that affect your view of him? Donnelly said that there were two types of question. The first is to ask, 'What was the chance of this happening, given that the archbishop was honest?' The answer: a probability of 70,000 to one against him getting a royal flush. The second asks, 'Is the archbishop honest, given that he has just dealt a royal flush?' Most people would be inclined to give the archbishop at least some benefit of doubt.

Drawing the analogy back to the court case, Donnelly said that DNA evidence could be viewed in two ways: 'What is the probability that the defendant's DNA profile matches that of the crime sample, assuming that the defendant is innocent?' or, 'What is the probability

29. Heisenberg's uncertainty principle states that it is impossible to know the position and the momentum of a particle (e.g. an electron) simultaneously. The more accurately you know the position of a particle, the less accurately you can determine its momentum, and vice versa. This is because in measuring one feature, you disturb the other.

of the defendant being innocent, assuming that the DNA profiles of the defendant and the crime sample match?'[30]

It turns out that answering this conundrum is more than an amusing party game, because it is central to an argument about the power of genetic evidence. A crime sample is analysed and matched to that from a suspect. A probability will be quoted for the likelihood that this match could happen by chance with DNA from any randomly selected member of the public. Figures in the order of one in thirty million are not uncommon and can sound incredibly convincing to a jury. However, Donnelly argued that the court needed to take a piece of statistical theory called Bayes' theorem into account. Thomas Bayes was an eighteenth-century English Presbyterian minister who showed how prior beliefs could alter the way we view new data. In effect this shows that when considering the odds that a person is innocent, the individual odds from separate pieces of data must be combined. The effect is intriguing.

Imagine for example, a murder. No known motive, no indication of a suspect. But at the scene there is some hair, apparently pulled from the assailant's head. Chromosome analysis of cells at the base of the hair shows that it came from a male, and DNA fingerprinting reveals a particular profile. Police take a guess that they are searching for a man within a twenty-five-mile radius of the scene, and estimate that within that area live 50,000 men. The odds of any individual man taken in for questioning at random being innocent are 49,999 to one – his chance of being guilty is one in 50,000. However, one of the men is found to have a genetic fingerprint matching that of the hair cells. Forensic experts claim that the chance of this match being a coincidence is one in ten million. Taking this evidence alone would suggest that there is a one-in-ten million chance of him being innocent (i.e. very unlikely) – a ten-million-to-one chance of him being guilty (i.e. very likely).

Presented like this in court, the odds look very impressive. The prisoner must go down. However, Bayes' theorem says that when you have two sets of evidence you have to consider four possible outcomes:

30. Pringle, D., 'Who's the DNA Fingerprinting Pointing At?' *New Scientist*, 29 January 1994, pp. 51–52.

1. The suspect may be guilty and the test may indicate guilt;
2. The person may be guilty, but the test does not indicate guilt;
3. The person may be innocent, but the test suggests that he or she is guilty;
4. The person is innocent and the test suggests innocence.

If you believe in justice the key issue is that innocent people aren't found guilty. The forensic evidence alone says that there is only a one-in-ten-million chance of a genetic test incriminating the wrong person. However, once you consider that the person has been pulled from a population of 50,000 people, the chance of an innocent man having a positive genetic identification is close to one in 200 – not such an impressive degree of safety.

Faced with this argument, the judges at Deen's appeal overturned the initial guilty verdict and ordered a retrial. DNA fingerprinting might be good, but let's keep in mind that it is not infallible.

There is a keen debate as to whether it is appropriate to use Bayes' theorem. To start with, it is difficult to know what the real size of the population pool is that the equations should take into account. It is also unlikely that there is a simple relationship between the risk of saying that an innocent person's DNA matches that of the crime sample (a false positive) and of incorrectly saying that a guilty person's DNA does not match the crime sample (a false negative). Without a clear relationship, it is inappropriate to use the theorem.

However, while this mode of calculating the precise odds may not be perfect, it highlights the issue that genetic evidence on its own may not be as powerful as it first appears.

The question of who holds genetic information is also relevant to criminal inquiries. Some defendants have found that genetic-fingerprint data show that they are innocent because their genetic fingerprint differs from that found in evidence associated with the crime. While there is always a slight chance that a defendant's fingerprint coincidentally matches that found by the police, there is no way that tissue samples bearing a different DNA fingerprint could come from the defendant. In cases such as rape, on occasions when only one attacker is involved, this will prove the defendant's innocence.

However, if more than one person was involved in the crime, the defendant may still be guilty, because the forensic sample could have come from an accomplice.

If DNA forensic tools are going to aid our justice system, then it is vital that they are equally available to both prosecution and defence. According to the Innocence Project running at the Benjamin N. Cardozo School of Law in New York City, by October 1999 sixty-two convicts in twenty-two of the states in the USA, and five convicts in Canada, had gained their freedom after DNA techniques were used to re-examine evidence. Most of them had been found guilty of rape or murder.

In February 2000, British police dropped their charges against 49-year-old Raymond Easton. They had arrested him and charged him for burglary because his DNA fingerprint matched forensic evidence found at a crime scene. The odds against the match being a coincidence were said to be thirty-seven million to one. Compelling evidence. Easton, however, maintained his innocence. Suffering from Parkinson's disease he pointed out that it was unlikely he could travel the 200 miles from his home to the crime scene, and, in any case, he claimed to have been looking after his sick teenage daughter on the day of the burglary. Easton's DNA record was on the National DNA Database because three years earlier he had been cautioned by the police after hitting his daughter during a family row. There was no other reason for assuming that he was linked to the crime. 'They wouldn't even entertain the thought that they had made a mistake. They charged me and I was left to prove my innocence,' said Easton.[31]

It is worthy of note that a caution is sufficient grounds for the police to establish a criminal record and keep DNA data.

Easton was found to be innocent after his solicitor demanded that the police perform a more rigorous genetic test. The initial test had

---

31. Quoted in Chapman, J., and Moult, J., 'DNA-Test Blunder Nearly Landed Me in Jail', *The Daily Mail*, 11 February 2000.

found six key points of similarity between Easton's DNA and that in the crime evidence. When a ten-point test was used, the additional four criteria failed to match. This ten-point test is now part of the standard procedure, but it has only been used in the UK since June 1999, calling into question the convictions that are based on the previous less sensitive method. Easton's case highlights the need to treat all forensic evidence with caution, and points to the need for both parties to have access to the DNA samples and the ability to analyse them.

An extension of the power and accuracy of genetic-forensic analysis will come as the police start to be able to look at the genes found in a sample, rather than simply measuring the spaces between the genes. There is some indication that, along with identifying the sex of the wanted person, they will be able to make some assessment of the likely racial origin, and maybe even some aspects of the person's appearance. However, this will always have its limits: using genetic analysis to decide what hair colour, and even eye colour, the person has is obviously extremely limited thanks to the range of hair dyes, coloured contact lenses and plastic surgery that is readily available.

Finally, companies supplying DNA forensic services have found a lucrative money-spinner. Paternity testing is a burgeoning area of business, with companies springing up all around the globe to offer their services. Many stress the confidential nature of their operation and make provision for people to post samples to them, having ordered the test over the internet. Doing a quick internet search I discovered that twenty-five of the forty-two companies I found advertising genetic tests were primarily established to provide parental identification. In Chile paternity testing has seen a massive explosion, as new inheritance laws enacted in 1999 require fathers to acknowledge all their children, whether born in or out of wedlock. The scale of the situation can be seen by the fact that in 1998, forty-six per cent of children in Chile were disowned by one or both of their parents.

Again we face the question, who has a right to have access to your genetic code?

## Patenting

The last, but by no means least, area of ownership that I would like to consider is the thorny issue of patenting. Doing genetic research is expensive – seriously expensive. Huge amounts of time and money are invested and those involved feel they want to protect their findings so that they can make a profit from their investment. Enter the patent lawyer.

The initial concept of a patent was to enable inventors to gain by spreading their knowledge as widely as possible, for the benefit of as many people as possible. The first recorded patent was granted in 1421 to the Italian architect, goldsmith and sculptor who played a large role in developing the Renaissance style of Florence, Filippo Brunelleschi. Along with designing the then-largest dome in the world, he thought up a system for loading ships and was granted a patent by the city of Florence so that everyone, including the inventor, would profit and that the inventor would be encouraged to dream up even more useful devices.

In more recent usage, patents have become legal devices used to protect 'intellectual property'. They are effectively 'trespassers-will-be-prosecuted' signs and they have started to be staked in various parts of the human genome. Patents have become negative things. A patent does not give its holder the right to make, use, sell or import a given invention; instead it allows the holder to prevent others from doing so.

Each country issues its own patents, so if you want to stop a person taking your invention abroad and using it there, you have to file in every country you can think of. Within Europe there is a move to see if the process can be simplified so that a single patent application to either a national patent office, or the European Patents' Office, would provide protection throughout the EU. Judging by the pace of change within the EU I would be surprised if they pulled this one off quickly. When, on top of all this, you consider that in order to maintain a patent you have to pay an annual fee, you can see that establishing a comprehensive patent can be a complex and expensive business.

After all this effort, a patent only lasts twenty years, after which the information that it covers falls into the public domain and is free for anyone to make use of. However, it gives the holder a reasonable amount of time to recoup any investment. Very often, by the time the patent has expired the item or process covered by it is obsolete. And this may prove to be the case with many patents issued in the name of genetic technology; however, some, as we will see, cover genetic sequences – genes – and there will be a long-term interest in those.

I, along with many other observers, think it is bizarre that patents are being awarded for gene sequences. Patent offices defend this practice, arguing that there is no difference between the criteria needed to claim a patent for a piece of engineering and that needed for a piece of genetics. An application must provide a written description of the item being presented, showing what it does and that it has some useful function (its *utility*), that it is *unique* and that it is *non-obvious*.

Arguments have flared as to whether a gene that has been in existence for millions of years can ever be claimed to be unique or non-obvious. On top of this there are very few genes for which we fully understand the link between the sequence and all of its activity, so the description of its utility must be limited, incomplete or inaccurate. Nevertheless there seems to be a growing consensus in Western legislatures that the purification or isolation of a sequence, or its incorporation into some unit that is capable of moving it into cells – a vector – is sufficient.

Commenting on this, Jeremy Rifkin, president of the Washington-based watchdog, the Foundation on Economic Trends, said, 'Nothing in our patent laws allows this. Under US Law discoveries in nature are not inventions. The US patent office has been violating its statute.'[32]

The problem with allowing the genetic code to be colonised by patents becomes clear when we see the actions of a few dominant companies. In 1999 Craig Venter launched Celera Genomics, a company which made the ambitious claim that it would corner the market by sequencing and patenting vast stretches of the human

32. Reported in Borger, J., 'Bid to Own Gene Rights', *Guardian Weekly*, 29 October 1999.

genome. In October that year it applied for preliminary patents to some 6,500 genes, sending shock waves through the genetics community. The preliminary patents last for about a year and Celera Genomics hopes this gives it some time to identify the key 100 to 300 genes that are really likely to make money. These it then hopes to claim with full patents.

At the same time organisations like the Sanger Centre are pressing people to make any sequences that they discover available on the world wide web within twenty-four hours of making the discovery, destroying any notion of novelty and thus removing any chance of anyone laying claim to them.

At the moment this isn't stopping Celera, which is continuing to control access to the information that it is collecting and restrict the way it can be used. Anger is rising within the genetics community because a lot of Celera's information has come from the publicly accessible genetic databases that have been generated by publicly funded research laboratories.

To add to this boiling pot of legal activity, in January 2000 the Geron Corporation was granted a patent which covers the techniques used to create Dolly the sheep. Geron had already bought most of PPL Therapeutics, the company that originally owned Dolly. It's not just genes that are the subject of patents. In January 2000 PPL Therapeutics was awarded a patent to cover their cloning technology for sheep. The situation over who can use and profit from this patent is, however, somewhat complex because of the extent to which PPL Therapeutics and the Geron Corporation are entwined.

One question is whether giving people exclusive rights to areas of the human genome will encourage or restrict research. A letter published in *Nature* reported that of 525 working scientists who responded to a questionnaire, 508 (96.8 per cent) believed that patenting DNA sequences before any biological function was known would impede future development of medical diagnostics and therapeutics.[33] A prime reason for this is that once an area is claimed,

33. Glasner, P., and Rothmann, H., 'Patents, Ownership and Sovereignty', *Nature* **392**, 26 March 1998, p. 325.

the possessor can relax and proceed at their own pace, rather than pressing ahead to keep abreast of any potential competitors. For people who are anxious about the pace of change, this paradoxically could seem a good thing.

There are fears, though, that giving a company a patent for a gene could be granting a licence to print money. An article in *The Independent* in 1998 featured Wendy Watson, a 43-year-old woman who had just had both of her breasts removed to avoid the risk of succumbing to hereditary breast cancer. Close family members had died at young ages because of the disease and she had discovered that she had a mutation of a gene implicated in breast cancer. Her anxiety, however, was the cost of the diagnostic test. Patents for tests to identify the mutant breast cancer genes BRCA1 and BRCA2 are owned by Myriad Genetics, of Salt Lake City, USA, and it was charging £1,472 for each test performed. To add to the intrigue, Myriad Genetics' patent for BRCA2 was filed a matter of hours before the Institute of Cancer Research in Cambridge published its work on BRCA2 and the institute claims that they discovered the gene first.[34] 'Everyone should have the right to have a genetic test and take whatever action is necessary to save lives. By allowing companies to patent things like this and charge for them, we will in effect be denying some people the right to a cure,' said Wendy.[35]

The heat increased in February 2000 when Myriad Genetics started to make moves that would restrict fifteen publicly funded British laboratories performing tests to look for the so-called breast-cancer genes. The company claims that it is motivated by a desire to see a uniformly high standard of testing throughout the world, and points out that its test is more sophisticated. But the short-term result is likely to be a restriction of access to the test, because Myriad Genetics charges twice as much as the British laboratories for performing the test.

If anyone thinks an advantage of patents is that they will clarify

34. Reported in Meek, J., 'Attempt to "Patent Life" May Double Costs of Breast-Cancer Checks', *Guardian Weekly*, 20–26 January 2000.

35. Reported in *The Independent*, 13 May 1998, p. 7.

who owns what, they need to think again. While Myriad is planning to provide a global service, the UK's Cancer Research Campaign Technology claims that it, not Myriad, has the right to the patent. Confusion and argument reign.

The patent granted to Geron for mammalian cloning also caused critics such as Vivienne Nathanson, head of science and ethics at the British Medical Association, to say that such actions could inhibit medical research: 'A tremendous amount of research is small scale and doesn't lead to an expensive drug which might bring money back in, and organisations, including charities, may not have the money to pay to use this patented technology.'[36]

And money is the key issue. When Tony Blair and Bill Clinton released a joint statement calling for 'unencumbered access' to genetic information, the biotechnology stocks on Wall Street plunged. The Nasdaq index fell nearly 200 points, or four per cent of its total value – the second-worst point drop in its history.[37]

There are also people who want to restrict the use of regions of the genome to protect particular agendas. When Dean Hamer thought he had found a gene that played a role in determining whether a person would be homosexual he claimed that using this knowledge to test for the sexual orientation of an embryo 'would be an abuse of research'. To prevent it occurring, he says that if his laboratory discovers the gene and wins patent rights to it, he will use those rights to prevent anyone from developing such a test.[38]

The market-driven war seems set to intensify as genetic technology is brought to our homes and lives by companies making high-risk investments in the hope of high-geared gains. In the old world, where the consumer was king, there was at least some protection against exploitation, but now the shareholder reigns. The focus of commercial interest has become maximising shareholder

36. Quoted in 'Ethicists Query Dolly Patents', *BBC News Online*, 20 January 2000.

37. Quoted in 'Make Human-Gene Data Public', *BBC News Online*, 15 March 2000.

38. Reported in Holmes, B., 'Gay-Gene Test "Inaccurate and Immoral"', *New Scientist*, 5 March 1994, p. 9.

return. As shareholders can sell at the click of a button, this can cause a distinct element of 'short-termism'. Drug companies frequently sell drugs that are banned in countries with strict regulations to people living in less-regulated areas of the world. This increases the shareholder's profit, but it is unlikely to benefit the customer. We can already see the signs of protectionist tendencies leading to restricted access, as the shareholder's return becomes more important than the prospective patient.

Without care our developing, genetically informed society, which seeks to unite behind its new ability to interrogate our genome, will falter as our freedom to exploit genetic knowledge becomes restricted and directed with the sole purpose of generating wealth.

## Whose rights?

The problem with genetic data is that in almost every case there is a conflict of interest between an individual's right for privacy and another's right for disclosure. The problem is that no one can establish what the real potential for genetic technology is, so trying to legislate to limit any possible risks is proving to be impossible.

At the same time it is vital that everyone involved in handling genetic information realises the limitations of the knowledge that it currently affords. Damage can only be done to individual people and to public confidence when organisations and authorities make premature use of not completely tried, tested and established technologies. If the penalty for waiting is that a few people slip through the net or abuse the system, then that surely is preferable to causing harm.

# Chapter 10

# STEPPING OUT

*'The future is not what it was.'*[1]

The inhabitants of every age have marvelled at their inventiveness and the power springing from their creativity – the domestication of fire, the invention of wheels and bricks, the smelting of metals, the harnessing of steam and the discovery of antibiotics. There is every reason to believe that each generation has felt as if it has reached some ultimate point, some pinnacle of achievement.

At the same time there is the constant nagging fear that this time we have gone too far. When steam was harnessed, some feared that the human body would never survive the unnatural speed of thirty miles per hour. It's easy to cry doom. 'When I look at this present generation I despair for the future hope of civilisation,' cried Aristotle in the fourth century BC.

Entering the generation of the new Babel we again hear calls that the remarkable is achievable. Again there are cries for caution. Some plead that we backtrack and pack the technology away.

The genetic knowledge being amassed is truly remarkable and the scale is monumental. Like a helical tower, it stands as an icon marking the beginning of the new millennium and will undoubtedly have great influence over life from now on. You could no more remove genetic knowledge than you can uninvent the wheel, and in the same

1. Attributed to an anonymous professor of economics by Bernard Levin in the *Sunday Times*, 22 May 1977.

way, there is no reason why we should want to. The search to understand the mechanisms that support life is exciting and deeply fulfilling, both to the individuals involved and to the massed ranks of humanity who look on. Holding and handling this sort of intricate and complex knowledge is one feature that marks us out from other species.

But this towering achievement does have its dangers. It can serve people, or it can be used to make people serve it: it can enable or entrap. The tower can provide an ever-expanding place of wonderment, or it can become a virtual prison, trapping the technologist in its helical labyrinths. It can cause people to stand back and look up in wonder, or cause a shadow to fall on people so that all they see is a dark and overbearing monument to human self-aggrandizement.

Let's consider light for a moment, because you need light to cast a shadow. One thing about light is that it has to have a source. Personally I find the source of moral light to be the God revealed in the Bible. The light and its source will not be changed by the presence of the tower. Instead, the light illuminates the tower, so that its workings and beauty are clear for all to see. A decision to hide in the shadows could come from trying to ignore the fact that the tower is a created structure in the middle of a much larger created universe. One result of this is that you lose sight of any sense of purpose in life and in particular the sense of the unique value of human life.

Whatever your source of inspiration and illumination, one thing should unite all who look seriously at this area. If our new tower is going to fit into society it will need careful planning, and as with any other structure its builders should seek planning permission before embarking on any extensions or expansions. If we allowed 'market forces' to be the only guiding principle in conventional planning applications, there would be factories and housing estates springing up without any overall scheme to supply the required services. You can see the chaotic effect of this lack of control in the cities of developing nations where sewerage, clean water and power are poorly distributed; where the rich provide for themselves and the poor suffer.

If genetic technology is going to be the servant of humanity, rather than its master, we need to look and see what we would like to use it for and start to make plans that allow its implementation. Then we can step out from the fear-filled shadows and enjoy the benefits.

It is all too easy to believe that the shadow is a prison from which no one can escape. The horror headlines, that genetic technology is an unstoppable force, add to that pessimism. But this is an illusion. If, as a society, we wish to take control of the situation, we could establish guidelines and boundaries that mean that genetic technology is no more confining than a shadow.

Similarly, it is all too easy for the technologists to get so excited about their work that they forget it will affect the world outside. When challenged they seem to think that the science is the driving force and that they are merely passive observers, with no control over the direction the science is taking. Like people standing too close to a massive building, they have lost sight of the whole structure – they are entrapped by their own enthusiasm. They need to pause, step back from the tower and have a good look at the project and the effect it is having on those around. Then they will be in a position to take responsible charge of its direction.

Expressing it in a slightly different way, Jeremy Rifkin, president of the Washington-based watchdog, the Foundation on Economic Trends, said that genetic technology 'should force us all, this generation and the next, to ask all the big questions. What is the value of a human being? Does life have intrinsic or just utility value? What is our obligation to future generations? What is our sense of responsibility to the creatures with which we coexist? It really does force us, if we are willing and open to have a debate, to rethink our humanity and the meaning of existence. I mean that in a very sincere way. I don't know if we will have the debate, but if we do, it will be a great opportunity and, in the final analysis, genetic science will be well served.'[2]

I would add to the list of questions, *Who am I? What am I? What does it mean to be human?* Richard Dawkins would like to believe there is no validity to any question that seeks to establish why things are as they are. In his mind, all that we see and encounter is a product of

2. Reported in 'Apocalypse When?' *New Scientist*, 31 October 1998, pp. 34–36.

pure chance, with purpose being an illusion of our accidentally created imagination. I join the millions of people who find that view deeply unsatisfactory and believe that genetics, as it turns upside down many preconceptions, will force us to think again about why we exist.

If we don't have the debate, if we huddle in the shade, the issues will remain. They're not going to go away. As we have seen, genetics is now a part of prenatal screening and is making inroads into insurance assessing. This has occurred without any thorough debate and has already led to a situation where many people are fearful. There is a breakdown of trust within society with different interest groups accusing each other of coercion. The easy gibe given by those who see themselves as advancing the new technology is that any who ask for a pause for thought are 'Luddites', intending to cast a humorous slur in so doing. It's worth remembering that the Luddites weren't anti-technology; they were only keen that any new technology should serve, rather than damage, people.[3] They didn't reject all technology, but, in their words, 'put down all machinery hurtful to the commonality'. As far as they were concerned, any new invention needed to have a social and environmental benefit, not just an economic incentive.

The most extreme breakdown in human society would be the introduction of genes and chromosomes that in future years lead to populations of people who are no longer capable of breeding outside their own, newly established, techno-genetic clan – a far-fetched idea, but one that is not outside the realm of possibility. Paradoxically, a technology that has the hope of bringing people together, in an environment where we could conquer previously unconquerable disease and introduce unheard of prosperity, could be the very technology that scatters and destroys us. We have a deep-seated sense of the need for equality between all human beings. Genetics has the power to fundamentally undermine that equality.

3. Jim Thomas gives a review of the Luddites in *GenEthics News*, issue 24, June/July 1998, pp. 4–5.

## Boundaries

It is exceedingly untrendy to talk about boundaries and limits, but that does not mean they are wrong. Indeed it is part of our everyday life to place limits on one person's freedom in order to protect another person. Speed limits on roads are set so that one person is hopefully prevented from endangering another by exceeding their own capability in terms of the technical ability of the car and the person's own ability to react to changing situations, or demanding more than is reasonable of other road users.

Travel on most roads in the UK, though, and you will see the problem of setting legal limits: few people keep to them. And once the vast majority of people do not respect limits, they become virtually unenforceable. The same happens in medical legislation. Virtually all commentators agree that the law allowing abortion in the UK was not designed to allow the current situation, where it is all but supplied on demand. Indeed the wording of the law, with its requirement for two doctors to be convinced that this is the only workable solution, does not make that provision. However, the changing attitude in society means that it would be impossible to bring a prosecution against anyone involved in bending the rules.

For boundaries to work there must be a broad sense of agreement that they are appropriate. There will always be occasional breaches, but just because the law is broken there is no reason for abolishing it and leaving a free-for-all, or not establishing new boundaries where necessary. Murder and burglary still happen even though they are illegal, but there is no call to legalise them. Instead we build extra systems of protection and deterrent.

Speaking at the Royal Society, the late Rabbi Lord Jacobovits[4] suggested that boundaries are features which give special value to humankind. Far from being detrimental, they are positive. He drew inspiration for his comments from the creation story in Genesis,

---

4. Lord Jacobovits was awarded a Ph.D. by the University of London for his thesis on Jewish medical ethics. He was elevated to the peerage in 1988, and was awarded the Templeton Prize for Progress in Religion in 1991.

where, having brought the entire universe into being, God rested. The period of rest, the 'seventh day', was the part that was deemed to be sacred, not the period of industry. He pointed out that the Sabbath is a resting point, not a cessation of all further work. As God chose to pause and take a break, so humankind, as beings made in his image, should pause at frequent intervals. Christianity and other great religions have seen the rest days as a time to reflect on their creator. Any pause in the implementation of genetic technology would be well used in seeking to find God-given principles – some people might choose to call them practical guidelines – that can enable the new Babel to be constructed to a carefully considered plan.

It may be that we need to draw up moratoria, marking off various areas of research until the implications of them are more completely assessed. The idea would not be new. In February 1975 a meeting of lawyers, philosophers and scientists in a conference centre at Asilomar, California, decided that there were so many unanswered questions thrown up by the emerging science of genetic engineering that a voluntary moratorium on certain areas of research should be established. By 1978 many of the restrictions that had grown from the Asilomar conference were relaxed, as scientists learnt more and provided evidence that the caution was no longer necessary.

Any assessment of the Asilomar moratorium shows that it was imperfect, with a poor level of interaction between those who really knew about the science and policy-makers who had the public good to consider. However, it did serve to humanise science, as for the first time those involved took a bold decision to pause and think.

We need to be careful that we don't fall into the trap of leaving decisions to the 'free market', in the assumption that market forces will determine the best way forward. We've seen how the customer has been usurped from the throne and the shareholder enthroned as king. Consequently, market forces will determine the best way to make the shareholders wealthy, and that is not necessarily the same thing as delivering an ethically sound product.

## Globalisation

Markets have also become international entities. My school atlas made the world look a very simple place. Continents were divided into subunits – nation states. The legacy of colonialism meant that everywhere that had formerly come under British rule was coloured pink and everything that had been French was green. Political maps still exist, though the colours and the borders change with remarkable frequency, but as far as industry is concerned they are becoming increasingly irrelevant.

Power is switching from politicians and monarchs, who once dictated what happened, to the boardrooms of multinational companies. These organisations span borders and operate simultaneously in many different legislative areas of the world. The power they hold is the power to go elsewhere and take their wealth creation with them.

I believe it is most important that we don't allow the might of these mega-companies to set the agenda. They must exist to serve the global community; the global community must not be made to serve their shareholders. If being nasty to multinationals means that a few of them leave our shores it will, in the long-term, be a necessary and beneficial loss.

Big businesses aren't the only operations to act on a global scale. When the Wellcome Trust had their planning permission for a new business park on the outskirts of Cambridge refused, their immediate response was to threaten to take the project abroad.[5] Many observers saw this as an attempt to twist the government's arm. However, the plans were turned down, not because of fears about the technology, but because the local council felt that the development was larger than could be sustained by housing and transport. The council suggested that plans could be acceptable if the development was scaled down. There followed a row about whether local councils should be allowed to have the power to stand in the way of progress. I think this is a good example of local people looking at the supposed progress and saying that it would come at unacceptably high cost.

5. Reported in Hyland, A., 'Government Stands Firm on Wellcome Biotech Park', *Electronic Telegraph*, 25 August 1999.

It is important that when we look at the genetic tower, we the people have the power to refuse planning permission and not be swayed by the threat that the technologists will go elsewhere.

One way of helping the debate is to establish local seminars, focus groups and people's juries. These need to be created with great care so that they don't become places of persuasion, but they could be forums for gauging popular opinion and collecting ideas. However, there is a pitfall, in that finding that some behaviour or belief is the statistical norm is not the same as saying it is an appropriate moral standard for ethical behaviour.

There are people calling for a major international conference that could debate the issues being raised by genetics. George Davatelis, formerly a senior programme officer for the National Academy of Sciences, believes we need what he terms 'Asilomar 2'. Writing in *The Scientist* he suggests that we need a major symposium, which should involve scientists, policy-makers and the public.[6] It seems like a great idea, but I fear that it would become a toothless talking shop – all talk, no power.

## The scientists' dilemma

Mention boundaries to scientists and you soon meet a wall of hostility. First of all, they complain that if *they* don't do it, then *someone else* will. Consequently, claim the scientists, we will get left behind.

However, the questions to ask are, *Where is the science leading?* and, *Do we really want to go there in the first place?* If the answers turn out to be, 'No,' then there is no crisis in getting left behind. If, as a society, we decide that something is too dangerous, unethical or is likely to cause division, we should be confident in our decision to make a stand. For this reason, I think it is most unfortunate that the UK has not signed the European Convention on Human Rights and Bioethics, which seeks to establish ethical boundaries within which member states of the Council of Europe should operate. The call is

6. Davatelis, G., 'Asilomar 2: An Idea Whose Time Has Come', *The Scientist* **13**, 1999, p. 12.

often that in an increasingly global market place there is no way to regulate anything, but conventions like these offer ways of providing a unified set of standards.

Even if the answer is, 'Yes, we do want to go there,' I'm not sure the panic is justified. First of all, the implication is that there is only one possible route of exploration open at any one time. While science runs in trends with a particular area becoming popular for a few years, the history of scientific discovery is that these trends change rapidly. Blocking one area will be a great incentive to investigate others.

Remember the controversy about the ethics of therapeutic cloning? The problem highlighted was that while the technique could potentially deliver valuable therapies it always needs to start by creating an embryo–clone of the proposed patient. However, already the inventors of Dolly the sheep are saying they are developing ways of performing the same task without the need to start with an embryo.[7] There are many problems to be resolved, but if legislation banned the use of embryos in this research, then the incentive to solve them would increase.

One of the forces that could make such restraint harder to contemplate is the issuing of patents, as this rewards those who forge ahead without heeding any calls for restraint. Any territory that called for a moratorium on research would have to ensure that no one who has done research elsewhere in the world could gain an unfair advantage.

Secondly, scientists sometimes express the opinion that 'if we show caution, "they" will ban it'. Science and the technologies that lead from it feel distinctly under threat. The current state of the genetically modified (GM) food furore is a good example, with the international giant Monsanto so embattled that it has retreated from its advance into Europe and is facing severe pressure in the United States as sales of genetically modified soya come under scrutiny.

7. Reported in Coughlan, A., 'Cloning Without Embryos', *New Scientist*, 29 January 2000, p. 4.

All too often science agencies see their task as fighting their corner, rather than giving a completely accurate assessment of the situation. It's not an easy task, as in public communication there is often an incentive to give definite answers when in reality the situation is uncertain. The supporters of GM food are keen to point out that there is little, some claim no, evidence that it causes harm. Those who campaign against it point out there is no evidence that it is safe. The real problem is there is no clear evidence one way or the other. The work has not been done. When pressed, GM-food producers say this would take years and be very costly; environmental campaigners say that mopping up after a disaster would take years and be costly. It would clarify the debate if both sides admitted the exact situation with regard to the strength of their evidence.

## Agreement in a postmodern, pluralist society?

Because of the wide-ranging implications of genetic technology, stepping out of the shadow will demand that we move from dissension to decision. But that is not going to be easy. Freedom is the current god to be worshipped. I have the right to be free, free to be me, to do my own thing and not to have my decisions or values questioned. We see it as a basic component of human rights. Why shouldn't I use genetic technology to cure disease, to overcome infertility, to enhance my life, or to produce the child of my dreams if I want to? If I think it's OK, then who are you to say that it isn't?

Western society has moved from a position that, on the whole, accepted some form of biblical authority, through one that saw science as the great hope and saviour, to one that now has no single focus. Philosophers often talk of the current age as being one of postmodernity: we had a Christian age and then a post-Christian age; we had a modern age and now a postmodern age. The modern age was one where we believed that science could answer all the important questions and where technology could provide for all our needs. Postmodernity has grown from an awareness that happiness and a fulfilled life cannot be achieved by technical fixes alone. The problem with postmodernity is that, rather than being a philosophy that has something to offer, it offers nothing other than an absence of rules, regulations and responsibilities.

At times it is very convenient for people who want to act without restraint to use pluralism and postmodernity as tools to defeat any criticism. However, that is based on a lazy assumption that all religions, including Christianity, are dead, and that no one believes in science any more either. Both of these assumptions are plainly incorrect. Across the world there is a move towards people taking up religious beliefs, and science is clearly continuing to define how things work. Such anarchy would also deny that there is any continuing value in documents like the Universal Declaration of Human Rights, which clearly is not the case.

There are grounding principles that are established between the vast majority of nations, and the task of current and future policy-makers is to draw the emerging genetic technologies into these agreements. This will involve a critical assessment of what exactly we mean by human rights and their desire to enable people to be free. Australian theologian Charles Sherlock expresses the divergence of opinion like this:

*In the West, [human rights are] generally understood to refer to the rights of each individual. In other societies, in contrast, it is understood to refer to the right of a community to preserve its own identity... The fundamental Christian perspective seeks to hold them together by emphasising that 'personal' makes sense only in 'community', both terms finding their true meaning in the life of... God.*[8]

I believe that the next few years will be ones in which we will have to look again at the concept of community. A former UK prime minister, the 'iron lady' Margaret Thatcher, was famously quoted as saying that there is no such thing as society – that only individuals and families count. She may no longer be at the helm of British politics, but this concept continues to drive much of our current

8. Sherlock, *The Doctrine of Humanity*, pp. 90–91.

policy-making. However, in order for people to have true freedom, society has to provide a framework for support. In terms of people deciding what to do with genetic screening, in areas as diverse as insurance, employment and family planning, individuals only have the option of choosing the 'difficult' route if they have support.

If a society decides to make the insurance industry the main financial safety net and provider of support in a crisis, as is the case for healthcare in the USA, then this industry must not be allowed to discriminate against people with potentially expensive genetic mutations – the very people most in need of support. To do this removes any form of choice for these people. If insurance companies say that this is not possible, then we need to question the move away from the public provision of care. UK insurance companies conceded their role in the housing market when they agreed that no one should be restricted from having a £100,000 mortgage because of some feature of their genetic make-up, on the basis that home ownership is a part of membership of society. How much greater should be the entitlement to appropriate facilities, healthcare and education?

If a society decides to provide antenatal genetic tests, then it must also supply support to anyone who decides either not to use the tests, or to use them and then continue with a pregnancy, knowing that the child will have some genetic disease. Without this provision there is no real freedom. We need to beware of commentators like Francis Crick who say that we have to take reproductive autonomy away from humans to guarantee the advancement of humankind.[9]

Certainly patient- and parent-support groups are worried about this sort of sentiment. I was intrigued by a policy statement on genetics and deafness written by the National Deaf Children's Society in the UK. This maintains that 'Deafness is not an illness or a life-threatening condition. Therefore, the Society believes that if support is provided and positive attitudes are fostered, the challenge

9. Crick, F., 'Man and its Future', Ciba Gigy Symposium, 1962.

of deafness can be a rewarding one for deaf children and their families.'

At the moment medicine works on a basis of 'informed consent': people are asked to sign 'consent' forms, indicating that they are prepared to allow a particular procedure to occur. I would like to see a move towards the use of 'request' forms, where an individual asks for a procedure. We already agree that patients should be informed of their options before starting any treatment, so request is a more positive statement than consent. The difference might seem slight, but it acknowledges that the power to decide should lie more firmly with the individual patient. This will be even more important as genetic screening becomes more available and starts to be offered to people who, up to that point, considered themselves to be basically healthy.

Once again the National Deaf Children's Society is concerned:

*[We] do not support the genetic screening of whole populations for genetic conditions, with the consequent risk of moving towards a society in which difference is no longer accepted or tolerated. Nor does the NDCS consider that the eventual elimination of deafness, however unlikely, would be in the best interest of society.*

I'm not so naive that I believe we will ever reach total agreement on the positions of any boundaries. No democratic system has ever tried to do that. However, democracies set rules that prevent one person's actions damaging another and which seek to ensure that no one does anything that the majority considers to be ethically incorrect. There will always be borderline cases needing careful thought, and people who have certain options closed because of the restrictions. But that is an inevitable part of living in a mature community that desires to have a long future.

## Out of Eden

Running through the genetic technology debate is the question of whether we are exceeding our authority, whether we are 'playing

God'. As someone who believes in God, I have to take this issue seriously, and for me the route to solving it comes from looking to see what our authority is.

Contemporary theologian Walter Brueggemann points out that, in Genesis, humankind is created with a God-given set of principles: vocation, permission and prohibition. The vocation is to 'till and keep', to work and take care of the created world. The permission is enormous – everything is permitted, humankind is in control. There is only one prohibition, which is that humankind should not eat from the 'tree of the knowledge of good and evil' lest they should die.[10] Theologian, scientist and scholar of Hebrew Ernest Lucas points out that the term 'good and evil' is a common Hebrew idiom for summing up a single idea in two words, by stating the two extremes. 'Good and evil' is therefore the sum total of knowledge.

In his book, *Brave New Worlds*, Bryan Appleyard suggests this means the Bible claims that any search for knowledge – *logotaxis*, he calls it – is inherently evil: 'it distances us from God and condemns us to wander the earth, exiles from Eden, seeking salvation from our disastrously logotaxic selves'.[11] He sets this against the evolutionary story of life, where humankind's success is based on its acquisition of knowledge. 'The evolutionary story explains our success: the biblical story explains our failure,' he says.

I find this an unsatisfactory explanation of the Genesis narrative as the rest of the text indicates that God expects humanity to have intelligence and responsibility. This must, therefore, require our acquisition of knowledge. The problem starts to resolve itself if we ask what is meant by eating the fruit of the forbidden tree. The first thing to note is that following their act of rebellion neither Adam nor Eve fell to the ground stone dead. What died, however, was the closeness of humankind's relationship with its

10. Brueggemann, W., *Interpretation – Genesis*, John Knox Press, 1982, p. 46.

11. Appleyard, B., *Brave New Worlds*, HarperCollins, 1999, p. 146.

creator. The process that led to the taking of the 'knowledge of good and evil' was the starting point of being critical about God. It was the first moment when humankind felt on a par, or superior, to its creator. Brueggemann says that the serpent is the first character in the Bible to 'practise *theology* in the place of *obedience*'.[12] And obedience is the critical issue, not knowledge. Humankind is given permission, and that permission must include permission to learn, otherwise we would be incapable of caring for the world. The issue is whether we use that learning wisely, and, for the Bible, wisely means in reference to God.

In as much as humankind was made in the 'image of God', the Bible anticipates that we will be involved in learning, in understanding, in working with, creation. To that extent, we are very properly 'playing God'. If we must bring God into it, I would prefer to call it 'reflecting God'. I think it would be even better to describe it as being fully human. At times like this we should embrace the new Babel with grateful thanks for the release that it could bring from various forms of distress.

But 'playing God' is usually thrown onto the front pages when something disturbing happens. This I believe is false for two reasons. First, it is sad to assume that in doing something disturbing, we are in any way representing an all-loving deity. Secondly, even if we decide that the technology under discussion is good, then it is highly presumptuous of us to assume we have any capability equivalent to God's. In the Old Testament, God challenges Job with a series of rhetorical questions, designed to put Job and his companions in their places. Speaking poetically, he asks,

> *Where were you when I laid the earth's foundation?...*
> *Have you ever given orders to the morning?...*
> *Have you comprehended the vast expanses of the earth?...*
> *Do you give the horse his strength...? (Job 38:4, 12, 18; 39:19).*

12. Brueggemann, *Interpretation – Genesis*, p. 48.

Often we would do better to come clean and say that someone is acting irresponsibly or contrary to any ethical principle, rather than pretend to engage in some pseudo-theological debate.

## A new enlightenment

*There is a naive idea that there is only one choice – are you for this science, or are you a Luddite? Are you an advocate of change or are you scared to death of the future? That's not the debate. The issue is not whether you are for or against the science, the issue is how we can use these technologies so that they are commercially achievable and socially acceptable.*[13]

As I write, the new millennium has dawned amid speculation that this could give the world a chance of a collective fresh start, a chance to leave the conflict and grief of previous centuries behind. I wish I could believe that such optimism is firmly grounded, but I do believe that there is a chance for those in charge of genetic technology to show a grown-up sense of responsibility.

Are we going to concentrate on individualising treatments, or are we going to truly respect people as individuals? We have the opportunity to develop treatments that really can make a difference to the way people live in our society, building facilities and systems to meet the needs of the most vulnerable. Or we can design our society and then use every possible technique to try to force people to fit in. At a time when we are more capable of fighting disease, we are more frightened of it. We are so frightened of disease that we are more likely to avoid the person living with a disease than care for them.

Part of being human is the desire to care for the weakest and most vulnerable in society, to give dignity to people who may feel that they have no value and to supply their needs. Developed nations are richer than ever, and have never been in a stronger position to provide the care and to use genetic knowledge to enable

---

13. Jeremy Rifkin, president of the Washington-based watchdog, the Foundation on Economic Trends, reported in 'Apocalypse When?' *New Scientist*, 31 October 1998, pp. 34–36.

that provision. The question is, do we really care? Are we going to create our future by moulding and recreating individual people or by moulding and regulating our society?

Increasing the amount we understand about genetics will affect all future generations. Our generation is charged with the task of setting the foundations to the project and building the first few stages. It is important, therefore, that we think clearly and plan well. We need to encourage the scientists, technologists and financiers to step outside the tower and look at what they are creating. We need to encourage the public and policy-makers to stop moaning about the technology and the problems of containing it, and take the effort required to understand enough about it to make enlightened decisions.

Let's step out of the tower, move away from the shadow and enjoy the light. Let's make use of genetics and not let it make use of us.

## Twenty-first-century Babel: an enlightened scenario

Now the whole world had an amazing technology and a mass of genetic code.

As the people saw the potential use of this technology they paused for thought.

They said to each other, 'Come, let's make use of this skill that we have developed for the benefit of all people.' They used their intellect to harness natural processes and combat disease.

Then they said, 'Come, let us build ourselves an industry, with a database that encompasses all knowledge, so that we can serve our generation and build a future that gives dignity to every human being.'

The Lord came down to see the society and their genetically enabled technologies.

The Lord said, 'If as one people speaking the same language of "care" and "value" they have begun to do this, then nothing they plan to do will be impossible for them.

'Come, let us go down and make ourselves available to be beside them in this work.'

But the Lord warned that the people should not become proud and forget the source of their knowledge and understanding.

That is why it was called Babel – because out of all the confusion caused by a rapidly changing society, the people retained a unity based on honouring each other as beings made of great value – as made in the image of God.

# GLOSSARY

**allele:** *genes* can exist in a number of slightly different forms. Each form is called an allele.

**autosomes:** the *chromosomes* that are not involved in determining the sex of an individual.

**bacteriophage:** a virus that attacks bacteria. These viruses are used to transport sections of *DNA* into bacterial cells.

**chromosome:** strand of *DNA* and supporting protein.

**cloning:** process of producing populations of genetically identical organisms.

**chimera:** *see* **mosaic**.

**DNA (deoxyribonucleic acid):** a chain-like molecule that can store information in a form that is easily copied.

**enzyme:** a protein that enables specific biochemical reactions to occur, or increases the rate at which they can occur.

**eugenics:** the word literally means 'well born'. It is the ideology that a population should control its genetic future by regulating those individuals allowed to breed or be born.

**eukaryote:** organism with its *DNA* contained in a *nucleus*.

**gene:** unit of information stored on a *chromosome* that gives instructions needed to build a specific protein.

**HFEA (Human Fertilisation and Embryology Authority):** the UK body established in 1990 by Act of Parliament to oversee centres that use reproductive technologies.

**HGAC (Human Genetics Advisory Commission):** A body set up by the UK government to advise on developments in human genetics.

**HUGO (Human Genome Organisation):** An international organisation that aimed to create a pool of intellectual resources large enough to take on the task of cracking the human genome.

**lyposomes:** tiny globules of fat that have a piece of *DNA* suspended inside them. They are used to transport *DNA* into cells.

**mitochondrial DNA:** A small section of *DNA* that exists in the cells' mitochondria.

**mosaic:** an animal, or a tissue within an animal, that contains two or more genetically distinct cell types.

**mRNA (messenger RNA):** the piece of *RNA* that is the equivalent to a photocopy of a **gene** and carries the genetic message to the place where protein production occurs.

**nucleus:** discrete membrane-bound zone inside *eukaryotic* cells which contains the *chromosomes*.

**ovum:** Latin word for egg.

**penetrance:** the proportion of people who have a genetic risk of a particular genetically influenced feature (disease or other physical or even possibly psychological attribute), who actually succumb to the disease. If penetrance is high, then looking for the presence of a particular genetic mutation will give more useful information than if penetrance is low.

**plasmid:** a loop of *DNA* that can replicate without having to become incorporated into a *chromosome*.

**phage:** abbreviation of *bacteriophage*.

**PCR (polymerase chain reaction):** a method for amplifying specific **DNA** segments which makes use of certain features of natural DNA replication.

**PGD (pre-implantation genetic diagnosis):**

**primitive streak:** a structure that develops in human embryos by day 14 as cells differentiate into those that will go on to form the fetus and those that will be dedicated to forming the placenta and umbilical cord.

**prokaryote:** organism with *DNA* floating freely in the cell and not bound by a *nucleus*.

**RNA (ribonucleic acid):** a single-stranded molecule that is similar to *DNA*, except that it contains ribose sugars instead of deoxyribose sugars and has uracil as a coding unit rather than thymine.

**RNA polymerase:** an enzyme that travels along *DNA*, copying the code of individual genes by building a molecule of *mRNA*.

**stem cells:** embryonic stem cells that come from early mammalian embryos. They are capable of repeatedly dividing in a laboratory culture dish and producing seemingly endless supplies of cells that have the potential to give rise to any organ in the body.

**telomere:** the end tip of each *chromosome*, which contains specific repeated *DNA* sequences. These tips shorten in each cycle of cell division and consequently the *telomeres* in each cell reduce in length as a person increases in age.

**therapeutic cloning:** producing an embryo by techniques used for cloning, but rather than trying to grow the embryo to the point where it can be born, its growth is arrested after a couple of weeks. The intention is to use its cells to create a therapy to treat disease.

**totipotent:** a term used to describe cells that have the potential for developing into any cell type in the body: skin, muscle, nervous tissue, etc.

**transcription:** process whereby a section of *DNA* code is copied into a piece of *mRNA*.

**translation:** process whereby a section of *mRNA* is used to generate a protein by linking amino acids together in a specific sequence.

**vector:** an agent (*plasmid* or *bacteriophage*) used to transport specific pieces of *DNA* into bacterial or other cells.

# BIBLIOGRAPHY

Appleyard, B., *Brave New Worlds*, London: HarperCollins, 1999.

Bains, W., *Genetic Engineering for Almost Everybody*, London: Penguin, 1987.

Berry, R.J. (ed.), *Real Science, Real Faith*, Eastbourne: Monarch, 1991.

British Council of Churches, *The Forgotten Trinity: Parts 1, 2 & 3*, London: The British Council of Churches, 1989.

Bruce, D., and Bruce, A., *Engineering Genesis*, London: Earthscan, 1998.

Brueggemann, W., *Interpretation – Genesis*, Atlanta, Georgia: John Knox Press, 1982.

Cameron, N.M., *The New Medicine*, Sevenoaks: Hodder & Stoughton, 1991.

Cook, D., *The Moral Maze*, London: SPCK, 1983.

Dawkins, R., *The Selfish Gene*, Oxford: Oxford University Press, 1976.

Dawkins, R., *The Blind Watchmaker*, London: Penguin, 1986.

Dawkins, R., *River Out of Eden*, London: HarperCollins, 1995.

Feinburg, J.S., and Feinburg, P.D., *Ethics for a Brave New World*, Illinois: Crossway Books, 1993.

Griffiths, A.J.F., et al., *An Introduction to Genetic Analysis* (5th edition), W.H. Freeman & Company, 1993.

Jeeves, M.A., and Berry, R.J., *Science and Christian Belief*, Leicester: Apollos, 1998.

Jones, D.G., *Manufacturing Humans*, Leicester: Inter-Varsity Press, 1987.

Jones, D.G., *Valuing People*, Carlisle: Paternoster Press, 1999.

Jones, S., *The Language of the Genes*, London: Flamingo, 1993.

Jones, S., *In the Blood*, London: Flamingo, 1997.

Kimbrell, A., *The Human Body Shop*, London: HarperCollins, 1993.

Kolata, G., *Clone*, London: Penguin, 1998.

McCarthy, B., *Fertility and Faith*, Leicester: Inter-Varsity Press, 1997.

McFadyen, A.I., *The Call to Personhood*, Cambridge: Cambridge University Press, 1990.

Moltmann, J., *God in Creation*, SCM Press, 1983.

Moore, P.J., *Trying for a Baby*, Oxford: Lion Publishing, 1996.

Moore, P.J., *Pregnancy: A Testing Time*, Oxford: Lion Publishing, 1997.

Pellegrino, C., *Return to Sodom and Gomorrah*, New York: Random House, 1994.

Rose, S., *From Brain to Consciousness?* London: Penguin, 1999.

Sherlock, C., *The Doctrine of Humanity*, Leicester: Inter-Varsity Press, 1996.

Silver, L.M., *Remaking Eden: Cloning and Beyond in a Brave New World*, London: Weidenfeld & Nicolson, 1998.

Singer, P., *Rethinking Life and Death*, London: Oxford University Press, 1995.

Watson, J.D., *The Double Helix: A Personal Account of the Discovery of the Structure of DNA*, Weidenfeld, 1968.

Wright, L., *Twins: Genes, Environment and the Mystery of Human Identity*, London: Phoenix, 1997.

Wyatt, J., *Matters of Life and Death*, Leicester: Inter-Varsity Press, 1998.

# INDEX